*Anti-Foreign Imagery
in American Pulps and
Comic Books, 1920–1960*

Anti-Foreign Imagery in American Pulps and Comic Books, 1920–1960

NATHAN VERNON MADISON

McFarland & Company, Inc., Publishers
Jefferson, North Carolina, and London

Permission granted by Argosy Communications, Inc., for use of the following magazine cover images in this volume, which are protected by their respective copyrights and trademarks owned by Argosy Communications, Inc.: *Adventure, Argosy, Detective Fiction Weekly, Detective Tales, Famous Fantastic Mysteries, The Mysterious Wu Fang*, and *The Spider*. Copyright © 2012 Argosy Communications, Inc. All Rights Reserved.

LIBRARY OF CONGRESS CATALOGUING-IN-PUBLICATION DATA

Madison, Nathan Vernon, 1983–
    Anti-foreign imagery in American pulps and comic books, 1920–1960 / Nathan Vernon Madison.
      p.   cm.
    Includes bibliographical references and index.

    ISBN 978-0-7864-7095-2
    softcover : acid free paper ∞

    1. Comic books, strips, etc.— United States — History — 20th century. 2. Children's literature, American — History and criticism. 3. Pulp literature, American — History and criticism. 4. Xenophobia — United States — History. I. Title.
PN6725.M33 2013
741.5'973 — dc23   2012046911

BRITISH LIBRARY CATALOGUING DATA ARE AVAILABLE

© 2013 Nathan Vernon Madison. All rights reserved

No part of this book may be reproduced or transmitted in any form or by any means, electronic or mechanical, including photocopying or recording, or by any information storage and retrieval system, without permission in writing from the publisher.

On the cover: Cover art from *Headline Comics*, No. 11, Winter 1944 (Prize Publications)

Manufactured in the United States of America

McFarland & Company, Inc., Publishers
  Box 611, Jefferson, North Carolina 28640
    www.mcfarlandpub.com

Table of Contents

Preface	1
Introduction	13
Chapter I. *The Yellow Peril: The American Pulps Between the World Wars, 1919–1935*	41
Chapter II. *The Hun and the Nipponese Hordes: The American Pulps and Comic Books of World War II, 1935–1945*	88
Chapter III. *Russian Communists, Red Chinese and Nuclear Annihilation: The American Pulps and Comic Books of the Early Cold War, 1945–1956*	146
Conclusion	202
Chapter Notes	211
Bibliography	223
Index	231

Acknowledgments

There are a good number of people I owe thanks to following the completion of this project. My appreciation goes to my master's thesis committee members, who read the original version of what would eventually become this book: Dr. Emilie Raymond, Dr. John Kneebone, and Cindy Jackson.

I would also like to thank my family: my parents, James and Sylvia, and my sisters Natalie and Stacey, and my brother-in-law Kevin. Much appreciation also goes to the staffs of the Newspaper and Periodical Reading Room; the Rare Book Room; and the Microfilm Reading Room at the Library of Congress, as well as the Pulp Magazine Project, the Digital Comic Book Museum, and Phil Stephenson-Payne's Galactic Central archive of pulp magazine covers, all of which aided greatly in tracking down many primary sources.

Lastly, I would like to thank Sherry Corbin, who always insisted, against my doubts, throughout my time as an undergraduate student at the University of Mary Washington that I should do a senior, or even a master's, thesis concerning comic books.

Preface

> Europe is entering an era of twilight.... It is heading for a period of social and civil warfare which is likely to last fifty years and may last longer. It will emerge from this warfare a Socialist state. But the new Socialist Europe may be faced by a war greater and more crucial than any the world has yet seen — a war for the white man's right to leadership in civilization, a war with the yellow races of the world. — Georg Brandes, 1919

The preceding prediction by Scandinavian literary theorist Georg Brandes, published on the front page of the July 13, 1919, edition of the *New York Tribune,* spoke volumes to many Americans still reeling from the devastation of the First World War and on the verge of a Red Scare. While America was fortunate enough to avoid the destruction that had ravaged Europe, the reverberations of the conflict impacted America as violently as any military bombardment ever could. The Victorian ideal of sensibility and reason was brutally shattered, and in its place appeared an America very different from the one that had preceded it. Brandes elucidates perfectly the two central "terrors" that plagued America in the early years of the century and particularly following the Great War. Bolshevism was triumphant in Russia, which precipitated Red Scares at home, combined with a seemingly never-ending cascade of immigrants from Eastern Europe and Asia.

America was changing in many ways following the war, in every arena — from women's roles in society to Prohibition to literary experimentalism; not surprisingly, fear accompanied such change. Among the strongest fears of the time were those regarding the immigrant, the outsider, the "other," that had destroyed Europe or were slumbering in Asia waiting for their chance to "awaken." Immigrants that did not fit the traditional Anglo-American ideal had always been under scrutiny, such as the "uncivilized," "radical," and "atheistic" hordes of Eastern Europe, and the enigmatic "yellow" races of Asia. Such sentiments were not new and intermittently gained widespread support throughout American history, such as during wartime or severe economic downturns. Discriminatory imagery of foreigners, especially the Chinese and Eastern Europeans, appeared in excess throughout American publications in the late nineteenth and early twentieth centuries, due in part to economic uncertainties, as well as to concerns regarding cheap labor, steep climbs in immigration, and the expansion of America into a colonial and international power. After the end of World War I, however, assaults upon these groups soared to new heights — signifying, in many minds, a life or death struggle for the survival of what was considered American. Several factors contributed to the rise in anti-foreign sentiment following the First World War. A boom in nationalism that naturally follows the end of any war was certainly one reason, especially in a period of history during which "American" and "Anglo-Saxon" were understood to be one and the same. Anxiety over the possibilities of new conflicts arising out of strained international, and racial, relations also stoked anti-foreign feelings. A report on population and immigration control published in 1922 explains the connection between racial tension and the trepidation vis-à-vis renewed world conflicts:

> Around the Pacific is a new stirring of racial movements and aspirations. Russians, Chinese, Japanese, Malays, Dutch, British, Anzacs, Canadians and Americans are touching each other on the vast brim of the Pacific and are looking with apprehension at the many racial difficulties which are arising. Antagonisms are being engendered, politics are being pursued in this mighty caldron of conflicting forces which may in the future lead to another great war.[1]

Actors of foreign birth who had been beloved silent film stars before the war were forced to flee their adopted homes amidst nativist outcry. Anti-foreign rhetoric in politics and popular culture throughout the country rose, concurrent with an increase in isolationist policies that would last until America's entry into the Second World War.

The predominant forms of popular literature at this time, owing in large part to low costs both in production as well as in consumption, were first the dime novels of the late nineteenth and early twentieth centuries, followed by the fantastic pulps of the early 1920s and 1930s, and later, particularly with the advent of World War II, comic books. These mediums offered readers of varying ages many things: fast-paced action, travels to unbelievable and far-off worlds, miracles of modern science, and a reality in which good almost always triumphed over evil. What they also offered were definitions as to what that "good" and "evil" were; in many cases, the good was personified by a heroic, strapping Anglo-Saxon male and the evil by a villain of obviously foreign origin, either a sly and crafty Oriental or a brutish Slavic criminal — both of whom invariably held an alien-like disdain for wholesome American values. If, in the event that good was not triumphant, it was usually due to the hero's inability to cope with the foreign and alien nature of his opponent. The definitions of heroism and villainy reflected in what are now considered undoubtedly racist imagery were influenced and intensified by the horrors of the First World War. It was a time when America was undergoing fundamental changes in many aspects of its culture and identity after what was, until then, the most costly conflict in Western history. The intensity of isolationism and fear of the "other" from abroad on the part of politicians and the public alike were primarily responsible for the intensification of such imagery within the pages of popular literature.

The sheer amount of "yellow peril" and "European brute (or extremist)" narratives found in these mediums begs several questions that have never truly been approached satisfactorily. Why were pulp magazines, and later comic books, filled with "yellow emperors," "dragon ladies," opium peddlers, and sadistic, European barbarians? And how exactly did such stereotypes appear in these mediums; did they change over the course of years between the nativist turn of the twentieth century and the more inclusive society of the early twenty-first century? And if so, how? Investigative work into this question is lacking to a large degree. The manner in which many of these foreign characters were depicted does not support the most oft-cited reasoning — that outright racism was the sole agent. Racism undoubtedly played a role, but it does not account for the explosion of anti-foreign imagery and epithets in the early decades of the century. Orientalism, as described by Edward Said (*Orientalism*, 1978) in regards to both scholarly and novelized works, can only partially explain this phenomenon; just as racism cannot be regarded as the only factor, neither can orientalism, although both unquestionably played their part.

The historiography regarding pulp magazines is not as widespread when compared to the voluminous (some may say too much) amounts of research that focus on the history of comic books. Comic book history has become rather popular these days, with many academics finding all sorts of avenues of inquiry in the pages of these four-color fantasies, while pulp history has not received nearly as much attention. To be sure, one reason for this is the reputation the term "pulp fiction" has held, and continues to hold, in popular American imagination. In the past, as now, "pulp" suffers a connotation of trash, of vulgar tales full of horrendous violence and naked women. It is true that a good deal of pulp could be described in such a way, but to blanket the entire medium with such descriptors betrays an ignorance of the medium. Many of America's most famous writers began, or spent much of their career, writing for pulp magazines, and the fact that many pulp narrations (some of which appear in this work) were re-published in hardcover following their initial release speaks against the notion that they only exist for violence-seeking, sexually-frustrated young men. To find real pulp histories, one must first go to the authors who are (or were) a part of either the pulp or science fiction industry, pulp fandom, or some combination of the two, such as Mike Ashley, Sam Moskowitz, John Locke, Ron Goulart, Ed Hulse, and others. In-depth histories of the entire industry, its more popular (and lesser-known) creators, and even of specific titles and magazines exist and are wellsprings of information for those who know how to find them.[2] It is also safe to say that a great portion of pulp history exists as an oral culture among the former professionals and dedicated fanbase of the medium. Works of pulp history are many; works of pulp history that relate to nativism are lacking. Of the pulp histories, very few address the issue of racial depictions and caricatures. Editor Tony Goldstone, in his introduction to *The Pulps: Fifty Years of American Pop Culture*, devotes very little time to the subject, offering only that the heroic characters found in the pulps "took on all the known forces responsible for the plight of the country, and anything else that itched in the imagination, particularly 'red menaces' and 'yellow perils.'"[3] Other writers do approach the topic of race and nativism in the pulps, but only by quickly making good points that deserve further elaboration. In *Yesterday's Faces: From the Dark Side* (the third in a five-volume series concerning pulp magazines), Robert Sampson suggests that the origins of the "yellow peril" made popular by Sax Rohmer's *Fu Manchu* stories of the early 1910s (which saw a resurgence in the pulps of the '20s and '30s) can be found in white, Anglo-Saxon fears concerning what appeared at the time to be a terrifyingly belligerent Oriental race. The Boxer Rebellion in Qing China in 1900 and the victory of Japan over Tsarist Russia in the Russo-Japanese War in 1905 are two of the examples that Sampson gives as the impetus for the creation of the "yellow peril" genre of pulps.[4] While the popular memories of such events as the Boxer Rebellion are vitally important to this entire discussion, Sampson, unfortunately, offers very little in the form of further evidence, failing to see a deeper and long-lasting series of events that could have led to the need for such depictions; the later texts in his series offer more synopses of pulp stories than actual analysis. Similar to Sampson, Ron Goulart, author of *Cheap Thrills: An Informal History of the Pulp Magazines*, offers one recent event of the time, the Japanese invasion of Manchuria in 1931, as a possible reason for the popularity of the "evil Oriental" motif—again not taking into account many other events and far-reaching factors. Goulart only partially approaches the question of nativism, offering one small answer (albeit a very good one) before halting that avenue of discussion. One of the few works (possibly the only) that offers a detailed analysis of ethnicity and pulps, *Hard-Boiled: Working Class Readers and Pulp Magazines*, argues that it was the loss of traditionally "white" jobs by the American proletariat to "newer" groups, such as those of Eastern European origin, that fostered this animosity. Author Erin A. Smith asserts that such class and ethnic antagonisms facilitated the rise in popularity of much of the negative depictions found in pulps of both "Orientals" and "Huns" alike. *Hard-Boiled* explains superbly how nativist sympathies resulted in a wide range of discrimination, both within the pulps and without. That it does not stretch back to the earliest of literary ephemera — the pulps' predecessors the dime novel and story paper — does not detract from her analysis one bit, although a deeper analysis of them would help.

One problem with pulp historiography (more so a problem in recent years) is that in some cases the authors in question have not actually read (by their own admissions) many of the texts they claim as primary sources. William F. Wu's section concerning pulp magazines in *The Yellow Peril— Chinese American in American Fiction 1850–1940*, focuses on several pulp and periodical titles, such as *Fu Manchu, Dr. Yen Sin*, and the works of Dashiell Hammett. The problem lies in Wu's dependence on secondary sources for this entire section, as he deems actual pulp magazines too rare and difficult to find, which simply is not the case; a search on any number of online auction sites will provide a vast amount of pulps, many rather cheaply, spanning the entirety of the early twentieth century. Moreover, visits to the Library of Congress' Rare Book, Periodical and Newspaper, or Microfilm reading rooms argues against the scarcity of such sources.[5] In almost every region of the United States there exists some manner of depository, university-affiliated or otherwise, dedicated to pulp magazines and related ephemera. Erin A. Smith, in the article "How the Other Half Read: Advertising, Working-Class Readers, and Pulp Magazines," attempts to define the pulp magazine's audience (her conclusion: lower-class and under-educated) not by analyzing the actual stories but rather the type of advertisements found within their pages.[6] Problems arise with the fact that the same advertisements, such as those for correspondence schools (which Smith points out in particular), appeared in any number of more "sophisticated magazines" of the day. Also, according to sources contemporary with the pulps, publishers depended on newsstand and subscription sales for their income, with advertisements accounting for very little of the pulps' revenue. It would seem that the stories, not the ads, were the chief interest of both publisher and reader.[7] Even a superficial glance at many pulp magazine letter-pages argues against the stereotype of the ignorant, under-educated pulp reader as well.[8]

In particular regards to the subject of the depiction of minorities in comic books, most efforts focus on the subject of race relations within America, as opposed to long-entrenched American fears concerning those from outside the United States. Gerald Early and Alan Lightman's article "Race, Art and Integration: The Image of the African American Soldier in Popular Culture During the Korean War," and Jeffrey A. Brown's *Black Superheroes, Milestone Comics, and Their Fans*, are excellent examples of works that study the role comic books have or have not played in relation to the social history of African-Americans. Arie Kaplan's *From Krakow to Krypton: Jews and Comic Books* explores the vital role American Jews played in the creation of the comic book industry itself—as publishers, writers and artists.[9]

The majority of works that detail the history of comic books do just that—provide an overview of a particular decade, a certain company, or even the entirety of the industry itself—while only touching here and there upon issues of race and their importance in comics at the time. In actuality it is difficult to find any serious discussion concerning comic books and anti-foreign sentiments, with many authors preferring to praise comic books for sending heroes to battle foreign foes before war even broke out. In many works, if the topic of race (with the exception of African Americans) is approached, it is rather quickly addressed and just as speedily left behind. Les Daniels' *Marvel: Five Fabulous Decades of the World's Greatest Comics* attributes the depiction of Japanese villains in Marvel (in the 1940s, "Timely") Comics in one sentence: as the product of "racial prejudice and resentment over the attack on Pearl Harbor," which "created a climate in which it didn't seem out of line to depict Orientals as subhuman monsters."[10] In his introduction to Marvel Comics' inaugural volume of collected reprints of 1941's *U.S.A. Comics*, Dr. Michael J. Vassallo hurriedly touches upon the issue by stating that the "ethnic references we find offensive today ... were products of their time period, and should be taken as such," then moving off quickly to analyses of the stories found within the volume.[11]

Many works mention what the Second World War did to comics and how they changed as a result of the war — namely, the inclusion of foreigners as recurring antagonists. *Super Heroes: A Modern Mythology* by Richard Reynolds states that "America's entry into World War Two gave the superheroes a whole new set of enemies, and supplied a complete working rationale and world view..." that would allow for the creation of even greater numbers of superheroes, particularly those of the patriotic theme, such as Captain America.[12] While Reynolds' statement that often times superheroes served as "proxies of U.S. foreign policy" is true, it does little to explain the virulent imagery that accompanied the exploits of these heroes. Mike Benton's *The Illustrated History: Superhero Comics of the Golden Age* recalls that there was a patriotic fervor in the nation prior to Pearl Harbor that allowed for the creation of more "foreign" characters as foils, and that their proliferation after the attack on Pearl Harbor was purely for propaganda purposes. Benton quotes comic artist C.C. Beck as having stated that his superiors demanded he draw "anything to make the Japs look ugly or the Nazis look like punks."[13] Bradford W. Wright's *Comic Book Nation: The Transformation of Youth Culture in America* argues that the heroes and villains that appeared in American comic books during World War II were intended to "unite the American people behind their government for the purpose of waging war." In Wright's view, the foreign enemy was a rather "recent" creation, whereas the enemy before the Second World War, in the years of the Great Depression, had been the rich and the politically corrupt within America.[14] David Hajdu's *The Ten-Cent Plague* offers the view that the appeal of the superhero during the war years was as "a simple, democratic, home-grown symbol of American might and surety of purpose."[15] In *From Krakow to Krypton: Jews and Comic Books*, Arie Kaplan describes the depiction of German brutes and savages as the work of American Jews in the comic book industry of the time (of which there were many, if not an outright majority) who gladly depicted "their alpha-male superheroes sweeping the floor with Nazi spies and saboteurs," not to mention Nazi soldiers and, on more than one occasion, even Hitler himself.[16] Kaplan advances comic book historiography by giving the creations of the Golden Age more of a background rather than merely labeling them as simple answers to unbridled American racism and opportunistic propaganda. *Men of Tomorrow: Geeks, Gangsters and the Birth of the Comic Book* by Gerard Jones follows a similar trend by emphasizing the importance of American Jews to the creation and prosperity of the comic book industry. Jones' work focuses on the personalities (and eccentricities) behind the artist's easel and writer's desk, pointing out how many of the ideas that were floating about in the post–World War I landscape, including fascism, socialism and scientific innovation (as well as eugenics), influenced the mindset, and therefore artistic output, of the earliest comic book creators. It is interesting to note from these works the dual nature inherent in the Jewish creators of the comic book industry — that they were creating works that featured nativist imagery and themes, while at the same time often being themselves targets of nativist sentiments (throughout American history the caricatures of the radical European and covetous, treacherous Jew were interchangeable).

William W. Savage, in *Commies, Cowboys and Jungle Queens: Comic Books and America, 1945–1954* (one of the few works to specifically address comic books published during the Korean and Cold Wars), succeeds, where other works have failed, in assigning comic books a place as a kind of barometer of the confusion facing America after the Second World War. The main problem is that Savage, in using predominately the works of EC Comics (a company, even during the height of its popularity, known to be on the fringe on many levels and to be pushing limits) as the central focus of his discussion of war comics of the 1950s, assigns to the totality of the industry what he finds in the work of a singular company: a terrified, anti-war America who was emasculated and left impotent by the ambiguous nature of the Korean War, in comparison with the more traditional goals of World War II. Savage rightfully credits a great deal of 1950s comics' imagery to uncertainties about changing societal situations occurring at the time, such as divorce rates, but does not really relate such changes to fluctuations in modern American sentiment in regard to nativism and "Americanism."

Works outside of those solely focused on the pulps and comics offer better avenues of analysis as to how anti-foreign sentiments can affect popular printed media. Examples include Sam Moskowitz's *Strange Horizons: The Spectrum of Science Fiction*, which dissects science fiction pulps' relation to everything from anti–Semitism to civil rights, and Sheridan Prasso's *The Asian Mystique—Dragon Ladies, Geisha Girls, and Our Fantasies of the Exotic Orient*, an excellent examination of modern "orientalism." Neither work, however, tackles the object of nativism in pulps and comic books, with Moskowitz's concern being specifically science-fiction magazines, over a particular length of time, nor do they address international relations to any large extent. Prasso's work, brilliant in its analysis of the exotic fetishism that permeates Western preconceptions of the East, does not mention pulp magazines or comic books for the most part; nor should it be expected to, as that is not its purpose. Titles such as these are valuable in that they help the reader "fill in" what the pulp and comic historiographies leave out, but some sort of combination of the two is warranted.

The preceding works of pulp and comic history are not "wrong," and no inference is intended to that effect. There has not been a great deal of academic inquiry concerning the depictions in pulps and comic books of foreigners and wartime enemies, and certainly none that make an effort to connect such imagery to any multifaceted reasons other than simple racism or the needs of American propaganda during wartime. A reason, and a review, that stretches back to the earliest examples of American popular literature, displaying a continuity that extends throughout modern American history, is lacking. This book is an attempt to fill such a void.

An Understanding

> The horrible massacre of foreigners in China has shocked the whole civilized world. An insurrection, attended by unparalleled atrocities has aroused the deepest concern in America and Europe.— Henry Davenport Northrop, *China; the Orient and the Yellow Man* (1900)

In addition to demonstrating what forms nativist and anti-foreign feelings took in pulp magazines and comic books during the previous century, it is hoped that this work also conveys what nativism is exactly, outside of simple racial bias and prejudice. The purpose for bringing to light the following two definitions (neither mutually exclusive but rather overlapping) is to inspire the reader to think about what exactly was going on at a particular moment in history when viewing instances of nativist language or imagery. Southern Nazarene University sociologist and author Brian N. Fry defines nativism as "a collective attempt by self-identified natives to secure or retain prior or exclusive rights to valued resources against the challenges reputedly posed by resident or prospective populations on the basis of their perceived foreignness."[17] In the case of the post–Great War worldview, the "valued resources" can be understood as the very meaning of the term "American" in the face of what appeared to many at the time to be a bombardment of foreign ills and corrosiveness upon the traditional American identity. On the floor of the United States House of Representatives on April 20, 1921, Lucian Walton Parrish of Texas, in arguing for the ratification of new limitations upon immigration into America, pleaded:

> Those who are out of sympathy with our Constitution and the spirit of our government will be here in large numbers, and the true spirit of American-

ism left us by our fathers will gradually become poisoned by this uncertain element.... There can be nothing so dangerous as for us to allow the undesirable foreign element to poison our civilization and thereby threaten the safety of the institutions that our forefathers have established for us.[18]

This understanding—that unmitigated and unassimilated immigration threatened the existence of the Republic—appeared in many forms over the course of the succeeding years. What came about in the wake of such arguments were the "Quota Laws" of the 1920s. The Quota Laws, passed in 1921 and renewed in 1924, placed numerical limits on immigrants allowed into the United States; three percent of a country's immigrant representation in the 1910 American census were allowed into the United States each year, with this percentage being lowered to two, and the census year pushed back to 1890, during the 1924 revision.[19] Such laws only added to earlier anti-immigrant legislation, such as that dating back to the 1870s which deemed Asian immigrants of any nationality "aliens ineligible to citizenship," barring them from becoming naturalized citizens for almost the next one hundred years.[20]

In *A Nation by Design: Immigration Policies in the Fashioning of America*, political scientist Aristide R. Zolberg argues that

> although reaction such as these are attributable in large part to prejudice and xenophobia that tend to exaggerate the problematic aspects of the situation, it should be recognized that the settlement—or prospective settlement—of any substantial group of people whose culture diverges markedly from the hosts' is likely to call the established "cultural compromise" pertaining to religious, linguistic, and racial diversity into question, and hence is a legitimate source of concern.[21]

In Zolberg's understanding, there is a clear demarcation between out-and-out racism and the fear that foreigners will subvert the traditional order of a society. This fear to some degree is "legitimate" only in the sense that change is indeed occurring. "Legitimate" may represent a poor choice of words, as it could be misconstrued as lending credence to nativism instead of its intended purpose: to simply clarify that changes, feared by some, are actually occurring during the time in question. Whether or not the traditional society is truly threatened is more dependent on the person feeling nativist tendencies, and on the level of racism and bigotry already present—something that xenophobia can only exacerbate further.

Applying Fry's and Zolberg's definitions and examinations of nativism to America after the First World War, and the isolationist and anti-foreign sentiment that were a major part of it, two things can be understood, or at least proposed. First, that after the Great War many Americans felt that a valued resource (the American identity and everything connected to it) was being compromised, in large part by the influx of foreigners and foreign ideas; second, that such a fear, while certainly containing elements of racism and xenophobia, cannot be completely defined in such terms. The fear pertaining to the loss of this "valued resource" is, as Zolberg states, somewhat legitimate when it is threatened by new people (or ideas) being introduced to what was once (or imagined to be) a homogenous community. Again, whether anything (or anything worth protecting) was actually threatened is a different question entirely. The fear existed, and that is all that is needed for widespread phobias to spread.

This is not to suggest that early twentieth century racism in America is justified — then or at any point in the nation's history; such a belief runs counter to what a truly democratic society hopes to develop. Nor is it the purpose of this work, when analyzing the changes that occurred in American public opinion regarding race, to suggest that suddenly there was some sort of divine "explosion" of acceptance throughout America that left horrendous stereotypes like Fu Manchu completely disconnected from modern popular culture. What is being suggested, however, is that racism is not adequate enough as a sole explanation for the undeniably racist imagery that appeared during the post-war years in America; nor does an absence of racism completely explain the rescinding of nativist discussions. Only a full understanding of nativism and all of its varied elements provides an attempt at an explanation. Just as Japanese depictions of Americans as apes and barbarians during the Second World War drew on influences beyond a simple need for war propaganda (racism, Japanese-centric origin myths, a history of Western colonialism, repeated attempts to supplant native religions with Christianity, etc.), so too did American nativist imagery draw on several factors in addition to straightforward racism; as nativism, a part of American history since before the nation's founding, is just one aspect of the overall whole. European radicalism, Hunnish barbarism, Bolshevik violence, and Asiatic craftiness — these were the ideologies, centuries-old assumptions, and exaggerated stereotypes that the popular culture of the time used to define the enemy who seemed to be encroaching upon America's "valued resources." The quotation earlier, referring to the "unparalleled atrocities" of China's Boxer Rebellion, is an example of the image many Americans had in their minds concerning Asia, due in large part to a sensationalized press. When combined with uncertainties domestically (only heightened following the Great War and the

Great Depression), the spread of nativist mentalities was almost a certainty. To quote Zolberg again, "[Nationality and nationalism] entails the elaboration of a boundary between 'us' and 'them': thus, we are who we are by virtue of who we are not."[22] The stories found in the popular literature of the time, under close examination, can be shown to elucidate the threats Americans believed to exist in the form of the foreign "other," and Zolberg's emphasis on a question of "religion, linguistic, and racial" differences can be seen in these works. An assessment of the stories found within the pages of America's popular pulp magazines and comic books reveals that, while racism and a tendency to "orientalize" the East certainly had their effects, it was rather the "otherness" of what Americans considered to be inherent in foreigners, and what threats they (supposedly) posed to the American system of values and society, that drove the growth of such caricatures and imagery. So it was not only simply racial prejudice in and of itself that allowed for the spread of nativist popular literature. Such a point is important to make because ascribing nativism to simple racial prejudice is really a misunderstanding of American history, culturally and socially.

INTRODUCTION

A Brief History of American Nativism and Anti-Foreignism

EUROPEAN BRUTES, CATHOLICS AND RADICALS

A (severely) truncated history of nativism in America is in order before reviewing its appearance in pulp magazines and comic books; again, it is stressed that this is a very brief overview, and a much more thorough understanding may be attained through the works listed in the notes (Higham and Curran in particular). Nativism is a problematic term, as it is a combination of several ideologies on the one hand, yet is slightly divergent from all of them on the other. Commonly today, nativism and racism are used interchangeably, which is something of an error; likewise, nationalism and nativism are often substituted one for the other, which is also not quite accurate. Nativism, on many levels, sprang from the combination of both ideologies and other influences. Paradoxically enough, it has also co-existed with a sense of multi-racial egalitarianism and pride that spoke to the United States' self-image as a haven for all.

Nativism did not begin as the racist, predominantly White-supremacist movement that it is usually identified with today. Racism, as an accepted and widespread method of reasoning behind legal discriminations and segregations, did not appear in America until the latter half of the nineteenth century, although it would be in error to disregard America's early ideas concerning race. Benjamin Franklin himself often separated different groups of people by what he considered intrinsic characteristics, such as the "tawny" Asians, and "swarthy" Italians and Russians.[1] Many British colonists and later American citizens approached the Native Americans as uncivil savages, due in part to their pagan beliefs — and the fact that they happened to occupy land that "belonged" to the ever-expanding Anglo-Americans. An illustration from a 1877 children's school book demonstrates the differences between "The Races of Men" (as the image is titled): swarthy, dark colored men (representing Asian, African, Native Americans, and inhabitants of the South Pacific), with cowardly, averted eyes look away from the reader, while an angelic woman, symbolizing the Caucasian race, gazes directly out towards her audience.[2] There was, since the earliest settlers, a belief in some sort of hierarchy of races. An attempt to graft biological and scientific theories onto prejudices that had existed for centuries, and thereby create laws based on them, was a product of later years.

Nativism's original point of demarcation regarding persecution was not race but rather religious and political differences — the strife between Catholicism and Protestantism in particular. Although anti–Catholicism does not feature prominently in this work, it is nonetheless important to note its existence. A sense of anti–Catholic nativism reaches as far back into American history as the nation's existence itself, and even before it. British colonists often found enemies among the Spanish or the French, two Catholic European powers also hoping to attain a foothold in the New World. Within twenty years of its founding, the colony of Massachusetts had enacted laws that made it extremely difficult for anyone that could not be classified as a Puritan to settle in its lands.[3] Despite an eventual break with Britain, the colonies, and later United States, of America were mostly Protestant and still held reservations towards minority faiths, specifically Catholics, in their midst. The earliest recognized, organized nativist movement that attained national and political prominence was that of the Know-Nothings (invariably known as the American Republican Party or the Native American Party, depending on the region), which set its sights first on Catholics (mainly the Irish) but later expanded its range of persecutions to other groups. Appropriating age-old stereotypes and rhetoric, the Know-Nothings spread propaganda predicting a Catholic takeover of America, slandering the Pope as an Old World despot biding his time until his minions in America rose up to destroy the Republic. Despite winning numerous seats in state and national elections (including several governorships), the Know-Nothings fizzled out after a few years of existence, while their nativist message persisted.

Anti-Catholicism remained a staple of nativist thought following the Know-Nothings, but was soon joined by an anti-radical fervor that targeted immigrants from Eastern Europe who hailed from those kingdoms most associated at the time with revolutionaries and anarchists. The revolutions that rocked Europe in 1848, the Paris Commune of 1871, and other attempts at socialist reconstructions of society fueled anti-radical rhetoric. Recent events on the home front also seemed to offer evidence of the uncivilized nature of the Eastern European "barbarians." The Haymarket Affair of 1886, wherein a number of anarchists were charged with (and executed for) participating in a public bombing that killed several police officers; the attempted assassination of Carnegie lieutenant Henry Clay Frick by anarchist (and Emma Goldman intimate) Alexander Berkman; and the murder of President McKinley by anarchist sympathizer Leon Colgzoz all (among others) cemented the late nineteenth and early twentieth centuries as a home for anti-radical nativism. The anti-radical version of nativism actually fit quite well with the established anti–Catholic view; both socialist radicals and stereotypical Catholic myrmidons were regarded as violent, barbarous holdovers of Old Europe, incapable of understanding democratic institutions and determined to plunge America, if not the entire globe, into another dark age under the rule of foreign, unequivocally un-modern tyrants. Since the two are inextricably intertwined throughout the better part of American history, the anti-radical/communist/anarchist strain of nativism will be combined with the anti–European (Eastern in particular) strain for the purposes of this work. The belief in one automatically assumes the belief in the other, creating a system of circular logic that makes the two inseparable. Why were radicals not to be trusted? Because they were violent, barbarous Europeans with no understanding of republican values. Why did they not understand republican values? Because they were atheistic radicals bent on destroying civilization who could not be trusted. The anti-radical/anti–Eastern European agenda of nativists was realized through the various laws introduced over decades that curbed immigrants from particular European countries, as well as the Red Scare of the early 1920s.

The Heathen Orientals

Owing to fears of inexpensive labor and pagan rituals, along with a distrust and lack of understanding that has permeated Western interactions with the East for centuries, immigrants from Asia also bore the brunt of nativist attacks throughout American history, beginning in the mid-nineteenth century. Chinese immigrants suffered the most from this, although all Asiatics, at one time or another and for one reason or another, were also victims.

For more than half a century following the founding of the Republic, Chinese immigration to America could barely be called even a trickle, with

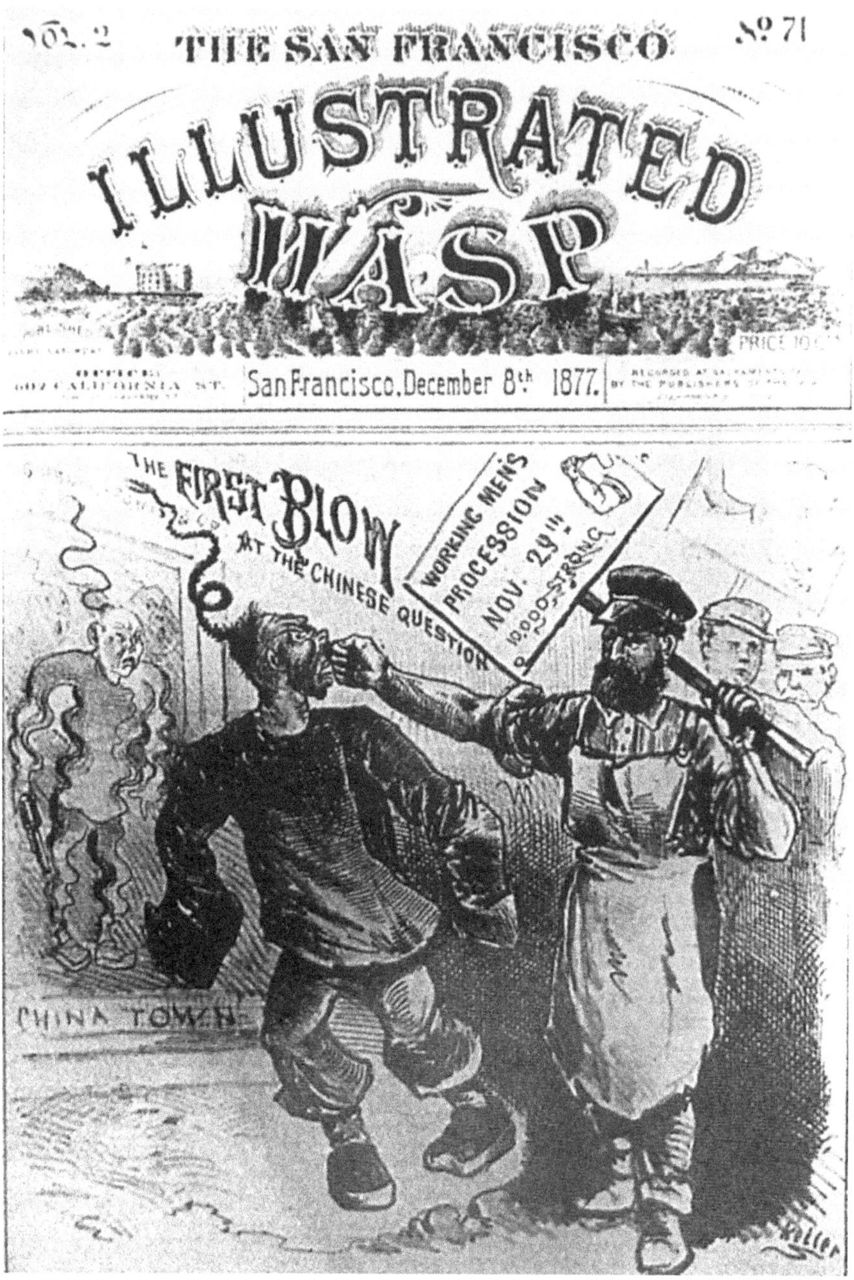

Ever since the first Chinese immigrants arrived, many in America saw their presence as a threat to American labor (from Philip P. Choy, Lorraine Dong, and Marlon K. Hon's *The Coming Man—19th Century American Perceptions of the Chinese*).

literally only a handful of émigrés appearing in official records of the time; these numbers, however, heightened quickly following the onset of the California Gold Rush in 1848, and a flood of Chinese laborers poured into the southwest. While the Gold Rush was a major impetus, it is important to note that this general time period was a point of convergence for several events in Chinese history that spurred emigration, such as the failure of the Qing Dynasty in the Opium Wars with Britain, and the political, economic and agricultural instability brought on by the Taiping and Nien Rebellions.[4] Almost as soon as they arrived in the American Southwest, Chinese immigrants were reviled by a predominantly White workforce, due particularly to their willingness to work for lower wages and endure longer, more strenuous hours than others. Labor unions targeted the Chinese as a central threat to the American workforce; the Knights of Labor, one of the most powerful unions of the late nineteenth century, specifically barred Chinese from membership.[5] Despite the Burlingame Treaty of 1868, which provided for an amicable understating between China and the United States in regards to immigration, numerous bills, laws and taxes were proposed or enacted in various states with the sole purpose of discouraging the immigration of Chinese laborers to America. The Chinese "coolie" became a favorite target for any politician or periodical seeking to assign blame for this sit-

A late nineteenth century publication showcasing several stereotypes of the "exotic" East (*Aladdin or the Wonderful Lamp*, 1889).

uation or that circumstance, particularly during the severe economic downturns that wracked the nation near the end of the century. Following an economic panic in Austria that rapidly spread across the Atlantic, the boom in industry that had defined post–Civil War America halted abruptly during the Panic of 1873. Multitudes of Americans suddenly found themselves thrown out of work, while the hard-working, lower-wage "Joe Chinaman" was always readily available for employment. If White America saw a threat in Chinese immigrants prior to the Panic, such animosity was only heightened by the onset of financial depression.

The Page Act of 1875 further restricted the flow of immigrants from the East, and the Angell Treaty of 1880 undermined the good will brought by Burlingame (which was written at a time of economic prosperity, when railroad barons lusted after the inexpensive Chinese labor workforce) by suggesting possible limits that could be placed on the supposedly free immigration promised in 1868.[6] Such legislation was only a precursor to one of the most un–American, most nativist-inspired works of legislation ever to pass the American Congress — the Chinese Exclusion Act of 1882, which stipulated

> that from and after the expiration of ninety days next after the passage of this act, and until the expiration of ten years next after the passage of this act, the coming of Chinese laborers to the United States be, and the same is hereby, suspended; and during such suspension it shall not be lawful for any Chinese laborer to come, or, having so come after the expiration of said ninety days, to remain within the United States.[7]

After decades of attempts, nativist sympathies won out at the federal level, and the first ban on a particular race and nationality emerged. The Exclusion Act seemed to achieve its intended purpose — the curtailing of Chinese immigration into the United States. According to Census records, the number of Chinese in America went from 89,863 in 1900 down to 61,688 in 1920 — a difference of almost 30,000.[8] While the difference could be attributed to other factors, including more Chinese immigrating illegally to circumvent the Act, sustained drops in the number of Chinese immigrants in the following years speaks to the effectiveness of the policy. In time, successive laws were passed that extended the initial ten year moratorium indefinitely.[9] While nativists had succeeded in stemming the tide of (legal) immigrants, there were still thousands of Chinese (naturalized and otherwise) that had arrived prior to 1882, and attacks on them continued, regardless of the Exclusion Law. In 1885 a mob of White workers, spurred on by the vitriolic urgings of a local labor leader, attacked Chinese settlers in a coal-mining community, killing 15 residents and causing thousands of dollars' worth of damages; the involvement of the Knights of Labor was suspected but never definitively proven.[10] Anti-Chinese violence and sentiments continued into the twentieth century, particularly following the attacks on American citizens and missionaries during the Boxer Rebellion of 1898–1901; pamphlets, periodicals, books, and religious treatises were printed explaining the depravity of the "heathen Chinese." One example:

> In one of China's remote provinces, John Brooks, a missionary, fell into the hands of the Boxers and was subjected to peculiar tortures.... Knives in hand, they stood over him and taunted him. They waved their weapons and laughed at him, circling about him like vultures, sprung upon him from different directions. They then stabbed him until he fell dead when they cut off his head and bore it back to their companions in triumph.[11]

Social and reform issues began to dominate the "Chinese question" in the early 1900s. Popular magazines and literature propagated the squalid, crime-ridden, opium addict–infested Chinatowns of New York, San Francisco and other American cities, perpetuating the idea of the Chinese as something wholly unfamiliar and un–American. "Mott Streets," Pell Streets," and "the Mongolian Quarter" became the only descriptors necessary to describe locales of depravity and vice.

Ultra-Nationalism, Darwinian Survival and Racism

A second major economic depression that struck America in the early 1890s produced a resurgence in anti-immigrant opinions (against Europeans and Asians alike), with underemployed and disillusioned Americans blaming their ills on new arrivals, whether the accusation was job theft or radical subversion. Hard economic times have always brought out the most nativist of American voices, and obviously the nineteenth century was no different. This anti-immigrant sentiment in turn helped introduce a new component to American nativism: that of ultra-nationalism or jingoism. There was a concerted effort on the parts of many Americans to trace their lineage back to the "original" Americans of the Thirteen Colonies in an attempt to substantiate their credentials as "real" Americans; it was during this period that groups dedicated to preserving ancestral testimonials, such as the Sons of the American Revolution and the United Daughters of the Confederacy, were formed. Groups that were unabashedly nativist in their messages and actions, such as the American Protective Association, the Loyal Knights of America, and the American Patriotic League, also

During the Boxer Uprising, many reports appeared in America describing the chaos and bloodshed of the event (cover of *Massacres of Christians by Heathen Chinese and Horrors of the Boxers*, 1900).

appeared. Warhawks were to be found rallying behind every international situation wherein American prestige was seemingly threatened. America flirted with going to war with several nations, including Britain, at the height of jingoistic fervor — for reasons that would be considered rather trivial today; in other cases, such as America's conflict with Spain, jingoism won out.[12]

This ultra-nationalism also encouraged America's acquisition of foreign colonies and territories in the late 1890s. The American overthrow of Queen Liliuokalani and subsequent annexation of the Hawaiian Islands was praised as a civilizing act on the part of the Republic. America's occupation of Cuba and other Caribbean lands was understood to be an aspect of "the White Man's Burden"— the responsibility of the Anglo-Saxon to bring civility and modernity to his "little brown brothers," whether the "brothers" asked for it or not. Cultural and ideological exports were seen as the most important gift America could offer, and the East (and China in particular) seemed ripe for the implantation of American Anglo-Saxon systems of belief, government, and daily life — at the expense of the indigenous, "uncivilized" cultures. Economic imperialism was another factor of this jingoistic push for American dominance abroad, with President Theodore Roosevelt emphasizing the importance of spreading American monetary influence further — into the very heart of China — during his first State of the Union address to Congress.[13] The belief in an American people that were responsible for bringing civilization to those lacking was bound to create, and bolster, any ideas that attempted to scientifically prove such an elevated status.

As the twentieth century dawned, an inherent distrust of foreigners, combined with ardent nationalism, was soon coupled with Darwinian theories concerning competition and species survival, wherein "species" was often substituted with "race" when speaking of human beings. The notion that the Anglo-Saxon was the pinnacle of human existence had existed for quite some time, but the infusion of Darwinian competition brought the racist aspect of nativism into play. This was the period during which "race" attained a meaning that it had not, for the most part, held previously — that of a proven, scientific and biological demarcation between one species of human being and another. Everything that had been "wrong" with the foreigner (circumstances ranging from physical to cultural to religious dissimilarities) could now be explained as the product of deficient genetics and "backwardness" on the part of that race as a whole. The Eastern European was bent on revolution because he hailed from a racially-inferior branch of the human family tree that simply was not capable of learning anything beyond brute force and violence. Likewise, all the negatives attributed to Asians, from criminality to deceit to devil-worship, could now be traced to defects genetically inherent in the race. All other victims of discrimination, from African Americans to Jews to any other ethnic or religious minority, were branded as an utterly distinct strain of humanity that served only as competition for Anglo-Saxon hegemony and even survival.

This multi-faceted nativism (composed of anti-radical, anti–Eastern European, and racist tendencies, among others) grew in the early twentieth century, then subsided somewhat during America's involvement in the First World War (although German-Americans still faced a nativist backlash), only to return, reinvigorated, following the war's end. This work covers, via the pulp fiction magazines and comic books of the time, this reinvigoration of nativism in America after World War I, and the changes in its strength and message during the ensuing years.

Paradoxically, throughout American nativist history there were periods during which the phenomena lessened in strength and popularity, and at times was acknowledged for the prejudice it propagated. Between the end of the American Civil War and the economic depression of the 1890s, when productivity and industry were flourishing, many championed immigration not only as proof of the Statue of Liberty's claim to the tired, poor and huddled masses of Old Europe, but also as an impetus for the creation of an "American race." The new American man was to be an amalgamation of the best qualities of a variety of immigrants (Asians, however, were still often removed from this "melting pot"), who would lead the rest of the world into enlightenment, civilization, and peace. Prominent industry leaders and financiers who were largely responsible for much of America's prosperity and cultural growth throughout the late nineteenth and early twentieth centuries, such as Andrew Carnegie and Joseph Pulitzer, were immigrants (from Scotland and Germany, respectively). Among the many nativist groups that formed during the height of American jingoism at the close of the nineteenth century were also some patriotic societies (although not as large as those fervently nativist, and usually isolated to specific regions) that appealed to the concept of the "new American man" and welcomed all races and ethnicities, regardless of nation of birth. One such group was the Order of the Little Red School House, formed in 1895, which demanded only loyalty to the United States from its members: "The Order welcomed all, whether American or alien, black or white, Jew or Gentile, Catholic or Mohammedan, if they could 'stand shoulder to shoulder with us and take our solemn oath.' Devotion to the American flag and American institutions was to characterize its demand of applicants."[14] There were voices, such as the following in the popular magazine *The Outlook* (August 18, 1906), that protested the "Americanization" programs that were intended to replace immigrants' cultural and ethnic heritages with "100 percent Americanism":

> The newcomers bring with them a rich variety of gifts. Someone has said that the greatest country will be the one containing the greatest possible differences compatible with unity.... Indeed, one of the special dangers of the present moment is that we may rush a superficial Americanizing process so fast that much of value be lost.... Despising one's forefathers is not a strong foundation on which to build up good citizenship,

and the boy who says with flashing eyes that Ziska was the George Washington of Bohemia has a good deal better chance of understanding what George Washington really stood for than his schoolmate whose conceptions include nothing broader than a flashy, pretentious Americanism.[15]

After the Boxer Rebellion and the posting of American troops in Peking at the turn of the century, many newspapers and periodicals created permanent offices in the Far East, allowing for (relatively) more objective and less vituperative information concerning China and the Chinese to be disseminated in the States.[16] The outcome of the 1904–1905 Russo-Japanese War also provided for the expansion of American media outlets in the East, in addition to shifting the image of the threatening Asiatic enemy from China to Japan. Owing in part to, as well as helping to further, a shift in attitudes towards China was a renewed sense of romanticism on the part of American businessmen and politicians, who saw the Qing Empire as a gateway to an untapped potential trade bonanza — the teeming millions that previously had threatened American industry were, at times, viewed as a near-guarantee of its future success. Even as businessmen greedily eyed the potential market in China, such ventures unquestionably also brought doctors, missionaries and others who attempted to better the lives of the kingdom's inhabitants — not out of some distorted notion of national or ethnic superiority, but out of the simple human desire to help others. The notion of the welcome immigrant, arriving to help broaden America's horizons and create a new, amalgamated American man, as well as ideas of international brotherhood, appeared mostly in good times, with nativism rising to its highest peaks during the bad times. This paradoxical dichotomy between disdain and acceptance is important to this work, and invaluable to an understanding of American nativist history as a whole.

The Mediums and Their Roles in Nativism

The pulp magazines, so named for the cheap pulpwood paper on which they were printed, were the descendents of the nineteenth century's popular youth literature and dime novels, and continued their tradition with tales of adventure and excitement, while also crossing over into a wider spectrum of genres, including romance, western, horror, war, and science fiction. The pulps' heyday was in the years immediately prior to and following the First World War; their success as cheap, popular fiction began to diminish in the early 1940s due to the rising popularity of comic books, the availability of inexpensive paperback novels, the ever-growing motion picture audience, and other avenues of entertainment.

One of the most common "foreign" threats to be found in this popular literature is that of the "yellow peril"—the fear of the ancient Far East, envisioned as an eternal puzzle to the Westerner. Many pulp magazines, such as *The Shadow, Oriental Stories, Adventure* and others, featured images reflecting the yellow peril theme on the covers of their inaugural issue, demonstrating the popularity of such stories. Any publisher betting a great deal of capital on the success of a new publication would have started with a genre among the highest in commercial appeal. There were other titles, such as *Oriental Tales*, whose contents catered solely to tales of the exotic East. The "otherworldliness" of the Orient is what many popular literature authors fostered in the minds of their readers. While pulp magazines and other media of the day certainly, and somewhat unsurprisingly, depicted either Europeans generally or Germans in particular as villains, such caricatures were not as exaggerated and loaded with racial imagery as the yellow peril (possibly due to white America's aversion to depicting someone so similar racially in a negative light, despite past aggressions), and were, for the most part, found in only two roles: German spy and/or soldier, or the European radical. The return of the brutish "Hun," depicted in countless American propaganda posters from World War I, would occur, for the most part, only with the rise of fascist Germany in the mid–1930s, a period to be examined in Chapter II. For reasons that are probably more racial in nature than anything else, Anglo-America did not harbor the level of disgust and hatred for the White German as it did the "Oriental." The most common avenue of discrimination concerning "undesirable" Europeans came in the form of ideological differences; "reds," "anarchists," and "socialists" defined the majority of characters of Central and Eastern European descent. Whether from the eastern edges of Germany or the shores of Vladivostok, the Eastern European's "otherness" was due to his radical agenda, which was only augmented further by his often brutish nature and appearance. The fact that Asian characters were defined, more often than not, by their physical differences from Caucasians is important to note when examining the popular depictions of the "Oriental" and the European "savage."

To begin an analysis of this nativism one should start with the pulp and comic books' predecessors, the dime novels of the mid-to-late nineteenth century. As with their successors, the dime novels contained nativist imagery that was influenced by recent events, both foreign and domestic. There appears in the dime novels nativist imagery unarguably virulent and discriminatory, but still not as augmented by xenophobia as the popular fiction after the Great War. As the pulps would be influenced by events such as the Chinese gang wars of the early 1900s and the ongoing Chinese Civil War, the dime novels were influenced by contemporary events such as the fate of missionaries when traveling to Asia, or memories of the Taiping Rebellion. The Boxer Rebellion in particular was one event which managed to affect the image of the East for decades and prejudiced imagery that appeared from the dime novels of the 1900s to the pulps of the 1940s.

Similarly, the manner in which Bolshevism and the rise of Nazism influenced the pulps and comic books, the activities of radical groups throughout Eastern Europe, and the "anarchist scare" here in America in the early 1900s adversely affected the image of Europeans in dime novels and story papers. Beliefs in biological factors determining racial superiority (while being dismissed by many actual experts in their fields) were also prevalent and popular at the time; works claiming to explain the nature of such "race-hierarchies" sold quite well in the early twentieth century and would not be largely dismissed until years later. The centuries-long fascination with an exotic and "orientalized" Far East also contributed to American interpretations of the Ori-

In both popular literature and the news of the day, the Boxer Rebellion (or Uprising) was seen as an assault upon civilization itself (from Philip P. Choy, Lorraine Dong, and Marlon K. Hon's *The Coming Man—19th Century American Perceptions of the Chinese*).

In both the popular Wild West of the imagination and actual reality, the Chinese laborer was seen as enemy to "forty-niner" and cowboy alike (*The Nugget Library* No. 111, September 17, 1891).

ent. Decades — in some cases centuries — old notions concerning racial hierarchies; the spread of information regarding "transgressions" against White civilization on the part of other ethnic groups; and the human tendency to fear what is different to the point of absurdity all combined to form nativist sentiments alongside racism in its most basic form.

Taking note of how far back such representations reach serves to establish continuity, in both imagery and the possible reasons for such imagery, as well as to better show the change, gradual as it may be, in popular American thinking that eventually would cast disapproval upon such depictions. Further descriptions and new avenues of nativist imagery will appear as the chapters proceed; for now, establishing a history for such images is required. For this section and Chapter I, the nativist reaction to Asians will feature heavily, while attacks on the "undesirable" populations of Europe will wait until Chapters II and III. The fact that I have chosen to focus on the yellow peril when speaking of the pulps should not suggest that other symptoms of nativism were absent from them, but rather that the yellow peril, in my research, was the most predominant form of nativism to appear in such works. One of the most difficult aspects of attempting a work such as this is the multitude of sources available, and, consequently, the number of those that must be excluded for lack of space. It is important for the reader to keep in mind that all of the examples offered throughout this book are just that — examples of a much larger whole. The number of titles that feature "saffron devils," "Teutonic monsters," or "godless anarchists" is simply staggering. For every story or piece of art that is mentioned, it is no exaggeration to imagine that there are dozens upon dozens of similar items contributing to the sheer magnitude of pulps and comic books that carry the narrative of American nativist sentiment. It is also critical to note that some genres factor into a discussion of this nature more than others; stories of action, adventure and even science fiction featured anti-immigrant prejudices more often than other fields, such as romance, westerns, or sports. Such titles are just as important to the overall history of popular literature, and feature nativist imagery themselves, but do not necessarily warrant a great deal of attention regarding the topics discussed here. As a result, adventure, science fiction, detective and weird fiction titles comprise the majority of sources cited in this work.

Dime Novels and Story Papers

> Great God! It is terrible to think of that pure girl in the power of that yellow devil. — *The Nugget Library* No. 146 (March 24, 1892)

"Dime novel" is something of a problematic term, as it is usually used to denote any cheap literature printed around the turn of the last century, while, technically, there were several different media formats in which this literature appeared. Aside from the dime novel proper, as popularized by Beadle and Adams and imitated by others decades afterwards, there were the story papers and weekly juvenile fiction titles. Usually containing tales of virtuous young Americans overcoming near-insurmountable odds — and generally becoming rich in the process — juvenile fiction was a booming industry in the later half of the nineteenth century (Frank Munsey's *Argosy* began its existence as a juvenile literature paper prior to its 1896 conversion into the first pulp magazine). For the sake of consistency, the entire cheap literature of the time will be referenced as "dime novels," though if a source is a story paper or juvenile fiction or anything else, it will be duly noted.

The dime novel has its origins in a 128-page, 6 × 4 inch publication entitled *Malaeska, the Indian Wife of the White Hunter*, dated June 9, 1860, and published by the Beadle and Adams Co. under the headline of *Beadle's Dime Novels—The Choicest Works of the Most Popular Authors*. Written by Ann Sophia Winterbotham Stephens, a popular name in magazines of the day, *Malaeska* was originally serialized in the periodical *Ladies Companion* and was purchased for the first issue of their new publication by Erastus and Irwin Beadle, two young printers who had recently found a partner in Irwin's friend, Robert Adams.[17] *Malaeska* was an instant success and led to decades' worth of *Beadle's Dime Novel* installments, as well as other publications by the trio—*Pocket Novels, Boy's Library of Sport, Story and Adventure, American Tales, New Dime Novels, Dime Library, 20-Cent Novels*, and others. More importantly, a host of imitators appeared within months of *Malaeska*'s release. *Ten Cent Novelettes*, by Elliot, Thomas and Talbot; *DeWitt's Ten Cent Romances*, published by Robert M. DeWitt; and the Richmond Company's *Richmond Novels* were among the numerous imitators to appear. And with their appearance an industry was born. Just as was the case with later inexpensive "peoples'" literature, the dime novels since their inception were attacked as "trash" and accused of corrupting young minds with fancies of danger and adventurism.

It is extremely important, especially for the purposes of this work, to note that nativism appears in inexpensive American literature at the very birth of the medium itself, with *Malaeska*. As ridiculous as it may be for descendants of European settlers in America to feel "nativism" in regards to Native Americans, such feelings are nativistic in the most basic sense that it promotes Christian and American (and, to some degree, white) characteristics over all else. Furthermore, it is a nativism that is contrasted with a sense of tolerance and of tragedy brought on by prejudice and discrimination. This dual nature of nativism in *Malaeska* acts almost as a harbinger of the conversation the dime novel and its successors would unintentionally carry on regarding the evolution of modern ideals of American racial tolerance and multiculturalism.

As the title implies, Malaeska is the wife of a Caucasian hunter—William Danforth, who has married the local chief's daughter and settled in New York's Catskill Mountains. Malaeska is described in vivid detail and given an attractive appearance that seems to betray the mentality towards Native Americans prevalent in most tales of the Wild West:

> A young Indian girl was sitting on a pile of furs at the opposite extremity. She wore no paint—her cheek was round and smooth, and large gazelle-like eyes gave a soft brilliancy to her countenance, beautiful beyond

expression. Her dress was a robe of dark chintz, open at the throat, and confined at the waist by a narrow belt of wampum, which, with the bead bracelets on her naked arms, and the embroidered moccasins laced over her feet, was the only Indian ornament about her. Even her hair, which all of her tribe wore laden with ornaments, and hanging down the back, was braided and wreathed in raven bands over her smooth forehead. [She spoke], in a sweet, mellow voice....[18]

A great amount of affinity is expressed between both Malaeska and her white husband, as well as between the parents and their newborn boy, a child of mixed ancestry whom the father expects great things from in the future. Unfortunately, he will not live long enough to see his son mature, as Danforth is killed while hunting, and Malaeska is left a widow. Malaeska and the child are never truly accepted by Caucasian society nor by her tribe, and she remains a widow, dedicated to the memory of her husband until her death.

The attitudes towards Native Americans created by an Anglo-centric worldview are obvious throughout the narrative by the stereotypical "You White Man, Me Indian" manner of speech Malaeska and others use in the novel, as well as the "barbarous" treatment she receives at the hands of her own kind. One of the tragedies of the tale the author impresses upon her readers is that Malaeska's husband died before teaching her the ways of Christianity, damning her to an uncivilized and pagan existence. And certainly the penultimate event of the novel is evidence of the view concerning the relation between the "Other" and Caucasians of the time: the death of William Danforth, Jr., who had been told of his parents' supposed death by his "handmaid" Malaeska and, upon discovering his mixed ancestry, commits suicide rather than live with "tainted" blood. There are, however, minute kernels of racial co-existence and tolerance that appear within the story that seems to counter-balance such racial prejudice, such as the love shared between the elder Danforth and his wife. Malaeska's ongoing sacrifices and deep love for her son are a focus of the novel, with Malaeska obviously intended to be the most sympathetic figure in the story. Her last scenes are written to evoke the most emotion from the reader. The secondary emotional "heartstring" to be plucked is the poignant loss suffered by Danforth Jr.'s Caucasian bride following his suicide. This "back and forth" between revulsion and sympathy appears throughout the popular American literature of the nineteenth and early twentieth century, and represents the change that would occur over the years, both in the literature itself and in the greater American mindset.

The second predominant form of published escapism of the time, the story papers, were among the most popular of inexpensive American literature. Usually printed on newsprint and costing between five and ten cents, these weekly periodicals often featured a short novel (sometimes in addition to several smaller novelettes and serials), with either new, unrelated stories appearing each issue or a recurring character (frequently also credited as the author) starring in multiple issues. The story papers grew out of the serialized fiction appearing in many city newspapers in the early-to-mid-nineteenth century; with a rise in literacy brought about by public education and a rise in circulation due to new, cheaper postage regulations, the fiction sections of these newspapers eventually became their own stand-alone titles.[19] Many story papers, such as *Frank Leslie's Boys and Girls Weekly* (1866), *Golden Hours* (1869), *Golden Days* (1880) and *The Golden Argosy* (1882), were aimed at juvenile audiences and contained "up by your own bootstraps" tales and adventure yarns by the likes of Horatio Alger, Jr., Edward S. Ellis, Oliver Optic, and Harry Castlemon, while other titles could be enjoyed by readers of all ages. *Tip Top Weekly* featured the adventures of young all–American Frank Merriwell; Motor Matt appeared, surprisingly enough, in *Motor Stories*; and *Secret Service* chronicled the adventures of those New York sleuths Old and Young King Brady. As is to be expected, all of these feature characters exemplify the Anglo-American ideal. Merriwell is a young, attractive and educated socialite whose adventures usually revolve around his mastery of collegiate sports; and the Bradys are detectives of Holmsian ability, able to temporarily "downgrade" themselves via disguises in order to meet their nefarious (often foreign-born) enemies in their own environs. Actually, it is quite fair to say that the Bradys battled "heathen Orientals" far more often than any other group in their stories. As has been demonstrated via *Malaeska*, nativism in literature-for-the-masses appeared with the birth of the industry itself; while the original dichotomy was between Native American and White settlers in Wild West tales, the growth of multi-ethnic communities near the end of the century gradually shifted the spotlight to encounters between Americans and those representing the most recent of immigrants to appear in larger numbers—Central and Eastern Europeans, and especially Asians.

The first "yellow emperor" character, the first of many whose characteristics would come to be embodied in Sax Rohmer's Fu Manchu decades later, made his appearance in the pages of an American story paper, in the burgeoning genre of science fiction long before it was ever called science fiction. In the February 11, 1892 (No. 134), edition of *The Nugget*

Library there appeared the story "Tom Edison, Jr.'s Electric Sea Spider: or, the Wizard of the Submarine World" by Philip Reade, a writer credited with helping to popularize early science fiction in America. This short story is part of a genre popular at the time now referred to as *edisonades*, in which incredible (often ridiculous) exploits were credited to Thomas Edison himself, a distant relative, or someone else who was obviously modeled after the Wizard of Menlo Park. "Electric Sea Spider" features the young inventor matching wits with a devilish pirate of the Pacific Ocean, a mastermind who has created his own submersible weapon of war. Kiang Ho of the Golden Belt, who was "educated and trained in American universities [and] has terrorized the world's shipping with the Sea Serpent, a submersible vessel," has also affronted American sovereignty by taking several American sailors hostage. The jingoistic temperament emerging in America at the time is apparent, as is the suggestion of a racial antagonism between White America and "Yellow" China. "The Chinese are advancing rapidly in the arts of warfare, and it will not be long ere they take a leading part in such matters," the narrator of the tale explains. "It is not generally known that in several things they have even outdone our own proud America, and Captain Tom is to find this out to his cost."[20] It

The first appearance of a "yellow emperor" in American popular literature — "Tom Edison, Jr.'s Electric Sea Spider: or, the Wizard of the Submarine World" (*The Nugget Library* No. 134, February 11, 1892).

is only the Boy Genius Edison Jr., and his multi-legged, ocean-floor-crawling Sea Spider who can liberate the American captives, which he readily accomplishes, managing to kill Kiang Ho in the process as well. This early "yellow emperor" tale is important for a variety of reasons; not only does it feature the first appearance of a Fu Manchu–like archetype in popular American fiction, but it also presents two plot points that would continue to reappear in the coming years — the fear that "Asiatics" would somehow be "educated and trained" in the use of modern (i.e., Anglo-American) technology and, in turn, use it to overthrow Anglo-Saxon hegemony; and the notion of an intrinsic, natural antagonism between the two racial groups themselves. Tom Edison, Jr.'s liberation of captured Yankee sailors, representing the preservation of White freedom in the face of an Asiatic Horde, is a theme that will appear time and time again in future works. The fact that such a story as "Electric Sea Spider" appeared at a time when fears of Chinese immigration into America, and its effect on American labor, was at a height is not a coincidence.

The story papers did not only feature Asian villains of Kiang Ho's technological capabilities; the stereotypical "coolie" and "opium fiend" characters would appear more often than those of Kiang Ho's stature. Tom Edison, Jr., had, among other supporting characters, his Chinese cook and manservant, Chang Bang, who spoke in stereotypical "Engrish": "'Ugh!' exclaimed Chang Bang, with a Celestial shiver, while peeping into the great camp-kettle that he was getting to boil. 'Melican man's torpedoes no good for John Chinaman. Makee one think of helle fire!'"[21] *The Nugget Library* No. 146 (March 24, 1892) told the tale of "Dick Ferret — Detective, and the Opium Fiends; or Saved from a Terrible Fate," written by A. L. Pinkerton. This short story centers upon the kidnapping of a young white girl at the hands of a notorious opium den owner named Chu Yon, who (through Chinese craftiness) lured the child into his trap under the guise of wanting to attend her Bible study classes. Only fifteen pages of small type, the tale wraps up rather quickly, with Dick Ferret and his city-wide band of agents using disguises and brute force to expose Chinatown's underbelly, and return the victim to the waiting arms of her uncle and, more importantly, White society. The notion that White purity may be tainted by contact with Asian captors is inherent in the plot: "He knew that Ethel were a prisoner in some of the dens of the city," the author informs the reader concerning the distraught uncle's mindset, "subject to the insults and barbarity of Chu Yon and his gang of yellow-faced devils."[22] The captive niece pleads with Chu Yon to be released — not into the streets or into open society, but specifically into the protection of her own race. The Chinese and Caucasians of the story are described as worlds apart; Dick Ferret is youthful, lean, agile, and the very ideal of Western virility, while the Chinese are all devious, lustful and physically weak, to the point of Chu Yon actually being physically pummeled in the story's conclusion — not by Ferret but by a teenage girl. The adventures of Old and Young King Brady, as featured in the story paper *Secret Service*, repeatedly dealt with the criminality that was seemingly inherent among those of Asian descent. Stories such as "Ching Foo, the Yellow Dwarf; or the Bradys and the Opium Smokers" (No. 66, April 27, 1900) and "The Bradys and

The ever-present opium fiends of American Chinatowns (*The Nugget Library* No. 146, March 24, 1892).

the Drug Slaves: or, the Yellow Demons of Chinatown" (*Secret Service* No. 157, January 24, 1902) featured stalwart, strapping Anglo-Saxon males battling against Chinese opiate peddlers and users, "the lowest and most depraved specimens of humanity."[23]

Criminality also carried over from the story papers into another form the "dime novels" took — the so-called "thick books" of the early 1900s, which offered between two and three hundred pages of adventure and escapism for ten to fifteen cents a copy. These books were closer in both size and form to modern paperback novels, as opposed to the somewhat flimsy periodicals that had preceded them. Many stalwarts of the story papers and early dime novels, such as Detective Nick Carter and collegiate hero Frank Merriwell, transitioned to this heftier format. In 1907, *Nick Carter's Close Call: or, the Way of the Doomed* featured the Master Detective (apparently not having aged much since his 1882 debut) battling a secret society of "Celestials" and their semi-mute, gargantuan killing machine — a Japanese slave named Kara. Over the course of the story, Carter and his team of sleuths repeatedly don disguises in order to infiltrate the "Tong of the Tailless Dragon" (a group Nick had infiltrated while in China, showcasing his prowess in masquerade) and uncover a plot filled with blackmail, opium smuggling and Chinese murderers-for-hire (or "hatchet-men"). The eponymous character, time and time again, showcases Anglo superiority in rela-

In the popular detective dime novels, to infiltrate a Chinese secret society was almost certainly a death sentence for any Occidental foolish enough to do so (*Nick Carter's Close Call; or the Way of the Doomed*, 1907).

tion to supposed Oriental weakness: "But if he was a giant in strength, so also was Nick Carter. The detective," the author informs us, "had never yet met his match for strength and agility, and he did not believe that he would find it in a Chinaman."[24] Chinese gangs (or tongs) spoke to a long-time stereotype of Asians as criminal, sneaky and subversive, and such depictions would appear for decades to come.

The title character of the Jeff Clayton series of detective novels also regularly featured villains of a "Mongolian" nature. Actually, the Jeff Clayton titles are prime examples of how far collective memories of international events are capable of influencing popular culture.[25] In *Jeff Clayton's Fatal Shot; or, Solving the Great Chinatown Mystery* (1911), Clayton is hired to discover the whereabouts of a priceless pearl, only to be drawn into an international plot of intrigue involving rebellions, secret societies and hatchet-men. The stealing of the pearl is discovered to be part of a plan to reinvigorate a Chinese revolutionary movement and overthrow the Manchurian Qing dynasty. Upon discovering a pair of conspirators, Clayton is informed as to whom he is speaking: "...the Princess Kan-su, of the famous house of Hung-sew-tsenen, the great leader of a great rebellion so many years ago, aiding us to make of our faith, a world religion."[26] Later speaking to one of his detectives, Clayton explains the Princess's impor-

The "Far East" featured prominently in many Christian publications as a land of heathens bereft of Christ's influence (*The New Sabbath Library*, 1898).

tance: "One of her husband's ancestors ran a big insurrection years ago in China.... There is [sic] a lot of Chinamen think her husband's ancestor is the man who should have been Emperor of China."²⁷ The individual to which Clayton refers is undoubtedly an allusion to Hong Xiuquan (or Hung Hsiu-ch'üan in the Wade Giles system of Romanization, used in a majority of works on the Taipings), the founder and spiritual, military, and secular head of state of the Taiping Heavenly Kingdom, a rebellious movement that engulfed Qing China from 1851 to 1864. The Taipings followed a religion created by Hong himself. After several attempts at passing the Confucian civil service exams that would have placed him within the Qing bureaucracy, Hong deliriously fell in and out of consciousness following his most recent failure. Upon awakening, he spoke of dreams wherein the Christian God and Jesus (whom he had learned of via Christian missionary texts given him in the port city of Canton several years prior) explained that he was in fact the second Son of God, younger brother of Jesus, whose mission was to return to Earth and "slay demons" (in his mind, Manchurians) and spread his new religion across the globe.²⁸ What started as a localized, predominantly peasant-supported movement quickly gained legions of followers from all facets of Chinese social and economic strata, creating a state inside China larger than most European nations. The Taipings took the ancient Ming Chinese capitol of Nanking in 1854, proclaiming it as the center of their new, quasi–Christian empire. The kingdom was subdued only after more than a decade of warfare and at least twenty million Chinese dead, making it the bloodiest rebellion in world history. The Taipings were extremely nationalistic (later seen as forebears of both the Kuomintang and Chinese Communist parties), but there was another factor that made them unique, and one which brought them the indignation of the West: their religion. What was first hailed as a Christian rebellion in "heathen" China was soon understood upon closer inspection to be a bastardization of Christianity, a melding of Confucianism, Taoism, Christianity and other belief systems that was intolerable to the West. It was in large part due to Western support that the beleaguered Qing eventually suppressed the Taipings. Scores of reports from the West, both during and after the war, blasted the rebels for their "demonic" understanding of Christianity. The fact that a rebellion, one that brought such an affront to Christendom, was linked to the villains of an early twentieth century dime novel is significant; it shows yet another instance, as would be the case with the Boxer Rebellion and other events, in which Americans looked back to previous (perceived) attacks on their traditional beliefs as a manner of justification for any demonizing of Asians that appeared in popular culture. The foreign enemy in Jeff Clayton's case is made even more evil by her association with a movement that, in Western minds, made an abomination out of the Christian faith. In a manner similar to the indignation expressed over the killing of Westerners during the Boxer Rebellion, memories of the Taiping Rebellion were able to exert considerable influence over the outrage felt by Americans in relation to the movement's "misappropriation" of traditional American beliefs. A presumed assault on Christianity was not entirely forgotten even forty years after the movement's collapse.

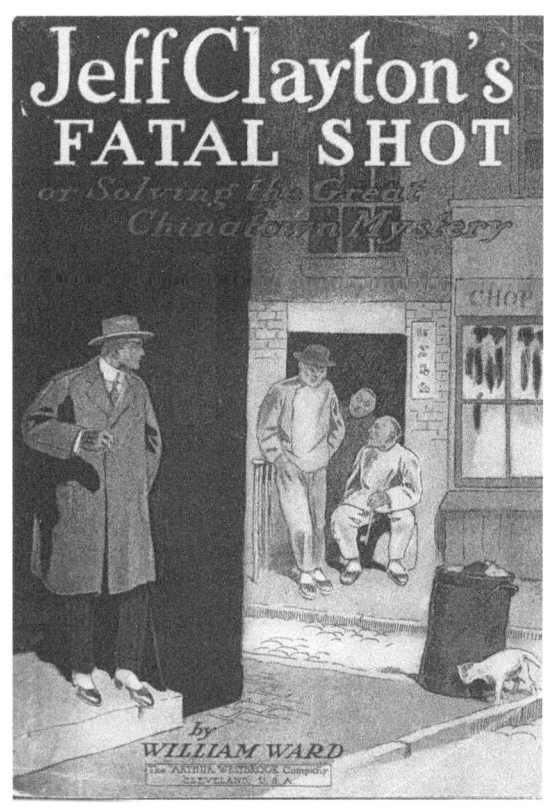

American Chinatowns, regardless of location, were often depicted as nothing more than hives of scum and villainy (*Jeff Clayton's Fatal Shot; or Solving the Great Chinatown Mystery*, 1911).

What should be apparent following this rather short overview of nativism in dime novels and story papers is that there are three main avenues such depictions take to further demonize (and separate White America from) immigrants of Asian descent. First, the supposed predisposition of Asians toward criminal activity is emphasized, whether it is in regards to assassinations, opium smuggling, or their widespread illicit enterprises facilitated by numerous Chinese secret societies. Nick Carter encounters a "mob of fanatically excited Celestials" after being discovered as an infiltrator during a meeting of Chinese gangsters. "Death, death, death, to the white-skinned enemy of the cause!" they shout as they chase the detective through the streets of Chinatown. Whether in New York or San Francisco, Chinatowns in dime novels, pulps, and comics are always depicted as the seediest places possible, inhabited only by thieves, cutthroats and scum. "If there is a hellhole on earth, Chinatown is that place," Dick Ferret explains to a client. "It swarms with murderers and thieves of every grade. There the law is a joke, and its officers are powerless."[29]

Second, the mystical, anti–Christian nature associated with Asia throughout the last few centuries made its way into popular literature. Every one of the afore-mentioned secret societies are mystical and esoteric in nature, praying to dragons, demons, ancestors, obscure Eastern deities, or some sort of combination of these. Explicit descriptions of the barbarism practiced within these fictional cults, appearing in the form of human sacrifice, ritual suicides, and the asking of divine favor in the carrying out of assassinations aided in the setting apart of Asians from mainstream, predominately Christian, America. In *Nick Carter's Close Call*, the members of the sinister "Suey Sing Society" dance in a frantic, untamed manner around a "hideous god-idol in a cavernous temple," while planning the ritual murder of a traitor. The "heathen" and "uncivilized" manner of Asian religions are deemed barbaric and exponentially inferior to the civilizing and compassionate acts attributed to Christianity (the Inquisition and Crusades notwithstanding, apparently). Some works display this understanding of Chinese religions as an animosity between Eastern and Western faiths, while others praise the "civilizing" nature of Christianity upon the "heathen." Religious-fiction periodicals, such as *The New Sabbath Library* and its July 1898 story "The Victory of Quang Po" feature Chinamen that have been "brought up" to Christian moral standards, as opposed to "falling" into the pagan lowliness of their polytheistic peers.

Third, and perhaps the most evident (especially by the time of the comic books), is the focus placed on physical and linguistic discrepancies between denizens of the East and West. "Yellow," "Saffron," "slant-eyed," "sing-song language," "almond-shaped eyes," "tawny," "No sabe!" and numerous other epithets pepper the popular literature in every era, from story papers and dime novels up through the pulps and the comics. Yellow skin, long fingernails, shuffling feet, hunched backs, and emotionless faces — all (and more) are descriptors used to segregate Asians from the rest of America. The Bradys of *Secret Service*, lacking fluency in any Eastern dialects, must maneuver through the "harsh guttural laughs of derision [that] came from the Chinese"; and "Engrish" is spoken by almost every Asian character, with the exception of those educated in the United States, who are by definition (slightly) more "civilized." When referencing Asians, no distinction is made between one ethnic group or another; "Mongols," "Mongolians," "Celestials," "Oriental," and "Yellow men" are used interchangeably, whether the character is of Chinese, Japanese, Korean or any other Asian nationality. The rationale, apparently, was that by simply looking Asian, one was placed into a large, homogeneous "rabble" of "Easterners."

This collection of descriptions includes various other subsets, branching off into even further avenues of nativist imagery, and these will be analyzed as they appear in the pulps and comic books of the early-to-mid-twentieth century. It is important, however, to show this continuity before delving into the "meat" of this work, to demonstrate that the pulps and comic books did not create such imagery but rather inherited it from their predecessors. The fact that popular literature seems to be invested with such nativism from its very creation is important to note as well. As the twentieth century advanced, a sense of nativism that was originally encouraged and fostered by delusions of perceived threats and actual events (however unfounded and racist the tying of the two together may have been) is remade over the decades, via domestic and international situations, into increasingly tolerant, liberal, and accepting definitions of American diversity and nationality. What is considered to be "American" undergoes a drastic change, and the popular literature of the century displays such a transformation more clearly than any statistical chart or public poll ever could. Popular literature

The American hero against the magic and mysticism of the unknowable "East" (*Jeff Clayton's Surprise; or the Lure of the Red Dragon*, 1909).

was not influencing the rise or fall of nativism in America, but it, in addition to other mediums (films, television, music, etc.), can undeniably be seen as a barometer of such thought.

The first chapter serves as a model for the second and third. It addresses the methods of differentiation and, at times, dehumanization of Asians via the pulp magazines of the 1920s and 1930s; the possible reasoning on the part of the nativist mindset to justify such imagery; and the kernels of tolerance that were visible, even among such rhetoric. The second and third chapters follow such a three-tiered formula regarding the Japanese and Germans during World War II, and the Chinese, North Koreans and Communist Russians during the Cold War, respectively. As far as this work is concerned, the "cut-off" date for the pulps will be the early 1950s, the period when titles such as *Argosy, Adventure* and others radically altered their formats and had little semblance to the all-fiction bonanzas they were previously. As a result, the amount of time dedicated to the pulps is not quite as extensive in the second chapter as it is in the first, and is very small indeed in the third, with a majority of space given to the pulps' successors in terms of inexpensive escapism — the comics. Obviously, this is not the first work to address nativism; it is, however, the first to do so with a focus on pulp magazines and comics for the purpose of demonstrating a continuity between the two mediums regarding nativist and xenophobic discourses, and American popular thought as a whole.

Two American archetypes: The boys who rise from rags to riches, and the nefarious foreigners who would thwart them (*Might and Main Library—Stories of Boys Who Succeed*, No. 63, May 4, 1907).

I

THE YELLOW PERIL

The American Pulps Between the World Wars, 1919–1935

Dime novels and story papers would survive into the early twentieth century, but they had begun to encounter competition as early as the mid-1890s. The pulp magazines, deriving their name from the cheaply-produced pulpwood paper on which they were printed, provided tales of the fantastic that appealed to an ever-growing audience. The pulp magazine originated with *The Golden Argosy*, first published in 1882, the creation of future newspaper magnate Frank Andrew Munsey. As biographer George Britt explains, Munsey's *Argosy* appeared at just the right time in American literary history:

> As yet there was no popular literature for them [the average American], no middle ground of periodicals between the Augusta [or penny] dreadful and the ponderous reviews dealing in subject matter the average man cared nothing about at a price he couldn't afford to pay.... And the country's non-magazine buying millions were ripe for anyone who could interest them in reading.[1]

The Golden Argosy was a story paper initially, a work of juvenile fiction filled with Horatio Alger, Jr., tales about American youth, "freighted with treasures for boys and girls," as the tagline proclaimed. It was in 1896, after realizing that the future lay in periodicals as opposed to juvenile story papers, that Munsey revamped his title, making it a thick, all-fiction, 10-cent magazine for adults simply titled *The Argosy* and printed on pulpwood paper.[2] While adventure and action stories comprised the bulk of the title's offerings, *The Argosy*, the first pulp magazine, was a showcase for all genres of fiction, from scientific speculation to westerns, from comedies to romances, and more. As was the case with the dime novels beforehand, the popularity and profits generated by Munsey's periodical inspired a host of imitators, and an industry was born. Hundreds of titles appeared in the succeeding decades, and millions of stories were told, all inspired by the success of that first pulpwood periodical. The Frank A. Munsey Company produced a host of successive titles once *The Argosy* had inaugurated the "pulp boom," one of the most important being *The All-Story Weekly*, which began in 1905 and featured the first published fiction by Edgar Rice Burroughs, and is remembered as the home for a large amount of early science fiction writers. The ship that had launched an entire fleet, *The Argosy* would see several changes throughout its long life, with many under-performing companion titles folded into its pages (such as its change to *Argosy All-Story Weekly* following Munsey's decision to merge *The All-Story* and *The Argosy* in 1920).

One of the most prolific pulp magazine publishers other than Munsey was Street & Smith Publications, founded in 1855 (one year after Frank Munsey's birth, no less) by newspapermen Francis Scott Street and Francis Shubael Smith. As was the case with Frank Munsey, Street & Smith found initial success in publishing story papers after Smith's narratives, which originally appeared in the duo's *New York Weekly Dispatch* newspaper, became increasingly popular.[3] The Street & Smith Company emulated *Argosy*'s pulp formula early on and produced dozens of titles, including *Astounding Stories, Clues, Detective Story Magazines, The Shadow, Doc Savage*, and *The Thrill Book*. Westerns, espionage, detective, and general adventure stories filled the pages of the fresh medium. Something new called "Scientification" (later renamed science fiction or simply SF) was one of several new genres the pulps would nurture, appearing in several of the anthology tiles and later in the first SF-centric title, *Amazing Stories* (1926). General fiction titles, such as *The Argosy, Adventure, Blue Book, Popular Magazine* and *Short Stories* (which helped to popularize Sax Rohmer's "Fu Manchu" in America), shared the newsstands with genre-specific titles like *Wonder Stories, Dime Detective Stories, Western Romances,* and *Weird Tales*. As with any medium, the pulps have their share of drivel and, by contrast, their masterpieces. For every painful cliché or uninspired work that was obviously vomited forth from the depths of authorial squalor (again, pseudonyms were used quite often) for the sole purpose of meeting an editor's deadline, there are works worthy of literary notice, from both recognized masters of fiction such as Edgar Rice Burroughs, Robert E. Howard, Isaac Asimov, H.P Lovecraft and Dashiell Hammett, and the more obscure authors who assuredly put just as much of themselves into their work as their more illustrious compatriots, and who hopefully will eventually be rescued from the literary limbo in which they now reside. Similarly to the dime novels, nativism was a part of the earlier pulp magazines, as seen in *Adventure*'s 1910 debut-issue story, "Yellow Men and Gold," or *The All-Story*'s "The Invisible Empire — A Celestial Romance" (1913) and "The Yellow Lord" (1919). While such examples exist, it was only after the conclusion of World War I that such imagery exploded in volume, and that pulp magazines became the principle media for inexpensive literature and, indirectly, for nativist narratives. Nativist fiction appeared before World War I in the pulps, to be sure; after 1919, however, the chances were quite high that one would find a "yellow peril" or "evil Orient" story or two in any number of titles, issue after issue, regardless of whether the cover suggested such contents. The plethora of titles that appeared, beginning in the early twenties, ensured the proliferation of such literature. The pulp magazines were not "nativists-only" products, as later readings will show, and it should be kept in mind that they were no more nativist than any other popular medium at the time. The pulps should be examined not because they are "more nativist" than other media, but rather because they provide easily-recognizable examples of mindsets and worldviews that were prevalent at the time, and are found in many other narratives and formats.

Immorality, Criminality and Torture

> That Jap. Never did like his looks. Bet he'd kill his own mother for the gold in her teeth.—"The Tallow Devil" (1934)

By means of Zolberg's observations as to what can produce nativism, the first "difference" to be examined is how the pulps portrayed Asians in relation to morality and criminality. Via an examination of Asian religious and moral beliefs as characterized in the pulps, two trends can be noted rather quickly. First, the "Oriental" is a godless pagan who worships only idols, demons or ancestors. Second, the Asian is depicted as a person in whom any sort of moral creed is nonexistent — with the Asian character (usually Chinese, but not always) claiming devotion only to criminality and the furthering of violence and murder in the pursuit of riches and power. The more "civilized" characteristics assumed to be inherent in Anglo-Saxon Protestant populations has been excised. For the pulps, life in the Orient was something to be disposed of quickly, especially if it got in the way of any profits or criminal gain. "The yellow man," says one pulp protagonist, "on the other hand, comes from a country where there is an excess of population, where life is held cheaply, and where the criminal element will butcher for next to nothing."[4] Religion (or lack thereof) and an innate propensity for crime and violence made up most of the Asian characters to be found in the pulps. Fu Manchu, the Oriental Emperor of Crime and arch-nemesis of two British adventurers (and, by default, of the Anglo-Saxon world itself), was the most popular of the yellow peril characters, and his heirs in the American pulps follow his lead to the letter. Originally published as a British magazine serial in 1912, Sax Rohmer's *Fu Manchu* stories saw publication in a number of subsequent magazines and books. They would eventually come to America, where their popularity was only heightened through both pulp serialization and film adaptations, in addition to a multitude of literary imitations.

Asia in the popular American imagination (*Adventure*, August 18, 1920, Argosy Communications).

"Here's the kindest race in the world, and yet the most callous; the noisiest and yet the most silent; the most beautifully ugly barbaric civilization that ever contradicted itself," begins the story "The Escape," by Robert J. Pearsall, from the August 18, 1920, issue of the pulp fiction magazine *Adventure*.[5] *Adventure* was founded in 1910 by Trumbull White, an adventurer whose exploits were as wide and as varied as those of the characters that appeared in his periodical. Published by the Butterick Company, a conglomerate already deeply entrenched in the magazine business, *Adventure* outlived many of its contemporaries, not ceasing publication until 1971.[6] In "The Escape," two heroic Anglo-Saxon males, Hazard and Partridge, in the fashion of Sherlock Holmes and Dr. Watson (or, more appropriately, given the subject matter, Nayland Smith and Dr. Petrie of Sax Rohmer's *Fu Munchu* stories), are hot on the trail of Koshinga, the evil "spirit of the East, past all Western understanding," in an attempt to upset his plot from behind bars to destroy the fledgling democracy in China and establish "his despotic rule on the ruins of the republic." Partridge (Watson to Hazard's Holmes, in the role of both sidekick as well as narrator), is constantly perplexed and dumbfounded both by the evil of their nemesis and the unspoken deductions made by his adventurous companion. After following several clues, convinced they are close to foiling a heinous plot, the pair are led into a secret cave in which the evil Koshinga dwells and unintentionally releases the madman from imprisonment, having played into his hands the entire time.

Two references found in this story provide an indication of how contemporary events could have influenced the manner

The Blue Book (November 1921).

in which this villain in particular, and a multitude of Asian antagonists in general, were characterized. One such allusion is to Koshinga's dealings with "old Boxer underground workings," a reference to the Boxer Rebellion that ignited in the late 1890s. The Boxer Rebellion, which saw its highest levels of violence in the summer of 1900, was retaliation on the part of Chinese nationalists against the foreign legations and Christian settlements that had encroached on Chinese sovereignty for decades.[7] The term "Boxer" is the Western name given to the Fists of Harmonious Righteousness (Yi Ho Chuan), a secret society that blamed the opium epidemic and other ills (rightfully so) on foreigner infringement. The Yi Ho Chuan often performed martial arts demonstrations in public and, given their name, used a clenched fist as their standard, thus garnering the name "Boxers."[8] The Boxer Rebellion (or, more accurately, Uprising), certainly would have been in the memories, both first-hand and second-hand, of many Americans (and Caucasians in general). It was viewed at the time, and later remembered, as a savage Oriental attack on the "civilizing" Western population of the foreign legations. The Boxers materialize as villains in many pulp stories, just as they did years earlier in the story papers and dime novels with which the Uprising was contemporaneous. The appearance of the Boxers in "The Escape" and other similar stories serves the same purpose as the presence of Taiping rebels in the dime novel *Jeff Clayton's Fatal Shot*— it appealed to Americans concerned with the ramifications of Asian immigration and served as a reminder of past "violations" upon Americans (and Christendom). Koshinga's tie to the Boxers is interesting in what it shows concerning America's memory (or, rather, what the nation chose to remember) concerning recent Chinese history and China's interactions with the West; it also helped to make the character undeniably anti–Christian and therefore anti–American.

The second important characterization of Koshinga — his position as "the head of the Asiatic Ko Lao Hui, maddest of the revolutionary tongs"— is a categorization that really moves beyond this character in particular to encompass the majority of Asian villains appearing in the pulps. The tongs were a collection of Chinese secret societies in America, predominantly found in the nation's "Chinatowns" that first appeared in the mid-nineteenth century. Secret societies are an intrinsic part of Chinese history, be it political, religious, or otherwise; their history stretches back thousands of years, with patriotic groups in China forming to overthrow usurpers as early as 9 A.D. From their inception, the societies were fiercely patriotic in nature and often saw the height of their political activities during times of foreign occupation. "The White Lotus Society" aided both in the removal of the Mongols from the imperial throne and in their replacement with the ethnic Han Chinese Ming Dynasty in 1368 A.D. Following the overthrow of the Ming by nomadic invaders from the North, the Manchu, and the founding of their Qing Dynasty (1644 A.D.), the multitude of secret societies that existed at the time were an integral part of anti–Manchurian activities, giving monetary, military and personnel support to various groups, including the Taiping and Nien rebels of the mid-nineteenth century. In the earliest years of the twentieth century, Chinese secret societies participated in attacks on Western interests and Christian missionaries during the Boxer Uprising, deciding that Manchurian domination was the lesser of two evils (at the moment) when compared to Western encroachment upon the sovereignty of the Chinese Empire. Secret societies participated in the events that led to both the 1911 Xinhai Revolution that overthrew the Qing and the last Chinese emperor, Pu Yi, and the establishment of the Republic of China.[9] The secret societies reaffirmed their nationalist leanings as a major supporter of the policies of "the Father of Modern China" and provisional first president of the Republic, Dr. Sun Yat-sen, as well as his protégé, and future leader of

The Occident meets the Orient (*Argosy All-Story Weekly*, May 28, 1921, Argosy Communications).

both the Republic of China (mainland) and the Republic of China on Taiwan, Chiang Kai-shek. During the decades-long civil war that erupted following President Yuan Shikai's attempts at reinstating the Empire, and the ensuing warlordism that tore China apart, many societies divided their allegiance between the two main powers vying for control of the fractured state — the Nationalists (led by Chiang Kai-shek) and the Communist Party of China, eventually headed by Mao Zedong. The role these societies played in both China's domestic politics and in America's Chinatowns from the late 1890s through the 1930s were reflected in the pulps.

During the late nineteenth century, when immigration from China was at its peak, the American understanding of the Chinese secret society, or "tong," first appeared; tong is an Americanization of the Chinese *tang*, which, among other things, can refer to a gathering hall similar to the ones frequented by society members. Amid the rising number of immigrants entering the United States in the late 1800s and early 1900s, there were undoubtedly members of various groups who, upon their arrival, kept the secret societies alive in their new home. In America, these groups, while offering assistance programs and services to newly arrived Chinese immigrants (such as aid in finding housing and employment, and in maintaining contact with the homeland), were, in the eyes of many Americans, connected more with crime and vice than anything else.[10] In short, they were seen as a Chinese mafia, and, for the better part of the early 1900s, rightfully so. The aura of banditry and political upheaval surrounding these groups, brought to America along with news of the Taiping and Boxer movements years earlier, unquestionably helped form public opinion of the tongs as agents of radical revolution, joining anti–Asian and anti-radical nativism together. By 1920 the tongs had relinquished a good portion of their hand in the criminal and vice trades in favor of the burgeoning tourist interest in Chinatowns.[11] However, as is often the case, what reality is and what the public perceives it to be can be two very different things, and the press and the public at large could always see any isolated incident as a resurgence of tong violence. As late as 1925, *Time* magazine was publishing articles detailing the violence in America's Chinatowns on the part of the dreaded tongs:

> Authorities throughout the country tried hard last week to end the animosity of the two great Tongs — the On Leong and the Hip Sing — which broke out two weeks ago.... That night Que Yee, a Hip Sing, was met by three pellets of steel as he walked upstairs in his house. He rolled to the bottom and died. Wong Hong, a young Hip Sing gunman, was entering

his lodging house. A hatchet came down on his head from behind and his brains were crushed. They found a revolver lashed inside his vest.[12]

Similar reports appeared throughout the 1920s. Despite the fact that by the time of the preceding article's publication the tong "threat" had mostly disappeared, it is obvious that the imagery it presented still held a firm grip on the mainstream American imagination. Many of the tongs that appear in pulp fiction (and even earlier in the dime novels), such the Hip Sing, On Leong, the Suey Sing, and the Four Brothers, were actual groups that existed in Chinatowns across the country. In nativist fiction related to Asians, from the 1890s through the 1930s, stories involving tongs, secret societies and hatchet-men (hired assassins) always, to the point of predictability, occur on "Mott Street" or "Pell Street" and others — all names of streets that "real-life" tongs ruled in their respective Chinatowns across the nation. The Chinatowns themselves (also alternatively referred to as "yellow streets" or "Mongol quarters") are often given as much characterization as their denizens; they are dank, filthy, lawless places where murder is an expected fact of life. As a March 1935 *Blue Book Magazine* short story ("Pell Street Blues," by Achmed Abdullah) describes it:

The looming, animalistic Oriental always ready to steal the innocence of Caucasian American womanhood (*True Mystic Crimes*, April 1931).

> Streets of Chinatown, squatting, turgid and sardonic and tremendously

alien! Not caring a tinker's dam for the White Man's world roaring its up-to-date, efficient steel-and-concrete symphony on all sides. Rickety, this Chinatown; moldy and viscous, not over-clean, smelling distressingly of sewer gas and rotting vegetables and sizzling, rancid fat.

Numerous pulp stories featured the tongs as agents of "white-slavery"— the abducting of pure, virginal Caucasian women for the purposes of becoming sexual slaves to Oriental masters. The April 1931 cover story of *True Mystic Crimes*, "I Rescued Slave Girls from Chinatown's Underground Dens," and its clawed "Celestial" looming over the partially disrobed white female, is a prime example of this particular plot device. Such illustrations were fueled by tong activities in the real world that reached back to the early years of the century. An example is the 1909 murder of Elsie Sigel, the 14-year-old granddaughter of famed Civil War veteran General Franz Sigel. Murdered by a man named Leong Lung, to whom she was giving Bible lessons, Elsie's murder helped create a great deal of animosity towards Chinese-American communities and further spread the fear of tong violence.[13] *Argosy*'s companion title, the general-interest *Munsey's Magazine*, provided a lengthy article on the event in its September 1909 edition: "Slumming in New York's Chinatown — a Glimpse into the Sordid Underworld of the Mott Street Quarter, Where Elsie Sigel Formed Her Fatal Associations."[14] Depravity on the part of Asian tongs against women was not limited to interracial situations, however; a real event chronicled in the pulps (that also occurred in 1909) sensationalized the supposed treatment of Asian women by Asian men, and also served to raise even more fears concerning tong violence and Chinese gangs in the early twentieth century. The "Bow Kum" (Bow Kim in some versions) incident in 1909, what historian Herbert Asbury calls the "most disastrous war the tongs ever fought in New York," left over fifty dead and further cemented in the public's mind the notion of Chinatown as a criminal den inhabited by misanthropic degenerates.[15] The tragedy began with a young Chinese immigrant named Bow Kum (or "Sweet Flower") who was sold in San Francisco's Chinatown to a tong member. This marriage was subsequently voided by the authorities, with the young girl later (legally) remarrying to a member of a rival tong. A gang war soon erupted between the two groups, which resulted in a multitude of deaths, including that of young Bow Kum, barely twenty-one years old, stabbed to death in her husband's home and her body horribly mutilated.[16]

Accounts of the Bow Kum incident left an imprint on America's understanding of tongs, as evidenced by its appearance in books and peri-

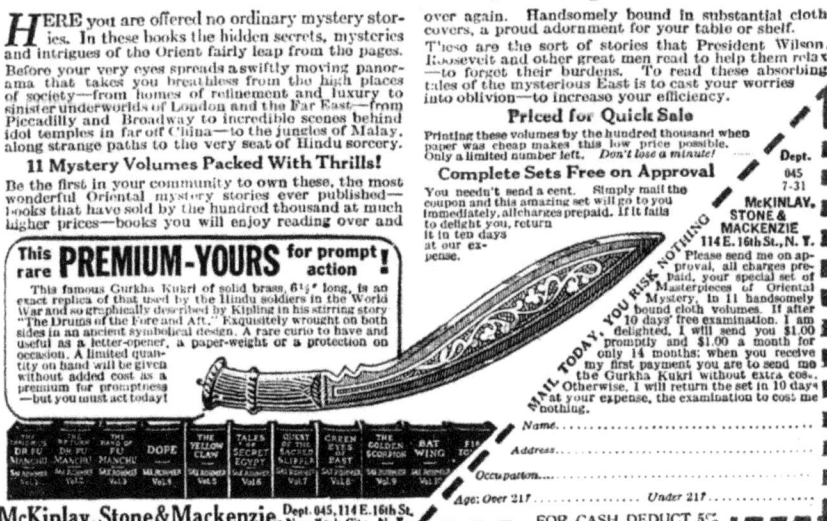

The "yellow peril" genre was quite popular in the early years of the twentieth century, enough to support the growth of book clubs devoted specifically to it (advertisement from *Oriental Stories*, Autumn 1931).

odicals decades later, including the November 1929 edition of the pulp *True Strange Stories*. Despite its cover featuring a Caucasian woman threatened by a menacing Oriental, *True Mystic Crimes* (April 1931) also detailed the horrors Chinese women endured at the hands of the tongs. Convinced to journey to America under false pretenses, the women are sold into sexual slavery immediately upon arrival, with no reprieve possible even if they happen to be rescued, due to the tongs' penchant for retaliation. The activities of the tongs by the mid–1920s may have diminished greatly, American popular culture retained the image of the bloodthirsty, criminal "hatchet-man."

While the pulp vision of the tongs appeared before World War I, as evidenced by *Detective Story Magazine*'s 1916 publication of stories detailing the exploits of the criminal-villain Li Shoon, the atmosphere of isolationism and xenophobia that existed after the war aided in the flourishing of such caricatures.[17] The idea of the tong, and the overall criminality and lack of (Christian) morality in the Oriental character, can be seen throughout the years of the pulp magazine's primacy. Sheriff Braintree battles tong criminals hiding out in a stereotypical Chinese laundry-mat in "The Chariot of Sing Lee," by Frederick Davis (*Argosy All-Story Weekly*, October 24, 1925). In the December 27, 1930, issue of *Street & Smith's Detective Story Magazine* (another long-lasting pulp, running from 1915 to 1953), A.E. Apple's "Mr. Chang's Tong War" appeared. In it, two heroes (or, rather, protagonist and deuteragonist, as neither is depicted as very "heroic"), Chinese Doctor Ling and his partner, the "Mongolian torture specialist" Doctor Hip Yee, seek to capture the diabolical Mr. Chang, "the notorious ... archcriminal king of the hatchetmen of the man-killing tong."[18] Mr. Chang, through "Oriental craftiness" discovers a secret passage between his hideout and that of a rival tong, and enters in the hope of stealing the society's treasure that has been saved to aid in the Chinese Republic's defense against "the rising monarchist movement, headed by war lords of Mongolia."[19] Mr. Chang eventually does succeed in stealing the loot, after killing one of his pursuers and escaping capture by the other, to thwart justice and plan countless future attacks upon civilization. The year 1932's "Fireflies of Death," by Sidney Herschel Small, featured recurring Chinatown detective Jimmy Wentworth in one of his many battles with tong lord Kong Gai. "This meant only one thing to Wentworth; Kong Gai was the brains behind the affair! Kong Gai, with whom he had so often crossed swords. Kong Gai, the Evil One, spreading out his snake-like influence to wherever money could be made in unlawful, profitable ways."[20] In the

May 26, 1934, issue of *Argosy All-Story Weekly*, Singapore Sammy, Anglo-Saxon adventurer in the Far East, matches wits with several Asiatic criminal organizations in "Buddha's Whisker," by George F. Worts, a pulp fiction writer known for the *Singapore Sammy* series as well as a multitude of other tales dealing with the criminality of the "yellow menace." Worts, Small and others were among many pulp authors of the day whose works of "Oriental" fiction were voluminous and comprised a large amount of their creative output.[21]

At the height of the pulps' success, the genre of the "pulp hero," the costumed vigilante sworn to fight crime (and precursor to the comic book super hero), appeared. Like his generic counterpart in the general fiction pulp titles, he too had to contend with what the popular culture considered to be the intrinsically criminal world of the Orient. Such characters are found in "The Tomb of Death," published in the November 1934 issue of *The Phantom Detective*, one of the many "hero-pulps" popular at the time (the most successful being *The Shadow*, a character to be discussed later and whose own title *The Phantom Detective* was created to contend with). Written mostly by Robert Wallace (a pen name utilized by a host of authors who worked on the magazine), the

Many pulp narratives featured recurring characters whose "enemy of choice" was usually Asiatic in origin (*Argosy Weekly*, May 26, 1934, Argosy Communications).

Phantom Detective was actually wealthy playboy Richard Curtis Van Loan, who, after witnessing the horrors of battle during the First World War, vowed to battle the criminal element as a masked master detective. In the twenty-first issue of his own magazine, the titular character is pitted against Li-Hung, a villain who "other by reputation, no white man knew the mysterious leader of the underworld forces of Chinatown, the undisputed leader of the lawless element of the Orientals in the city."[22] In the story the Phantom Detective is called upon to investigate the death of a famed aviator who died under mysterious circumstances after crashing in China during an attempted flight around the world. From the very beginning of the tale, almost as soon as China is mentioned, the criminal tongs make their appearance, with the Phantom being captured and taken to the tong headquarters, where torture by a "vicious crowd" of "cruel, beetle-browed, slant-eyed men who had gathered at the orders of their leader" awaits him. After escaping such a menacing collection of villains, as well as a giant, ax-wielding "Oriental," the Phantom continues in his quest to bring the murderer of a fellow white man to justice. As expected, in the end the Phantom prevails against the "King of these slant eyed thugs."

In some stories, such as the weird fiction genre of fantasy and horror, the foreigner's (typically Asian's) lack of morality and innate criminality combined to produce a type of devilish magic that threatened the civilized world in general and that of the white race in particular. Such tales of magic stemmed from the popular understanding of tongs also operating as secretive religious cults; indeed, many tongs did have specific deities or spirits from whom they sought guidance and protection. Sensationalized, often exaggerated news stories about tong activities combined with a general ignorance concerning Eastern religions to form a connection between a perceived inherent Asian criminality and non–Christian practices. This genre found a large number of readers in the long-running, and appropriately named, *Weird Tales*, which began in 1923 and has continued, with varying occasion and through various publishers, up through the present day. *Weird Tales*, fittingly, focused on narratives of weird fiction — a mix of science fiction, fantasy and horror that was, and is, in a class all to itself. *Weird Tales* was later joined by a companion title, *Oriental Stories* (first issued in 1930 and later renamed *The Magic Carpet Magazine*), which, as the name suggests, often provided escapism with a mystical and Eastern flair. Both titles, as well as a multitude of others, often supplied situations wherein the alleged criminality of the Orient produced otherworldly, mystical dangers. *Weird Tales* featured the writings of several "weird fiction" authors instantly recognizable today, such as Robert E. Howard, Clark Ashton Smith, and Howard Phillips (H.P.) Lovecraft. These three men formed a kind of "triumvirate" of weird fiction (knowing Lovecraft's predisposition for antiquity, he would certainly relish such terminology) and often contributed separately to Lovecraft's menagerie of monsters, collectively known as the Cthuhlu mythos.

The January 1927 edition of *Weird Tales* featured the Lovecraft short story "The Horror at Red Hook," wherein a New England police detective named Thomas Malone is sent to investigate the large amounts of immigrants that seem to be flooding into the area via the notorious and seedy "Red Hook" district of New York. Lovecraft discusses the Red Hook area thus:

> The population is a hopeless tangle and enigma; Syrian, Spanish, Italian, and negro elements impinging upon one another.... It is a babel of sound and filth ... from this tangle of material and spiritual putrescence the blasphemies of an hundred dialects assail the sky.... Visible offences are as varied as the local dialects, and run the gamut from the smuggling of rum and prohibited aliens through diverse stages of lawlessness and obscure vice to murder and mutilation in their most abhorrent guises.[23]

Over the course of his investigation, Malone encounters a plethora of suspect foreigners: "unclassified, slant-eyed folk," "squinting physiognomies," and those of "Mongoloid stock" who reminds the detective "of the Yezidis, last survivors of the Persian devil-worshippers." Following a suspect's trail, Malone uncovers a subterranean dock where both recent immigrants and demonic monstrosities from alternative, hellish dimensions gather for hideous ceremonies and the sacrifice of "blue-eyed, Norwegian" children.

At this time it should be pointed out that there are particular circumstances pertaining to H.P. Lovecraft that need to be taken into account when reading this and other pieces of his work, the latter of which are considered masterpieces of modern American horror. Lovecraft, at best, was a devout Anglophile and a lover of classical education; at worst, he was what a modern reader may call an overt racist and bigot. Evidence suggests that even the majority of Caucasians did not fit into Lovecraft's hierarchy of races, which placed those of the British Isles at the pinnacle. Lovecraft belonged to a once-influential Rhode Island family and regarded himself as something of a patrician floundering in an era that no longer recognized the nobility of aristocratic New England. One of Lovecraft's biographers and fellow fiction writers, L. Sprague De Camp, credits Lovecraft's views on racial hierarchy to both "the general ethnocentrism of Old Americans of his time" and his reading of such Anglo-Saxon–centric works

Advertisement from *Oriental Stories* (February–March 1931).

as Houston Stewart Chamberlain's 1912 publication *The Foundations of the Nineteenth Century* and Madison Grant's *The Passing of the Great Race* (1916).[24] Lovecraft was known for having a particularly hierarchal view of races and societies, even among his contemporaries, and his rather extreme views should not be applied to all pulp writers or even the majority of pulp readers. The fact does remain, however, that Lovecraft's work and others in a similar vein found an audience among readers of pulp magazines in general and of weird fiction in particular. It is important to note as well that the macabre ceremonies and unholy masses found in Lovecraft's stories do not differ a great deal from many of the pagan ceremonies attributed to Orientals in many other pulp stories; while the acolytes may be other-dimensional monsters in Lovecraftian tales, all that is needed is to replace these creatures with Asians and one would have any number of the horrendous rituals that appeared in "secret societies" and "tong" literature.

The pulps also depicted Asian immorality through characters' predisposition to torture and the use of it in almost any situation, whether necessary or not. Ancient torture devices, and an Asian predilection for using them as a first resort, appears throughout the pulps as one of the most common of descriptors, and also stems from sensationalized news stories of the day. Lemuel L. De Bra's 1920 short story "The Mystery of the Missing Hands" chronicles acts of torturous violence enacted by a pair of Chinese brothers in return for atrocities they themselves endured at the hands of a bloodthirsty Chinese pirate. The brigand proudly exclaims that he "was sired by a dragon and born of a typhoon; and the sharks whom I feed with fools like you worship me as their ancestor."[25]

Even the first of the "Scientifiction" (later redefined as "science fiction") pulps depicted Asian antagonists as masters of inhuman torture. In April 1926, inventor/scientist/publisher Hugo Gernsback released the first issue of the first science fiction–only title, *Amazing Stories*, following the success of such stories printed in two of his technology magazines, *Electrical Experimenter* and *Modern Electronics*. Gernsback's hope for *Amazing* was that it would be a home for fiction that examined modern sciences and technology, and extrapolated from them machinery and situations that could carry mankind into the future. All stories, as published by Gernsback, were required to have some sort of real scientific notions at their core, from which the fiction of the future could be based. The March 1928 issue of *Amazing Stories* contained W.F. Hammond's "Lakh-Dal, Destroyer of Souls," a tale of futuristic Eastern torture machines that also provided the issue's cover art:

Certain things are transpiring today, both in this country and abroad, which can only be accounted for by the existence of a living, breathing Embodiment of Evil — a creature half-human, half-demon, whose diabolic designs and ruthless will are carried out through a secret organization, with ramifications in every part of the civilized world.... We do know, however, that he came from a spot in the remote fastnesses of the Himalayas, near the sacred city of Lhasa which ... is not only the capital of Tibet, but also the residence of the Dalai Lama, supreme head of the Lamaist [sic] hierarchy.[26]

True to the Gernsbackian formula defining "true" science fiction, Lahk-Dal utilizes the most modern of technology to further his goals — in this case, torturing his victims under the light of his "lunacy ray" to the point they are transformed into raving madmen intent only upon carrying out their master's orders:

> The screams of the doomed man changed to a howl of pure anguish.... Under the malign influence of those mysterious rays, the man's face changed horribly. The light of intelligence faded from his eyes and his lower jaw sagged weakly. In five minutes those watching beheld a hopeless lunatic, whose vacuous grimaces and grotesque mouthings were fearful to behold.

Early science fiction (in this case, the first SF-centric magazine) was not immune to exaggerations influenced by the yellow peril (*Amazing Stories*, March 1928).

One particularly interesting example of this presupposed Asian fascination with torture can be found in the pulp magazine understood to be the "father" of them all, *Argosy*. In one of the many "real world" segments found in a variety of pulp periodicals, a November 1928 edition of *Argosy All-Story Weekly* contained an article entitled "Combating 'Crime Wave' in Tibet." The piece explains various systems of Chinese torture in an apparent attempt to offer a contrast to the more humane treatment one might expect in Christian (white) America:

> While America is not likely to adopt Oriental ways, it is still interesting to speculate on what the results would be were this country to model the criminal laws after those effective in the Chinese province of Tibet.... In that primitive country, beheading is not unusual ... while lesser crimes are punishable by the cutting off of a limb.... Murder is often punished by immersing the murderer in a boiling oil bath. However, the more common punishment is crucifixion.[27]

It is true that beheading and other forms of capital punishment were common throughout China's long history; such acts, however, had been forbidden since the Revolution of 1911, and later officially in 1927, with the establishment of the Kuomintang (or Nationalist) government in Nanjing.[28] Regardless of whether such events were (still) taking place in China, articles like this suggested that they were, and the writers of pulp magazine stories would incorporate such ideas into their works to further demonize the

Precursors to the super-heroes later found in comic books, the pulp heroes featured rogue galleries just as expansive as their successors, and often included villains of the tong variety (illustration from "The Tomb of Death," *Phantom Detective*, November 1934).

Eastern "other." The October 6, 1928, issue of *Argosy All-Story Weekly* contains the tale of "The Crime Circus," by George F. Worts, in which a lone Anglo-Saxon protagonist was warned by a criminal that, if cooperation was not attained, he would "first describe some of the methods of torture used by Orientals."[29] Worts' "The Silver Fang," published in a Winter 1929 issue of the same magazine, tells the story of Malabar Mackenzie, a wealthy American playboy who loses his inheritance and follows in his grandfather's footsteps as a pirate of the South Seas. "The Chinese," Malabar is told by one of his grandfather's former crewmen, "are a brutal race. They love torture, when it's applied to the other fellow."[30] In the previously mentioned "Tomb of Death," the Phantom Detective encounters the savage brutality of Oriental tortures, one such method being his suspension off the ground via piano wire wrapped about his thumbs, while a horde of starving rats gnaw away at his dangling feet.

His lithe body lifted in a long leap

Illustration from "The Tomb of Death," *Phantom Detective*, November 1934.

The Orient's seeming inclination towards criminality and violence was only one way that the nativist pulp literature of the 1920s and '30s demonized Asians. The inability to speak "proper" English, and the possible subversive acts the use of one's native language could conceal, was another method of vilification.

Language and Intelligence

Luby-Pagan...—"The Pagan Ruby" (1928)

"Luby-Pagan" are the last words of a dying Chinese man, uttered to pulp hero Jack Eastman (*Argosy All-Story Weekly*, October 6, 1928). This simple mangling of "l"s and "r"s would propel Eastman into an adventure of international proportions, and into the clutches of the evil Wily Chun Wah and his "Oriental cleverness."[31] The broken English found in J. Allan Dunn's "The Pagan Ruby" reveals another aspect of early twentieth century nativism's attack on the foreigner: linguistics, and its ties to intelligence and nationalism. The question of nativism, or, rather, the subject of language and its importance to nativism, can be seen throughout the early twentieth century, most visibly in a sociopolitical arena known as "Americanization." The speaking of the English language, or the lack of an ability to do so, instantly aided in the differentiation between someone who was native-born and someone who was not. Beginning prior to World War I and continuing with zeal afterwards, there was a drive throughout various parts of American society to "Americanize" immigrants in regard to language. English language schools appeared throughout the country, and many school districts enacted measures to teach children in English and English only, regardless of their primary language. Traditionalist groups, such as the Freemasons and the Daughters of the Confederacy, pushed for such acts to be sanctioned by federal legislation.[32] Henry Ford provided for his workers, many of whom were foreign in origin, Americanization schools within the walls of his factories. The first lesson in Ford's classes consisted of learning the phrase "I am an American."[33] While encouraging immigrants to learn a new nation's language and customs is not wrong in and of itself, the force placed on many immigrants to conform went far beyond "encouragement" and often times came at the cost of sacrificing their traditional language and culture.

In 1922 the state of Oregon passed a controversial law that required all children between the ages of eight and sixteen to be taught in public schools, as opposed to private schools (many of which were Catholic and were still distrusted in many circles as being part of a conspiracy to reduce America to a Papal State). Such legislation would have forced "Americanization" curriculum on all children affected.[34] On the subject of pontifical conspiracies, it is important to note that language was also understood to be an instrument not only of foreigners in general but of foreign radicals as well. Someone speaking only Italian could be an emissary for the Pope, and many of the radical journals and newspapers of the time, owing to their mostly immigrant membership, were printed in foreign languages. The well-known anarchist Emma Goldman, while being fluent in English, often presented her fiery orations in her native Russian or Yiddish.[35] English, and, most importantly in the case of depictions of foreigners in the pulps, "proper" English, was a sign of "Americanism," with anything less signifying possible (or even probable) foreign loyalties. So a lack of complete mastery of English could possibly make one a victim of anti-radical nativism as well. Furthermore, the inability to speak English correctly could also be seen as a sign of a child-like mentality on the part of the speaker.

In the majority of 1920s pulps, any Asian language is regarded as sub-human, a degeneration of human speech that is more akin to the grunts of wild beasts or an unintelligible "sing-song." The term "sing-song" was used almost to the point of exhaustion in pulp narratives to describe the language of Asian characters. The protagonist of Horace Howard Herr's "A Daughter of the White Star," serialized from May 28 to June 25, 1921, in *Argosy All-Story Weekly*, remarks on the "open vowels and singsong characteristics I had often observed in conversations of Chinamen." Later, in speaking of an Oriental he has just encountered, "his words were unintelligible to me, being in that vowel-marked sing-song language."[36] Instances of "sing-song phrases" and of an Asian "coo[ing] his broken English" abound in this story, and can be observed in many others of the time. Mr. Woo, an Asian detective in several pulp stories, while a sleuth of Holmes-like proportions, was still separated from his mostly White supporting cast by his appearance as well as his use of improper English. Mr Woo uses what has come to be known recently as "Engrish," so named because of the stereotyped understanding that many Asian speakers will jumble "r"s and "l"s in their speech. While speaking to a prospective client of his detective agency, Mr. Woo suggests, in order to get closer to a suspected murderer, "I will invite my miselable self to visit honolable mansion of Mist'l Meldon."[37] In "Crooks Is Crooks," a 1921 story by Lemuel L. DeBra about two American criminals attempting to run an opium ring between Mexico and the United States, an opium dealer with whom the crooks hope to do business says of their product, "Aw lite ... not numba one chop, but aw lite. I buy."[38] The hero of "The Tale of the Bat-Dragon," while investigating the scene of a crime, overhears the "expressionless, sing-song voice ... of two Orientals."[39]

The early twentieth century saw this separation of the "white" and "yellow" races along the lines of what each is capable of mentally and linguistically reach into the scholastic and public spheres of American consciousness. In the 1920s there was a good deal of discussion concerning "Mongoloid imbecility," a genetic disorder known today as Down Syndrome. In *The Mongol in Our Midst*, a work that gained quite a following in the United States following its 1924 publication, English physician F. G. Crookshank attempted to provide evidence that the reason Down Syndrome occurred in particular individuals was due to the presence of Asiatic, particularly Mongolian, ancestry within their bloodline.[40] Such an idea was not invented by Crookshank, but in the post-war world his seemingly authoritative work on the subject, which received praise from scholarly journals in both the United States and the United Kingdom, reached a new audience who had come to see nativism, and the protection of America's Anglo-Saxon heritage, as the only pathways to preserving civilization.

Pseudo-intellectual works and "scientific" research were not the only avenues in which the idea of the threatening or "devolved" otherness of the Orient manifested itself: educational tools, for children and adults alike, also gave such a notion a seeming air of legitimacy. Physical differences, especially those regarded as "primitive," could be construed as evidence of the mental and/or linguistic lacking on the part of the "Oriental." *Dodge's Advanced Geography*, written by Columbia University Professor of Geography Richard Elwood Dodge, presented "academia's" view of the "white vs. yellow" mentality in a

While still a protagonist, and much more intelligent than his Caucasian co-stars, pulp detective Mr. Woo did not differ much from Charlie Chan in the sense that his ethnicity was focused upon more than any of his other attributes (illustration from "Steel Skeletons," *Phantom Detective*, May 1935).

book of which "no better text-book in geography" could be found by a reviewer in the *Harvard Graduate Magazine*[41]:

> The largest number of people belong to the Caucasian or White Race ... they are the most active, enterprising, and imaginative race of the world.... The next largest number of people is found in the Yellow Race.... The people of the yellow race are shorter than those of the white race, and have coarse, black hair, small noses, and small black eyes, with the outer corners a little elevated. As a rule they are not progressive and include some of the most backward tribes of the world.[42]

Dodge's textbook, initially published in 1906, with reprints through 1920, was a part of many school districts' required reading, and can be found in a 1921 middle school "Course of Study" list of reference books for all public schools in Baltimore County, Maryland.[43]

Another "academic work" that placed "the yellow race" subservient to other races in reference to intelligence was Harmon B. Niver's *Complete Geography*, initially published in 1915 and reprinted through 1922, in which Asians' "broad faces, high cheek bones ... slanting eyes" and "short, broad noses" are emphasized over other characteristics, with the Japanese being described as "more active and intelligent than the Chinese."[44] Such an understanding is reflected in many pulp stories in which the Japanese are portrayed as "higher" ethnically than the Chinese, representing a more advanced "branch" of the Asiatic family tree that is highly mechanized and militarily capable of overrunning China, such as in W. Wirt's story "The White Warlords" (*Argosy Weekly*, December 9, 1933). As was the case with Dodge's book, Niver's work was used in school districts throughout America, and was even listed in a 1923 bulletin as being a recent acquisition of Ohio State University's Library for the Bureau of Educational Research.[45]

Adults, and specifically immigrant adults, did not escape the bombardment of such views. Nina Jay Smith Beglinger's 1922 text *Constructive Lessons in English for the Foreign Born* was a textbook made for recent immigrants, written to both aid in the user's understanding of the English language and to seemingly instill in them many of the views of race predominate in America at the time. "The Mongolian or Yellow race are natives of Eastern Asia and are recognized by their black eyes set slantingly, their straight black hair, and their yellow skin," writes Beglinger.[46] The positioning of such ideas in a language book for immigrants is actually quite devious; while recent arrivals to America are learning English in order to make themselves "better" Americans, they are also being educated in the finer points of racial hierarchies. Beglinger also makes a point to clarify that Chinese and Japanese immigrants "are barred from becoming citizens of the United States under present laws."⁴⁷ It is not unreasonable to see the inclusion of such a statement as something of an appeal to any of the "preferred" stock of immigrants (those of Anglo-Saxon or Western European origin) to see Asians in America, just as many native-born Americans saw them, as "lesser" and incapable of being "real" Americans.

The stereotypes concerning language and mental capacities had a two-fold effect — an external and an internal labeling. First, it delineated who was a "native-born" American, from someone who obviously was not. In a nativist atmosphere, such a demarcation implied the presence of not only a recent immigrant but an immigrant who was hostile to America. Why else would he or she not bother to correctly learn "our" language? Second, the lack of proper English implied an inability to understand it, or a physical incapability to pronounce certain phrases, reducing the mentality of the foreigner in question to that of a child or an invalid — in either case, someone who is not on "our level."

Physicality and Racial Antagonisms

> In our case ... civilisation ... forms the central point; a good characteristic, in so far as it promises durability, but a somewhat perilous one, in that we run a risk of becoming Chinese, a risk which would become a very real one if the non–Teutonic or scarcely Teutonic elements among us were ever to gain the upper hand.— *The Foundations of the Nineteenth Century* (1913)
>
> Wu Fang turned and let his green, slanted eyes rest upon her fondly.— "The Case of the Suicide Tomb" in *The Mysterious Wu Fang* (1935)

The most obvious and most-commonly employed descriptor of Asians found in the pulps is that of race, both in physical descriptions and in what are considered "Asiatic" bodily characteristics and mannerisms. "Yellow" terminology was used not only to distinguish "them" from "us," but, for many of the era, also as a line drawn, a kind of Rubicon that preceded an impending race war between the two. Such antagonisms can be seen in the years prior to the pulps of post–World War I America. In 1910, the celebrated author of *Call of the Wild*, Jack London, published "The Unparalleled Invasion," an early speculative-fiction tale set in 1976 that documents a war between the West and an awakened China, ending in the complete eradication of the "yellow race" via biological warfare.⁴⁸ The emphasis on the physical distinctions separating the races was a part of both scholarly and public discourse at the beginning of the twentieth century and continued with renewed interest into post–World War I America.

As shown in the previous section, the depictions found in pulp magazines, novels, films, and other media did not originate out of a vacuum. Racist and exaggerated to say the least, they appeared at a time not only when nativism and a fear of foreign "pollution" was at a fever pitch, but also when ideas concerning eugenics and "race suicide" were being published and widely read. Eugenics was a scientific discipline (or, rather, a scientific approach to a pseudo-scientific worldview) that sought to understand and then exploit differences in genes and breeding methods in order to evolve mankind into the better, higher race it is (theoretically) destined to become. For many followers of such a view, any "lower" races, which at the time consisted of nearly everyone who was not Anglo-Saxon, were to be driven to extinction. The idea of race suicide, not nearly as formal a science as eugenics, was simply the fear that if other races are not properly controlled (or destroyed, in some cases), the White race would disappear from the Earth. An understanding of the philosophies and writings that appealed to the nativist views of the time can better elucidate the atmosphere in which the pulps were created and thrived.

The idea of Anglo-Saxon supremacy was nothing new, and was an idea that filtered down through time, from the Enlightenment of the eighteenth and nineteenth centuries through to the years following World War I. Philosophers of the Enlightenment, such as Georg Wilhelm Friedrich Hegel, had written of Teutonic superiority and the backwardness of the Orient in works that had come to influence many ideologies and philosophers centuries after their initial publication (*The Philosophy of History*). The early 1900s saw the publication of many works which further espoused Anglo-Saxon superiority, works that, after the end of the First World War, saw higher levels of publication and popularity than had been the case previously. *The Races of Europe*, by economics professor William Z. Ripley, was among the first works to divide the races of Europe into specific categories (Teutonics, Alpines, and Mediterraneans), and to explain the basic differences between, and levels of superiority among, such groups. Ripley's book saw renewed interest in the early years of the twentieth century, along with Madison Grant's 1916 work *The Passing of the Great Race: or, the Racial Basis of European History.* Grant, a wealthy genealogist and amateur anthropologist, suggested that all previous successful (i.e. white) civilizations had succeeded only because of their ability to maintain Anglo-European stock, and that any large infusion of foreign (namely, Oriental) blood was the reason for their eventual downfall:

> With the expanding dominion of Rome, the native elements of vigor were drawn year after year into the legions ... while the slaves and those unfit for military duty stayed home and bred. In the present great war while the native Americans are at the front fighting, the aliens and immigrants are allowed to increase without check and the parallel is a close one.... In America we find another close parallel ... [the] Oriental races, who throughout history have shown little capacity to create, organize or even comprehend Republican institutions.[49]

Grant's view that "the Roman became ... less and less European and more and more Oriental until it, too, withered and expired" spoke volumes to a nation that was still reeling from the losses of a foreign war and the apparent loss of its traditional Anglo-American stock, or, at the very least, its values.[50] The book, initially published in 1916, saw several subsequent reprintings, with sales shooting noticeably upward after the end of the First World War.[51]

The overtly-prejudiced depictions of the physical traits of Asians, due in part to writings of such authors as Madison Grant and his followers, appeared in popular literature before the heyday of the pulps, and continued to appear in other media that were the pulp's contemporaries. Once again we may refer to Sax Rohmer's *The Insidious Dr. Fu Manchu* as containing many of the characteristics later Oriental pulp villains would follow:

> He wore a plain yellow robe, of a hue almost identical with that of his smooth, hairless countenance. His hands were large, long and bony, and he held them knuckles upward, rested his pointed chin upon their thinness. He had a great, high brow, crowned with sparse, neutral-colored hair. Of his face ... I despair of writing convincingly. It was that of an archangel of evil, and it was wholly dominated by the most uncanny eyes that ever reflected a human soul, for they were narrow and long, very slightly oblique, and of a brilliant green. But their unique horror lay in a certain filminess (it made me think of the *membrana nictitans* in a bird).[52]

This description, given by Dr. Petrie upon his first encounter with "the yellow devil," provides nearly all of the ingredients needed to compose the stereotypical yellow peril villain of the later pulp magazines. The emphasis on the color of the skin and the shape of the eyes; an appearance of stoic calculation and emotionless self-control; and a comparison of the Asian individual to an animal of some kind—all of these characteristics, and more, appear in the pulp periodicals. The Oriental villains

Wu Fang and Long Sin of Arthur Benjamin Reeve's 1916 novel *The Romance of Elaine* (which inspired a silent film of the same name, now lost) were described as having long "bony fingers" and of moving in a manner that is decidedly "monkey-like."[53] John Charles Beecham's 1920 novel *The Yellow Spider*, a contemporary of the pulp magazines, featured a character in the manner of Fu Manchu; a story that, once again, takes the Anglo-Saxon hero out of his element and places him deep in the depths of the East where "Ah Sing, the Yellow Spider, lay, watching events and spinning webs."[54] Works such as those of Rohmer's and Reeve's, written in a time of lower, yet certainly still existent, xenophobia and fear of a "yellow menace," set the foundation for the type of villainy that would appear in Beecham's and others' novels and the pulps, in which such fears were only heightened and inflated after the First World War.

A yellow, taut skin and bony, alien-like appendages were the most common and most exaggerated features ascribed to Asians in the pulps. Countless stories — too many to be fully enumerated here — contain references to "yellow devils," "yellow heathens," and "slinking Orientals." The term "yellow" is used as a descriptor of any Asian characters, whether applied to global masterminds in the vein of Fu Manchu or simply a humble Chinese "coolie." Many stories used such descriptions in their titles to give any prospective readers an idea as to just what type of tale awaited

Argosy All-Story Weekly, October 15, 1928, Argosy Communications.

them, as can be seen in pulp stories such as "Yellow Ghosts," "Yellow Men and Gold," and "The Tallow Devil." The "splash" (or opening) page of the T.T. Flynn story "The Evil Brand" alerted readers that the following story revolved around the "hall-mark of a saffron skinned terror tong that brought death to those who wore it."[55] The villain Koshinga of "The Escape" is described as having "yellowish eyes" set in a "huge, misshapen face ... black and diabolical ... utterly hostile to all that mankind envisages as good." Mr. Chang, villainous star of A.E. Apple's "Mr. Chang's Tong War," is presented in similar fashion to Fu Manchu, with the prerequisite emphasis on yellow skin and "inscrutable, black eyes [that] gave the impression of being thousands of years old." Li-Hung, the villain of *The Phantom Detective*'s "The Tomb of Death," had "a long, thin-fingered hand that loomed ghastly and evil in the moonlight" and "unseeing, almond-shaped eyes ... a face that was unmistakingly Oriental." In "The Kalgan Road," first published in the Winter of 1930–1931, Anglo-Saxon adventurer Jim Crane attempts to kidnap the Dalai Lama from his "yellow brethren" in a convoluted plot to secure ammunition for a besieged garrison of foreigners during (what is assumed to be, but never disclosed clearly as) the Boxer Uprising. Before Crane can get to the fortress, the wife of one of its commanders kills herself "rather than face these yellow devils."[56]

The practice of comparing Oriental characters to animals also appears in the pulps, in an obvious attempt to make them increasingly monstrous — men still in the grasp of some primeval, animalistic influence. Mr. Chang, the criminal mastermind previously referenced, was a regular villain of author A.E. Apple's stories. In an appearance in the October 25, 1924, issue of *Detective Story Magazine*, in "Mr. Chang, Man Trapper," the tong-man is not as cunning nor as highly placed in the tong underworld as in later stories. He is, however, depicted as being highly untrustworthy and particularly animal-like in both appearance and mannerisms:

> He ran a narrow red tongue around the edges of his dry parted lips.... Languidly Mr. Chang shuffled back and forth in the shadows at the far end of the veranda, keeping under cover from inquisitive Caucasian eyes. Somewhere in the distant woods sounded a shrill snarling scream; something in his catlike temperament quivered in response. He was half-tempted to answer.[57]

Throughout the story, in which Mr. Chang's first (printed) criminal enterprise involves the murder of a security guard and the theft of a local mine's gold shipment, the zoomorphism of Mr. Chang is rampant. Mr. Chang is "catlike" in his actions, his eyes "glow phosphorescently in the darkness," he leaps about "like a panther," and, at one point, he "hissed in his nostrils" like some sort of serpent. In fact, references to Mr. Chang in some sort of animal-like context appear in nearly every single paragraph in which he is mentioned.

Many Asian characters were compared with animals, apparently in an attempt to distinguish them even further from the rest of humanity. In Sidney Herschel Small's "Fireflies of Death" (*Detective Fiction Weekly*, January 9, 1932), the tong-master Kong Gai is described as having "snake-like influence" over the criminal underworld and sends one of his henchman to kill detective Jimmy Wentworth in his own hotel room, swinging "through the window like a yellow ape." In "The Warlords of Darkness" (*Adventure*, July, 1934), Mow Jie, the sidekick of Anglo-adventurer and All-American Man-of-Action Jimmy Harder, is also feline in appearance, to an almost superhuman degree. "And by some strange whim of subconscious suggestion," author Erle Stanley Gardner explains, "Mow Jie had grown into a human cat. He had eyes that could see in the dark, ears that were abnormally acute, a sense of smell that was more than human, and he moved through the night upon feet of velvet."[58] Such descriptions delve further into the nativist view of what separates "us" from "them." Perennial pulp villain Mr. Chang's reptilian mannerisms and bestial urges place him (and, directly, all of those like him) in a primitive, animalistic state bordering on humanity but still answerable to the savageness of beasts.

Detective Fiction Weekly, January 9, 1932, Argosy Communications.

The catlike aspects of many Asian pulp characters can be understood not only as a dehumanizing agent but also as the feminization of an entire race. Such feminization is also apparent in descriptions of Asian characters that involve extremely long nails, slender faces and figures, and clothing wherein robes are described more along the lines of dresses. Historian Robert G. Lee has noted that such feminization of a person (or entire race) was used in years past as a method of subjugation of that person, or race, in the mind of the reader. This is especially true when contrasted with a character of traditional, masculine composition, of which many of the heroic (white) figures of the pulps certainly were.[59] This was a time wherein women were quickly advancing in political rights, as evidenced by the passing of women's suffrage in 1919; and the conclusion of a world war that resulted in the depletion of the nation, and world's, supply of "old-stock" men in the eyes of many traditionalists. Combine such circumstances with the seeming passiveness on the part of many (according to nativists) in relinquishing the traditional American White man's hold on authority, and such a feminization of the enemy is not that surprising. Such a "reassurance" of masculinity can also be found in the pulps via the multitude of advertisements they published, promising everything from secrets to greater sexual abilities to courses in attaining Charles Atlas–like physiques and heightened levels of "manliness."

The pulps contained characters that are able to adopt disguises (sometimes simple, sometimes not) to better infiltrate Chinese tongs, Japanese temples or any other number of exotic locales that normally the White man is restricted from entering. Such plot devices speak to the importance that American popular fiction of the time placed on "physicality"— on the idea that among the most important aspects pertaining to a foreigner was his physical differences "from us." An example can be found in the April 15, 1919, edition of *The Thrill Book*, in the story "The Hidden Emperor," by George C. Hull. The story begins with two high-ranking officers in the American government discussing the threat posed by the reported creation of a "Pan-Asian" confederation, led by America's obvious enemy in the Pacific, Japan. Upon an intelligence officer's suggestion that they indeed have someone who can infiltrate the inauguration ceremonies of this conspiracy, a general asks, "And who is this man? Some two-faced Oriental taking money from both sides?"[60] At that moment, in a disguise of such completeness that the general is startled from his seat, in walks Captain Nullus Nemo, American adventurer and servant of Uncle Sam. With the aid of his Indian sidekick Runjeet Singh, Nemo embarks upon his journey to kidnap a descendant of Genghis Khan who is to be named emperor of this unholy alliance, assume his identity, and enter into the inner chambers of the mastermind of the operation, the dreaded "Yellow Pope," the Dalai Lama. "The Hidden Emperor" is but one of many tales in which a White man is able to "blend" in with the Asian (often criminal) community by simply altering his physical appearance.

Man Stories' 1930 short novelette "White Man," by Lyn Fox, takes the plot device of Caucasians masquerading as Asians to an absurd level; not only are the two eponymous characters able to first fool denizens of the Orient into thinking they are Buddhist monks, and later lowland bandits ("Bradford's white skin was stained with ocher, lending a surprisingly Oriental cast to his honest American face"), but one of them actually succeeds in convincing a frightful Chinese mob that he is the reincarnated Siddhartha Gautama, the Buddha himself.[61] In "The Hidden Monster," published in the Winter 1932 issue of *Oriental Stories*, an amateur sleuth is fascinated by the stories coming out of the nearby Chinatown of a new, golden deity that the local Chinese are flocking to in throngs, foregoing the traditional worship they have held for centuries. After a rejection by the local constabulary of his request for an investigation into this bizarre new religious practice, which involves the placing of the devotee's head into the gaping maw of the deity's statue, the sleuth decides to investigate the matter himself. "After an intensive and nauseating diet of carrots to yellow his skin to the appropriate shade," the amateur adventurer is able to ingratiate himself into the Chinese community and even becomes respected by many there who believe him to be a powerful tong leader.[62] Sev-

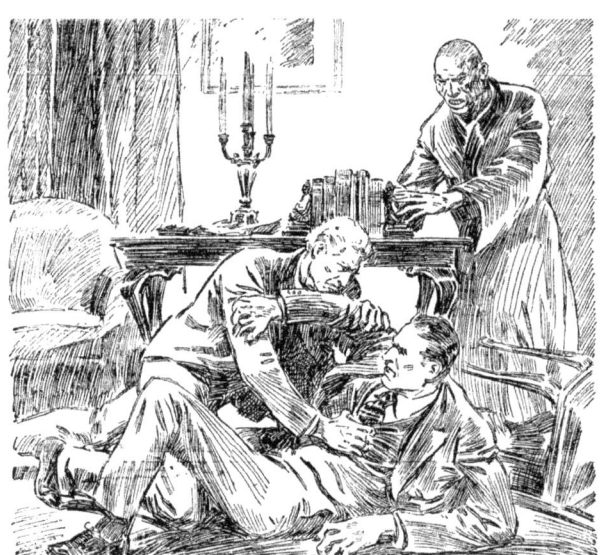

Illustration from "The Tallow Devil," *Phantom Detective*, October 1934.

eral months later, after faking the death of his tong alter ego, the former "Chinaman" reappears at the local police station, informing the astonished authorities that the "worship" is actually a cover for the smuggling of opium: the devout wear hats so that an unseen hand is able to place their pre-purchased amount of opium under their hat, freeing their hands from any incriminating evidence. Finishing his report to the police, the man proclaims, "I am tired of being a Chinaman. I think I will enjoy being a white man for a while." The pulp heroes, such as the Shadow and the Phantom Detective, often kept "Oriental" alter-egos in their repertoire of disguises in order to infiltrate secret societies and mystical cults.

The previously-mentioned "The Kalgan Road," which contains a scene wherein a Caucasian woman commits suicide rather than fall into the clutches of the "yellow devils," displays yet another aspect of the "white versus yellow" scenario — that of an antagonism not just between individual Caucasians and the Asians they encounter, but also of a larger "racial" resentment between the two. "Yellow Ghosts," penned by Robert E. Pinkerton for a 1928 issue of *Argosy All-Story Weekly*, uses not only "yellow" as a physical descriptor but also as a major narrative tool that emphasizes the loyalty that two white men are expected to share, dependent solely on the fact that they are both Caucasian. While prospecting for gold in Vancouver, rough-and-tumble outdoorsman Danny Sherburn serves as a guide to Vernon Kinnersley, a wealthy United States businessman who is interested in the rumors of a derelict Chinese junk that is said to have came to rest in the vicinity of Sherburn's encampment. Sherburn, who, throughout his time in the area, has seen "wraithlike, slant-eyed ghosts" creeping about near the shipwreck, has already unknowingly pilfered the treasure stored in the junk by removing planks he used for his shelter that were actually filled with gems from the court of the late Manchu dynasty.[63] When a group of tong-men arrive searching for the treasure as well, Kinnersley is kidnapped, while Sherburn and his companions flee into the nearby woods. Danny, however, decides to return to rescue Kinnersley. "He's a white man, and so are we. Those Chinks are capable of torturing him. There's at least ten, and they're armed," Danny admits. "But I never saw the time yet when a white man wasn't worth ten Chinamen, and there's two white men." The protagonist's rescue is cut short when it is revealed that there is more here than meets the eye, and that Kinnersley and the tong are actually working together to attain the loot. When things begin to turn sour between Kinnersley and his Chinese co-conspirators, he is once again left in the hands of the tong, this time not as a partner but as a prisoner. Upon realizing, once again that Kinnersley faces torture at the hands of the "Chinamen," Danny decides to aid the treacherous Kinnersley because it is a case of "a white man in the hands of those yellow devils ... he's white, whatever else he is."

Published in the August 1928 issue of *Amazing Stories*, "Armageddon 2419 A.D.," by Philip Francis Nowlan, was a work of fiction in which the superiority and righteousness of the Anglo-American would be displayed in contrast to the ruthlessness of the "yellow race" not in the present, but in the far future. Forgotten by most, thanks to the various adaptations, including television and comic series, which have appeared in the decades since his introduction, the exploits of space-hero Anthony (later "Buck") Rogers began as a singular novelette, foretelling a future overshadowed by a menacing yellow peril. Rogers, a Great War veteran who had fallen into a state of suspended animation after a toxic mine cave-in, awakes in the twenty-fifth century and finds America in ruins due to the ravages of "the Han":

> World domination was in the hands of Mongolians, and the center of world power lay in inland China, with Americans one of the few races of mankind unsubdued — and it must be admitted in fairness to the truth, not worth the trouble of subduing in the eyes of the Han Airlords who ruled North America as titular tributaries of the Most Magnificent.[64]

With the aid of future American survivors of the Mongolian invasion, Rogers fights to unite the scattered tribes of Americans and battle against the hegemony of the conquering Han.

A popular strain of the yellow peril theme personified this alleged Caucasian/Asiatic antagonism in the form of maniacal and tyrannical "yellow emperors," such as Rohmer's Fu Manchu and other similar characters. As previously examined, the yellow emperor appeared in American inexpensive literature as early as 1892's "The Electric Sea Spider" in the story paper *The Nugget Library*, and had remained a fixture in the industry ever since. The yellow emperor mixed the criminality associated with the Chinese tongs with the mystical and esoteric nature of the "Celestials" to create a being of base depravity and often paranormal abilities. Many, such as Fu Manchu or the previously mentioned Lakh-Dal, utilized futuristic technology in their plans of global domination, violating the West's supposed monopoly on science and modernity. Such archetypes appeared throughout the dime novels and later the pulps, especially in the mid-to-late 1930s, with some even receiving top billing in their own titles; Popular Publications released, in 1935 and 1936, respectively, *The Mysterious Wu Fang* and *Dr. Yen Sin*, two short-lived pulp series that borrowed heavily from Rohmer's fiction. In 1939, pulp hero the Shadow, who had begun as an announcer for *Street & Smith's Detective Story* radio show and proved popular enough to warrant his own series, first battled the evil of Shiwan Khan, an "Oriental mastermind who would conquer the world." Robert E. Howard, best remembered as the creator of Conan the Barbarian and one of the premiere weird fiction writers of the day, penned several tales of yellow-white racial antagonism. In the opening scene of "Skull-Face," first published in the October-December 1929 issue of *Weird Tales*, protagonist Stephen Costigan awakes from a dream-like state, having witnessed a supernatural horror of the "yellow" variety: "I thought at first it was merely a skull; then I saw that it was a hideous yellow instead of white, and was endowed with some horrid form of life. Eyes glimmered deep in the sockets and the jaws moved as if in speech."[65] Inside the opium-den in which he is currently a boarder, Costigan meets the bearer of this gruesome visage, concealed in the shadows, and is charged with a mission: to assassinate a British officer of great importance in the administration of the Crown's far-flung East African colonies. The one issuing these directives is the owner of the opium den and a reputed tong leader, feared in both Great Britain and throughout the civilized world. After at first refusing to comply with the assignment he had been given, Costigan is given the honor (or horror) of seeing his Master's face for the first time, the same demon-like visage he saw in his nightmares:

> [B]ut oh God, the face! A skull to which no vestige of flesh seemed to remain but on which taut brownish-yellow skin grew fast, etching out every detail of that terrible death's-head. The forehead was high and in a way magnificent, but the head was curiously narrow through the temples, and from under penthouse brows great eyes glimmered like pools of yellow fire.... A long, bony neck supported this frightful vision and completed the effect of a reptilian demon from some medieval hell.[66]

This Master, to whom Costigan owes both employment and the ending of his hashish cravings, which had brought him to the opium den in the first place, is revealed as the mystic and Oriental warlord Kathulos of Egypt.[67] Costigan, determined to release himself and the beautiful slave-girl Zuleika from the control of his Master, conspires with a veteran of Scotland Yard to arrange a situation wherein Kathulos may be apprehended. However, with the failure of his plan and his eventual capture, Costigan is shown the true nature of Kathulos, and his goal of white-servitude:

> Know you who I am? Kathulos of Egypt! ... I reigned in the dim misty sea lands ages and ages before the sea rose and engulfed the land. I died, not

as men die; the magic draft of life everlasting was ours! ... And you, you white barbarians, whose ape-ancestors forever defied my race and me, your doom is at hand! And when I mount my universal throne, the only whites shall be white slaves!

There were academic works of the time that enforced the idea of a perpetual "race-war," as seen in Costigan's battle with Kathulos and a myriad of other pulp narratives. A protégé of Madison Grant's, Lothrop Stoddard, in *The Rising Tide of Color Against White World Supremacy* (1921), echoed his mentor: "What is absolutely certain is that any wholesale Oriental influx would inevitably doom the whites, first of the Pacific coast, and later of the whole United States, to social sterilization and ultimate racial extinction."[68] While Grant saw the clash between races as a product of Darwinian battles for supremacy, Stoddard believed that the true tragedy of World War I was that it amounted to a civil war among the members of the white race, a war that left the white race demoralized and weakened, providing an enticing target for the unified hordes of the East.[69] The same year, William McDougall's *Is America Safe for Democracy* addressed the threat posed by the "yellow millions" of the Far East. McDougal also voiced his reasoning as to why exactly the white race was superior: the white race's survival and triumph in the Great War demonstrated, to McDougal at least, that it had passed a kind of litmus test for Darwinian survival, and was thus deserving of having dominion over the Earth. The fact that the First World War, for the most part (with the exception of fighting in Anatolia and other areas), was predominately a "white vs. white" war did not seem to enter into McDougall's thoughts.

As with other depictions, the exaggerated and monstrous physical features attributed to Asians by the pulps' authors worked to further alienate them from the "real" Americans, and to make them appear as subhuman if not outright bestial. The physical depictions, however, go one step further, as they are the most capable of providing a backdrop for a "race struggle" between white and yellow, the most basic interpretation of the yellow peril theme. The solidarity of whites and the yellow menaces bent on their destruction were the two factors at the very heart of the yellow peril.

Exotic Love Interests

"Red lips, half-parted, dark eyes like limpid seas of wonder, a mass of shimmering hair — framed in my drab doorway stood the girl of my dreams!"— *"Skull-Face"* (1929)

Zuleika, Costigan's love interest in Howard's "Skull-Face," provides another example of Asian stereotypes to appear in the pulps, as well as other media of the time. The majority of yellow peril imagery discussed thus far has been related to depictions of Asian males; there is, however, an altogether separate set of imagery where Asian women are concerned. Such imagery predates the yellow peril theme, stretching back to the earliest cultures of Western civilization. As Edward Said has pointed out, the "oriental-zation"—the exotic re-inventing of the East, and by direct association its women—has been a part of Western culture since the days of Aeschylus and Homer. Since antiquity, the exotic, mysterious nature of the Orient has been encapsulated in the form of the Asian female, an object of desire based solely on her deviation from "the norm," in a trend continued through the popular escapism of the twentieth century. What Western society (which, for the most part, means Western males) reviled and despised in Asian men— their "otherness"—was paradoxically what has made Asian females so appealing throughout American history and popular culture. Early film star Anna May Wong popularized such characters (predominately the cruel, manipulative, yet still exotic "dragon lady") in dozens

The demure "butterflies" are the Asian alabaster princesses of pulp fiction, whose exoticness, so hated in their male counterparts, provides their seeming irresistibility to the Occidental male (*Argosy All-Story Weekly*, December 8, 1928, Argosy Communications).

of films, roles that unfortunately led to her being typecast into such a singular corner of characterization. From the sympathetic, suffering Chinese mother in 1922's *Toll of the Sea*, to Fu Manchu's insidious heir in *Daughter of The Dragon* (1931), Anna May Wong ran the gamut of stereotypical Asian female roles. Even in such pigeonholed roles however, Wong was in the minority; Caucasian actresses (often in "yellow-face") usually performed such stereotypes. As with many things, the popular literature of the day, specifically the pulps, were not far behind in promoting what sold and, whether it is the case of inexpensive literature or big-budget motion pictures, the exotic femininity of the East obviously sold very well. The few examples that follow are only a sampling; just as the Oriental criminal or Chinese warlord appeared in the pulps issue after issue, year after year, so too did his female counterpart.

Do such depictions factor into the larger narrative concerning nativism to be found in this work? To some extent, no and yes. While such fascination with exotic women stretches back centuries, far longer than any of the modern circumstances related to post–World War I nativism, the depictions are born out of a belief that is concurrent with the larger, yellow peril themes found in anti-foreign sentiments; "they" are different, and are defined as such. Any discussion of nativist imagery that fails to mention "dragon ladies" and other similar Asian stereotypes is incomplete, and while perhaps not having the same origins as the masculine yellow peril, it still traverses the same path throughout the twentieth century, defined first by ethnicity and later, as geo-political situations (and American views concerning race and tolerance) changed, by reasons of ideology and socio-political realities. While one of the more recognized stereotypes of Asian women is the so-called "dragon lady," as far as the pulps are concerned this manner of characterization does not appear quite as often as another stereotype — that of the Asian "butterfly," the exotic love interest, or the "China Doll," to borrow a term from Sheridan Prasso's work *The Asian Mystique — Dragon Ladies, Geisha Girls,* and *Our Fantasies of the Exotic Orient*. "China Dolls" is refrained from use in this context, however, simply because the love interests to be found in the pulps did not hail only from China, but rather encompassed a larger area that "fit the bill" for Oriental exoticness — from China and Japan, and from the Middle East to the Indian subcontinent. Neither were all of these characters submissive and yielding to Caucasian dominance, as is typical among Prasso's "China Dolls"; rather, many show self-determination and toughness that, in its own way, was probably just as appealing to the pulp's male readership as was any appearances of servility.

It is not an exaggeration in the least to state that, while there were several titles and specific genres that were intended to appeal to both genders, the majority of pulps were aimed at a primarily male audience. As a result, many pulp magazines, regardless of genre, featured characterizations tailored to such a demographic. As is to be expected, horror and weird fiction titles, such as *Weird Tales* (where "Skull-Face" first appeared), often made use of the exotic female motif in stories that already had strange or unusual settings to begin with. Returning to "Skull-Face," Costigan's first sight of Zuleika describes perfectly the stereotypical pulp exotic love interest of the East:

> Her voice was soft and musical, with just a touch of foreign accent which I found delightful. As for the girl herself, every intonation, every movement proclaimed the Orient. She was a fragrant breath for the East. From her night-black hair, piled high above her alabaster forehead, to her little feet, encased in high-heeled pointed slippers, she portrayed the highest ideal of Asiatic loveliness — an effect which was heightened rather than lessened by the English blouse and skirt which she wore.[70]

One of Zuleika's predecessors in modern fiction was Kâramanèh, a servant of Fu Manchu, who often aids the protagonists and eventually betrays her Si-Fan master due to her love of Nayland Smith's partner, Dr. Petrie. Zuleika is the quintessential exotic love interest of the pulps — meek, submissive and (of course) attracted to Caucasian males, more so than to any member of her own ethnicity. Physical characteristics, most importantly any and all that may differentiate the character from "normal" white women, are emphasized and are often cited as the source of their beauty. Many, such as Kâramanèh and Zuleika, are eager to rebel against cruel masters in order to aid the hero and escape with him into Western civilization. Such characters do not appear solely in China proper but throughout the "non–Western" world. Fred MacIsaac's 1927 serial *Those Lima Eyes* revolved, to a large extent, around one of the main character's obsession with the exoticness of Peruvian women: "...very dark brunette, with midnight hair, and eyes like coals, an olive skin, a tiny foot, and a figure — oh boy!"[71] The exotic beauty of South American women is emphasized alongside the brutality of Spanish conquistadors in George M. Johnson's "Aztec Gold" (*Argosy All-Story Weekly*, January 1, 1927). As the history of the pulp magazines and the history of science fiction are intertwined, such imagery also appeared in SF tales, whether the stories took place on

Earth or on some distant world. This fascination with the "foreign woman" extended to aliens, robots, and beyond. While at first it may seem strange to include fictional races in a discussion of nativism, the same characterizations were used by many pulp authors, whether in Earthly or other-worldly fiction, to describe the exotic females; upon realizing this, the science fiction of the time has a good deal to more do with the "orientalizing" of "the other" than perhaps originally suspected. In the *John Carter of Mars* tales, penned by Edgar Rice Burroughs beginning in 1912 in *All-Story* before he rocketed to fame thanks to Tarzan, exotic beauties abound, and, while not specifically Oriental in ethnicity, they nonetheless feature many of the same physical characteristics of Zuleika, Kâramanèh, and the myriad host of other exotic love interests. The fact that Dejah Thoris and Thuvia, Maid of Mars, are denizens of the Red Planet only heighten their exoticness:

> Her face was oval and beautiful in the extreme, her every feature was finely chiseled and exquisite, her eyes large and lustrous and her head surmounted by a mass of coal black, waving hair, caught loosely into a strange yet becoming coiffure. Her skin was of a light reddish copper color, against which the crimson glow of her cheeks and the ruby of her beautifully molded lips shone with a strangely enhancing effect.[72]

Carter's description of his first encounter with Dejah Thoris, Princess of the Martian city-state of Helium, provides all of the needed attributes of the exotic, foreign beauty; if one were to replace "crimson" with "alabaster," the description could belong to any number of Far-Eastern "butterflies." While certainly a warrior of high stature on Mars, able to hold her own against the most dangerous opponents, Thoris quickly becomes reliant on the strapping, white Southern figure personified by John Carter.

Another "foreign beauty" of sorts appeared in the highly-misogynistic SF story "The Future Eve," by Auguste Villiers de l'Isle Adam. This English version of Adam's *L'Ève future* (translation from the original 1886 French, credited to Florence Crewe-Jones) premiered in the December 18, 1926, issue of *Argosy All-Story Weekly*. Similar to the *Maschinenmenschn* Maria of Fritz Lang's *Metropolis* (though pre-dating the film by several decades), "The Future Eve's" Andréide is a manufactured woman, intended to be the perfect woman as envisioned by man: beautiful, submissive, yielding and existing only to obey — the definition of many exotic love interests to be found in the pulps. Such characters as Dejah Thoris, the mechanized "Future Eve," and many more other worldly women factor into the nativist discussion simply because, despite their unorthodox origins, they contain the same attributes commonly ascribed to beauties from the exotic East, whether that be the cunning and ruthlessness of a dragon lady (Thoris) or the subservience of a demure "butterfly," the "perfect woman" (Andréide).

There exists examples of the exotic love interest that are not as submissive as Zuleika, nor as willing to escape into the West as Kâramanèh. The 1921, five-part serial *A Daughter of the White Star* features three protagonists — an American male, a girl of mixed Chinese and American ancestry; and her Chinese assistant, all of whom are fighting to aid in Sun Yat-sen's revolution for a free and modernized China. The heroine, while still the object of affection for the story's protagonist, is described as beautiful and alluring, but it is her bravery and dedication to her cause that fascinates the narrator. She does not throw herself into the arms of the hero as readily as other similar characters. Rather their bond is formed only after both have faced danger on equal terms. At the end of the story she chooses not to remain in America, instead rather returns to her mother's homeland in order to help build a new Chinese Republic. The fact that the male protagonist follows her on her quest, as opposed to the reverse, is telling in that this particular submissive-dominant dichotomy seems to be opposite what is normally found in such tales containing exotic love interests.

There also appeared stories of exotic beauties suffering under the control of their native, patriarchal societies, societies not benefiting from white civilization's "modernity." Stories such as "Della Wu: Chinese Courtesan" and "Flowers for Bow Kum," to be examined shortly, are examples of this sub-genre. There are instances of the Eastern beauty actually fearing being possessed by the white man; such stories, however, speak further to an "orientalized" East, mythic and mysterious, that seeks seclusion from the prying eyes of white civilization. A primitive, "Lost World" type of atmosphere accompanies such narrations; far from chastising readers for fantasies of tampering with a "forbidden culture," these tales depict eastern women as near-unattainable objects of desire, only enhancing their "exotic" allure. One such example is "The Dancer of Djogyakarta [sic]" (*Oriental Tales*, Winter 1932) — "The story of a lovely Javanese maiden, who called the Elder Gods of the Hindoos to aid her escape from the lust of white men who coveted her body."[73]

Many pulps featured short poems throughout the title, interspaced between the end of one story and the beginning of another. Such poems are often repositories for the pulps' fascination with the foreign, exotic beauty. Prime examples are the poems found in the pages of *Oriental Stories*, attributed to authors "Hung Long Tom" (obviously a pseudonym with sexual connotations), Clark Ashton Smith, and others. The poems act primarily as fillers in between stories, but are invaluable in their ability to convey what the pulp readers, specifically those reading *Oriental Stories*, wanted from their publication and, more importantly, from their fantasies of the exotic East. Poems such as "The Golden Girl," "Chinese Vase," and "Porcelain" demonstrate the fascination (some may say obsession) that permeates many pulp periodicals (and, honestly, a great deal of male-orientated fiction in general) in relation to exotic and foreign objects of enticement.

Regardless of the particular nature unique to each characterization, the over-arching theme of all is really very simple: the Oriental woman is a thing of exotic beauty, as befits someone hailing from the mythic East. She is something to be desired for her novelty, for her other-worldliness. It is, quite possibly, the most objectified understanding of a human being ever conceived, a system of stereotypes even more pervasive than those of the masculine yellow peril. While there are certainly dragon lady characters to be found in the pulps, the "orientalized" object of desire, submissive or not, was the predominant imagery used in regards to foreign women.

By the late 1930s the dragon ladies would appear more regularly in the pulps, and especially in the new comic books of the era. The nativist depictions of Asians, whether male or female, ultimately served the same purpose — to clarify the demarcations between "us" and "them" in the eyes of mainstream, Caucasian America. A humanizing and civilizing act is performed on the reader while reading, whether in the face of demonic characters such as Fu Manchu, or in the presence of fragile, submissive "oriental blossoms" who seek "us" for "our" civility and modernity.

As has already been demonstrated, American popular culture and politics were, at varying times throughout history, hostile to foreigners and in particular Asians. The Immigration or Quota Laws of 1921 and 1924 have already been discussed; the origins of these laws can be found in the xenophobia of the late nineteenth century and its own immigration laws, such as the Chinese Exclusion Act of 1882, which limited the amount of Chinese allowed into America. In 1922 the Cable Act was passed, which stated that the marriage of a foreign national to a female American citizen would result in the revoking of that female's citizenship in the United States.[74] In 1924, with the aid of eugenicist Harry Hamilton Laughlin, the state of Virginia passed the Racial Integrity Act, which made it a crime for members of one racial group to marry a member of another, and also provided state sanctions to the sterilization of "undesirables." This law stayed in effect in Virginia until 1967.[75]

I—*The American Pulps Between the World Wars, 1919–1935* 83

In such an atmosphere, what do the stories found in the pulp magazines of the 1920s and the 1930s tell us about Americans, and, specifically, about their views of Asians and foreigners in general? It is difficult, and rash, to simply assign racism to such a time period that differs from the current in so many ways. One reason for this difficulty, aside from the error of attempting to impose early twenty-first century political correctness upon those living in the early twentieth century, is the contradicting evidence of racial tolerance, and even racial acceptance, on the part of many Americans at the time. For every act of the federal government that attempted to impose immigration restrictions, there was an outcry from many denouncing the racial intolerance such acts legalized. While still using somewhat degrading terms ("Japs," "Chinese coolies"), G. K. Chesterton's *Eugenics and Other Evils*, published in 1922, presented warnings about the notion of the creation, or even existence, of an ideal, perfect human race.[76] In response to the 1922 Oregon law that practically enforced Americanization on all grade school children in the state, various groups, such as the Knights of Columbus, and, interestingly enough, a joining of the Catholic and Lutheran churches, argued against the legislation.[77] A number of United States senators were quite vocal in their opposition to the Immigration and Quota Laws of the 1920s on the grounds of intolerance; William E. Mason of Illinois argued that "if this bill had been passed 50 or 100 years ago hardly any of the House would have been here."[78] In 1924, the year of its publication, Crookshank's *The Mongol in Our Midst* was decried by the University of North Carolina's *Journal of Social Forces* as being based on "slim evidence" and only believable to those who were already committed to the idea of white superiority, a position the author of the review obviously did not hold.[79]

In response to the rallies against his 1915 epic *The Birth of a Nation* for its racially-insensitive depictions, director D.W. Griffith released the appropriately titled *Intolerance* (1916), which told of the devastating impacts that prejudice has wrought on humanity over the course of the previous two thousand years. Griffith's 1919 film *Broken Blossoms* portrayed its Chinese central character (albeit performed in yellowface by Richard Barthelmess) as sympathetic and full of "a pure and holy" virtue, with the murderous antagonists of the film all "Barbarous Anglo-Saxons, sons of turmoil" who hate "those not born in [their] great country"—a stark contrast to the yellow peril theme of its source material. Earl Derr Biggers, author of the 1925 detective novel *The House Without a Key*, which featured the first appearance of Charlie Chan, stated that his impetus in creating the Chinese sleuth was to combat the yellow peril imagery prevalent at the time and to portray a character of Asian ancestry that was just as capable of solving a crime as any of his Caucasian counterparts (while still, unquestionably, a bit too dependent on some stereotypes).[80]

Despite the amount of yellow peril and related themes that appear throughout the pulps, there were also instances of tolerance, kernels of understanding that saw the East as more than just a repository for yellow emperors and bloodthirsty tong-men. One such story is found in the November 1920 issue of *The Blue Book Magazine*. *The Blue Book Magazine* (also known as simply *Blue Book*) was one of the top selling general fiction pulp titles, alongside *Adventure* and *Argosy*. Often called the "King of the Pulps," *Blue Book* began its run in 1905, continuing throughout the decades, and in various forms, until its ultimate cancellation in 1975. "The Broker of Marriages," by Lemuel L. DeBra, provides (through the veil of a somewhat humorous and light-hearted tale) a sympathetic view of Chinese women, for whom arranged marriage was still common. When the local marriage-broker of a Chinatown hears the pleas of a young woman for release from the arranged marriage to which she has been "sentenced," the broker feels apologetic for imposing the traditional ways of her culture on this emissary of the next generation. "It was as though they felt but could not voice," writes DeBra, "the age-old cry of their sex — the cry of protest against 'the custom,' that custom which the tears of Chinese women for forty centuries have neither changed nor softened."[81] In the end, the young woman, who wants "to marry like the white women — for love," is removed from the obligations of the arranged marriage, in part due to the aid of the marriage-broker, and is allowed to marry the man whom she had personally chosen.

The heroine of "A Daughter of the White Star" extols her hope for China to join America in democracy. In reference to the Japanese fear of a strong, nationalistic China that could threaten the invader's hegemony in the region, the story's heroine proclaims: "And yet the foreign usurpers who rule the people of China would call it treason.... I am working for a free China, a China governed as the United States is governed. Liberty is for those who love her and dare for her, and if you are a friend of liberty there is no America, or China — there is only liberty![82] After unwittingly getting himself embroiled in the life-and-death struggle for Chinese democratic revolution, the main character, Thomas Munford, fights side by side with Asians "in whose veins flowed the blood of courage and devotion," those "doing yeoman service in the cause of Chinese liberty" who are "brave beyond the average man." In the form of Leota Jackson, the girl of biracial ancestry who has dedicated herself to the liberation of her mother's homeland, Munford observes that "it seemed to me the splendor of the Orient had been availed of by the modiste of the Occident to make her altogether elegant"; while certainly beautiful, there is also a sense of class and position in society that defines her. Despite the fact that "A Daughter of the White Star" does contain a few references to "singsong" speak and "hop heads" in an opium den, allusions of this sort are far and few between over the course of the entire story. These instances are nowhere near as prevalent, or derogatory, as are other references found in the majority of pulp stories that feature Asian characters. The hero fights alongside many Chinese to whom he has given a great deal of respect, and has, over the course of the story, grown less frightened and more interested in and respectful of the culture of the Orient, and has found it worth his life to fight for a republican China.

"Fifty Murders for the Love of Sweet Flower," by Clarence Reynolds (*True Strange Tales*, November 1929), is an account of the Bow Kum incident referred to earlier. Bow Kum, or "Sweet Flower," was "only a twelve-year-old Chinese girl, but her beauty wrung men's hearts." Through her unfortunate connections to the tongs of New York's Chinatown, she was murdered in one of the worst incidents of tong violence in American history, a death that hopefully, in the author's words, granted innocent Bow Kum "a peace that was denied her on earth."[83] While, to be sure, part of the story's purpose is to engender fear of the tongs, "Fifty Murders for the Love of Sweet Flower" is defined more by the sympathy it showers on the unfortunate figure of Bow Kum. The ill-fated girl is depicted as innocent and naive, happy in both of her relationships and heartbroken by their dissolution and the violence they wrought. Again, while the story does contain such phrases as "singsong" and "yellow-faced," and the cover of the magazine depicts a rather stereotypical view of "lustful Orientals," the story is overwhelmingly sympathetic to both Bow Kum and the men who loved her during her brief life.

Frank Owen's 1931 short-story "Della Wu, Chinese Courtesan" is another piece of pulp fiction wherein a female Chinese character is intended to be the object of the reader's sympathy. In China, where "a boy is cause for rejoicing, but the birth of a girl is looked upon ... as something approaching disgrace," Della Wu is born, the product of a loveless marriage, and is eventually put into service as a courtesan.[84] Through cleverness she is able to avoid the advances of many suitors — except one, who sees through her various ploys and steals her away from her home. Della Wu escapes her kidnapper through a final act of trickery — convincing him to cross a particular bridge while carrying her, a bridge she knows cannot hold a great deal of weight. Della Wu, along with her attacker, both drown, the author giving the suggestion that for a creature such as Della Wu, whose beauty and talents are praised throughout, death was more of a release than a tragedy.

From 1930 to 1933, in the pages of the quintessential crime pulp *Black Mask*, author Raoul Whitfield (sometimes writing under the pseudonym Ramon Decolta) provided tales of Jo Gar, a Filipino "private dick" who, much like Charlie Chan before him, was created to counter many of the yellow peril stereotypes then prevalent at the time. Twenty-four of Whitfield's stories feature Jo Gar, a character inspired by Whitfield's own time spent living in the Philippines. As pulp historian E.R. Hagemann makes clear, "No question about it. Decolta/Whitfield was an innovator in seriously using an Asian protagonist during this period."[85] Hagemann goes on to place Jo Gar in the upper echelon of Asian literary detectives in American fiction, followed only by Hugh Wiley's Lee Wong (much less stereotyped in print than in his cinematic portrayal, courtesy of Boris Karloff) and John P. Marquand's Mr. Moto.

Even the letter columns of the pulps provide evidence of tolerance in an otherwise nativist atmosphere. *Adventure* magazine, in an issue from 1920, published a letter written by a reader who was enraged by a previous reader's demand that a particular author be restricted from submitting works to the title on account of his name (Liebe) being Germanic in origin. The editor, in a reply to both letters, stated

Still an example of the stereotypical "Chinese butterfly," Della Wu's tale invites empathy from the reader on the part of the tragic heroine (illustration from "Della Wu, Chinese Courtesan," *Oriental Stories*, February–March, 1931).

that he "would not have discriminated against any German-named or German-born loyal Americans" in what can certainly be understood as quite a bold statement given the nativist atmosphere of the time.[86] In the editorial and letters column of *Oriental Stories*, for its February–March 1931 issue, the editor expressed dismay at the seeming loss of traditional cultures in the Orient, and that "modernization is slowly forcing the world into a common standard of customs."[87] In the Summer 1932 edition of the same title a reader wrote in to complain that he did not believe that a recent story's depiction of Muslims was culturally accurate. "But Timur [Tamerlane] was an Orthodox Moslem," Francis X. Bell, from Chicago, explains, "and consequently never drank at all. Mr. [Robert E.] Howard should know, if he has studied the history of Islam, that drinking alcoholic liquors is expressly forbidden by the Koran."[88]

Again, it must be noted that many of the stories that do present an overall positive (or at least not quite as negative) view of Asians still suffer from the terminology and views of the time, with language such as "yellow," "singsong," "hatchet-men," etc. It would be absurd to argue, in light of yellow-face acting and immigration quotas, that understanding and tolerance were widespread; but then again, that is not what is being suggested. When compared to the majority of stories in which the very humanity of Asians is called into question (and at times outright denied), a small collection of narratives can be considered fairly tolerant and sympathetic. These offerings of respect, or at least open-mindedness, reveal that, while feelings of xenophobia and nativism ran high, the foundations of such views were being questioned by some, lending a tolerant voice to an otherwise intolerant landscape.

By the mid–1930s, many such ideas, such as those of Madison Grant and F.G. Crookshank, had begun to fade from academic discussion (even though related depictions still continued to occur in the pulps and other media). This change was in part due to the rising threat of Japanese aggression in Asia, which created a sympathetic figure in the form of China as a victim of Japanese imperialism. As will be seen, by the time of America's involvement in World War II, the "Grantian" view of race collapsed under the onslaught of both academia and nationalism. The 1920s, especially the years immediately following the end of World War I, however, saw nativism in America, and its message of Anglo-Saxon sanctity, reach its highest level. As a result, the majority of both academic and popular publications concerning the "white" and "yellow" races appeared in the early years of that decade, with their influences lasting far longer.

II

THE HUN AND THE NIPPONESE HORDES

The American Pulps and Comic Books of World War II, 1935–1945

On December 13, 1937, the Empire of Japan launched an offensive against the beleaguered capital of the Republic of China, Nanjing. Having first landed on China's coast at Hangzhou Bay, the Imperial Army marched west to the ancient capitol, a passage that was strewn with the corpses of any man, woman, or child unfortunate enough to find themselves in its path.[1] Condemnation on the part of the world's governments followed the Rape of Nanjing, but little else. This was, after all, the era of appeasement. The following year the *Anschluss* of Austria, succeeded by the seizing of Czechoslovakia, saw Nazi Germany grow in territory and in ambition. Europe was not alone in its appeasement policies; isolationist America had long offered verbal objurgations, but not much else, in the face of Japan's aggression in China and imperialism throughout the Pacific.[2] The early and mid–1930s were not years that saw the world teetering on the brink of war; rather, war had already begun. Japan's desecration of Chinese sovereignty had begun years before Nanjing with its invasion of Manchuria in 1931 and the founding of the puppet state Manchukuo, with former Qing Emperor Aisin Gioro "Henry" Pu Yi as Emperor. Benito Mussolini, fascist dictator of Italy, launched an offensive into Ethiopia in 1935, and Hitler, having been granted the Chancellorship of Weimar Germany by a decrepit and politically-inept President Paul von Hindenburg, had been threatening war unless his thirst for Austria, Czechoslovakia, and ultimately Poland was quenched. With the signing by these three nations of the Tripartite Pact in September 1940, the long dreaded war that the failure of

Versailles had promised, and America had long feared, was a growing possibility if not an outright probability.

The Stock Market Crash of 1929 that had brought an end to the "Roaring Twenties" and inaugurated the Great Depression had dealt a staggering blow to the American psyche. Unemployment skyrocketed, and breadlines filled the streets of the nation as the future of the country appeared darker than it ever had before. As much as one may think such circumstances would draw America inwards to focus on internal dilemmas, such was the growing turmoil internationally that no amount of nativism present could keep America, or its popular fiction, isolated from transnational matters. Fictional predictions of invasion and subjugation in popular media appeared side-by-side with daily newspapers detailing the war mongering antics of Europe's dictators. The panic caused by the October 30, 1938, Orson Welles radio adaptation of H.G. Wells' *War of the Worlds* indicates the fear of a nation readying itself for invasion.

The nativist imagery of 1920s and early 1930s America was still very much alive during the years of totalitarianism's rise abroad and continued economic stagnation at home. What differed as the 1930s drew to a close were the targets of this imagery. The pulp magazines, with their yellow emperors and blood thirsty tong-men, began a slow but steady decline in popularity during the early 1940s. This growing void in cheap, popular literature was partly filled by a narrative media that, in many ways, had been inspired by the success of the pulps: comic books. Likewise, the imagery prevalent in the pulps, of "Fu Manchus" and "Mr. Changs," did not necessarily go away but rather underwent an interesting augmentation. In the late 1930s the comic books followed the pulps with imitations of Sax Rohmer's Fu Manchu and similar yellow peril characters; as the years went on, the formerly "generic" Asiatic villain (usually Chinese) was given a concrete nationality and, more importantly, an ideology. The yellow emperor was no longer Dr. Fu Manchu; it was the Showa Emperor, Hirohito. And his followers were no longer the teeming hordes of a "sleeping" China but instead the mad, fascist legions of the Rising Sun. As Japanese aggression mounted in the East and imperialistic advances were made throughout the Pacific, the "Nipponese" became the primary targets of the racist imagery previously reserved for all Orientals. Furthermore, Asian characters of other nationalities, such as Chinese and Korean, were depicted in a more positive light — as fellow democratic brethren fighting against foreign invasion.

In addition to the amalgamation of the "Yellow Peril" with the "Nipponese Peril," a second villainous depiction appeared (or, rather reappeared) in the form of the Hun, the monstrous (in both depravity and appearance) Teutonic brute of World War I propaganda. The Hun, having appeared here and there in the pulp magazines of the '20s and early '30s (mostly in the many war and spy-themed series that existed during the inter-war years) re-emerged once again in American popular literature, now sporting a Swastika as opposed to the Prussian Eagle of the Hohenzollern dynasty. The appearance of Hunnish (or, rather, "Nazi Hun") depictions, and the transference of the yellow peril from all Asians generally to the Japanese in particular, were contemporaneous with an overall shift in racial views occurring in America at the time. Most important to this shift was the decline in "scientific racism" in intellectual circles. A second reason was the fact that in the wider public sphere this "scientific racism" and its insistence on a biologically superior race proved too similar to the ideology of Nazi Germany. These two reasons overlapped, and either one can be considered a response to the other.

Despite the racially-charged imagery and rhetoric that appeared during the war years, popular and academic support for "scientific racism" and similar systems of thought were on the decline. Elazar Barkin, in *The Retreat of Scientific Racism — Changing Concepts of Race in Britain and the United States Between the World Wars*, points out that for many in academia an antagonism to the Grantian view of race had been mounting for quite some time (and in many cases had been held all along), but hindrances such as the weight of public opinion and political obstacles to publication hampered the printing of such sympathetic works for years, and possibly decades.[3]

The scholarly attack on ideas such as those of Madison Grant and Lothrop Stroddard had begun as soon as their works were published, but the critique did not reach truly effective levels until the late 1930s and early 1940s. By 1939, academic work on dismantling the "Great Race" understanding of anthropology had begun, with the closing of eugenics study centers at various schools. The Carnegie Institution had forced famed eugenicist Harry Hamilton Laughlin into retirement by year's end and ceased publication of the widely-read (among eugenicists circles, at least) *Eugenical News*.[4] One of the scientists most credited with helping to overturn the wide acceptance of such views was Ashley Montagu, an anthropologist who would eventually teach at Rutgers University and aid in the United Nations' codifying of accepted policies regarding racial distinctions and relations. In 1942, Montagu published the first edition of his attack on the Anglo-American superiority complex, *Man's Most Dangerous Myth — the Fallacy of Race*. In it he states:

> Not one of the great divisions of man is unmixed, nor is any one of its ethnic groups pure; all are, indeed, much mixed and of exceedingly complex descent. Nor is there any scientific justification for overzealous or emotional claims that any one of them is in any way superior to another.... Far from being "well-grounded," this is a view [speaking of Nazi-Aryan superiority] which no biologist and no anthropologist with whom I am familiar would accept. It is today generally agreed that all men belong to the same species, that all were probably derived from the same ancestral stock, and that all share in common patrimony.[5]

Montagu also attacked the work of Carleton Stevens Coon, an American anthropologist at Harvard who, in 1939, had written a new edition of William Z. Ripley's *The Races of Europe* (1899). Both versions of the text argued in favor of varying origins for the different "branches" of mankind (and, in many minds, varying levels of intelligence and teleological importance connected to each race).[6]

Another pioneer in the dismantling of the Grantian understanding of racial hierarchies was Franz Boas, a Jewish refugee from Europe and a member of Columbia University's faculty. Boas, a longtime critic of the "Great Race" mentality, pushed for the drafting of a "Scientist's Manifesto" that would hopefully expunge white dominance views from the center of academia and relegate them to the fringe. The Manifesto was eventually drafted in December of 1938 and signed by over 1,284 scholars and scientists, including three Nobel Prize winners and sixty-four members of the National Academy of Sciences.[7] This drive to rid scholarly American literature of the eugenicist vision of race hierarchies was in part a corollary to the widespread resentment Americans felt towards Nazi Germany. The regime's rhetoric concerning a "master race" was an ideal that contradicted the popular egalitarian notion of America itself. With the abhorrence of Nazi Germany accelerated by America's entry into the war and the need to cement an understanding of what separates "us" from "them," the push towards a wholesale rejection of a hierarchical analysis of racial and ethnic groups was a priority for both academia and American propagandists.

The purpose of this chapter is to demonstrate how the aspects of American nativism carried over into the "new" enemies of the Second World War, the Nazis and the Japanese (with the other Axis powers, such as Italy, usually being lumped together with the Nazis.) Assaults on the morality, language, culture, and physical characteristics of the "other" persisted, but with a narrower definition of "the other." What was once a largely imagined threat confined to the pages of popular literature suddenly became very real; the envisaged assault that nativism had predicted was now a possibility, as enemies across both the Atlantic and Pacific oceans readied for war. Nativist imagery survived (with some exceptions) in the depictions of the Nazis and, to a larger degree, the Japanese. Not only did the yellow peril transfer to the Japanese in particular, but this transition affected other Asiatic groups (Chinese and Koreans, for example) in that their depictions were less demonic, and in many cases noble and heroic. This chapter differs from the previous in that an examination of heroes (as opposed to primarily the villains) is undertaken to better elucidate what was considered "good" and "American." The existence of predominantly all-white heroes, followed by the (albeit painfully slow) introduction of non-white protagonists, is an essential part of understanding this phase in pulp and comic narratives. It is also the purpose of this chapter to show a shift in America's collective response to racial differences and to show an augmentation of the nativist view that had dominated the decades prior to the Second World War. The multiculturalism (or aspirations to it) that in part defines modern America has many of its origins, strangely enough, at a time during which the Armed Forces were segregated and the quota system of immigration was still enforced. This is not to say that Anglocentric racism disappeared as a result of World War II. The creation of internment camps such as Manzanar, and the continued use of "yellowface" acting in Hollywood, is proof of the longevity of such ideas. Nevertheless, taking into account a wider view of the period, a definite change can be seen if one compares the themes found in works from the earlier pulps, like "Yellow Men and Gold" (*Adventure*, 1910), with those of the 1940s, such as "How Japan Debauches Chinese Girls" (*Argosy*, 1942).

Pulps Before America's Involvement in the Second World War

Despite diplomatic overtures intended to reassure the Axis that America had no intention of getting involved in the escalating global conflict, United States participation was understood by many to be an eventuality by the beginning of the 1940s. America had already identified on which side sympathy officially rested, first by the 1940 oil embargo against Japan following the Empire's seizure of French-Indochina, and then by the initiation of the Lend-Lease program in the spring of 1941. In the popular culture, the battle lines were being drawn as well. Superman, Batman, and the other superheroes originally fought to right domestic and societal ills in the Great Depression; as the likelihood of American involvement in World War II increased, so too did the number of characters sent preemptively to the European and Asiatic fronts.[8] Such characters spoke to the rising patriotism evident in the months preceding Pearl Harbor. According to Captain America co-creator Jack Kirby, "Captain America was created for a time that needed noble figures.... We weren't at war yet, but everyone knew it was coming. That's why Captain America was born; America needed a superpatriot."[9] And, indeed, Captain America was only one of many "superpatriots" to appear in comic books in the years preceding 1941. This patriotism, however, also reveals a sense of idealism, a type of fantasy on the part of isolationist America — the idea that possibly America's involvement in the war could be avoided. It was the hope that someone would arrive in the nick of time (as many superheroes did) to avert the coming disaster. The fact that many superheroes first battled nationally ambiguous proxies of Germany and Japan, followed by those countries specifically named, reveals both this sense of idealism, and the pragmatic realization that eventually America could not avoid entanglement.

The majority of the 1930s and the early 1940s, however, still belonged to pulp literature. Some pulps presented short fiction that foretold near-apocalyptic levels of destruction in America's future as a result of the coming war. Others featured stories of valiant heroes either preventing such a conflict or emerging from the rubble to rebuild Western civilization. With a few exceptions (such as the Scientifiction pieces to be examined later), the pulps featured more realistic, albeit somewhat depressing, images of future war, such as scenes of American subjugation. While many pulps still showcased traditional Chinese tong villains up to the very start of America's involvement in World War II, as evidenced by the appearance of "the master of all brigands — Li Hoang" in "The Golden Pagoda," and the devilish mystery of "The Chinese Primrose," both appearing in the hero-pulp *The Shadow* (March 1, 1938, and February 15, 1941, respectively), such stories began to fade.[10] They were replaced in large part, beginning as early as the late 1930s, with stories featuring Japanese (or ethnicities implied, but not specifically mentioned, to be Japanese) as villains, not just in the back alleys and crime districts of America, but also as a threat to global Anglo-Saxon hegemony. At the same time, German aggression was beginning to find its way into the pages of the pulps.

Pulp narratives published in the years preceding the Second World War can be understood as fictionalized "warnings" to the populace, along with a healthy dose of sensational and adventurous fiction. As would be the case in 1950s comic books predicting a Third World War between America and the Soviet Union, these pre–World War II stories seemed, in addition to simple entertainment, to act as something akin to cautionary tales concerning America's possible future. As early as 1935, a stand-in for possible Japanese and German invasions appeared in the pages of pulp-hero magazine *Operator #5*. Secret agent Operator #5 often battled foreign elements in his adventures, and his magazine eventually became a collection of interlinked novels depicting attacks, invasions, occupations and battles of resistance against foreign aggressors. The March 1935 issue tells the story of the "Blood Reign of the Dictator," by Curtis Steele (actually a pseudonym for a host of authors), in which a madman has succeeded in taking control of a large portion of the American continent: "It was as though, for the moment, they had been transported to a European nation terrorized by the despotic power, the bloody purges of a militaristic dictator. Yet this spot was located just outside the capital of one of the forty-eight United States!"[11] The September 1935 issue's cover story featured a "Yellowese" villain that speaks more to a fear of growing Japanese strength than to a fear of hatchet-men and

As totalitarianism grew abroad, many pulps reflected the fear such circumstances wrought in the American psyche (*Argosy Weekly*, August 28, 1937, Argosy Communications).

tong-lords. In "Invasion of the Crimson Death Cult," Operator #5 and his faithful assistant Tim Donovan do battle against "The Son of Kasma," a Fu Manchu–like villain who is spreading a new religion across America in order to pave the way for his invasion of the nation and its incorporation into "the Yellow Empire":

> The Son of Kasma has not only plotted to seize control of the United States government. He has planned to establish Hako [a kidnapped Eastern prince Kasma is using as his tool] as the figure-head of this country. It is a scheme to spread the cult of Kasma from the United States into the Yellow Empire. That alone will give the Son of Kasma virtual domination of more than half the globe.[12]

The threat posed by the "Son of Kasma" is not that of a singular tong-lord hoping to spread his criminal enterprises, as would have been the case in pulps past, but rather an emissary of a ravenous and imperialistic "yellow" empire determined to undermine American sovereignty. *Operator #5* would continue to feature stories tailored to anxieties concerning growing belligerency abroad, such as "Liberty's Suicide Legions" (January 1937), "Revolt of the Devil Men" (May–June 1938), and "The Dawn That Shook The World" (December 1938). As Operator #5 and Tim sought to dislodge the "Yellow Messiah" and others' footholds in America, additional pulp magazines were beginning to feature stories that involved the invasion of America by foreign foes, from both the East and the West. The jack-booted, blonde youth giving a Nazi salute in front of a burning New York City below the words "Mailed Fist Over America" on the cover of *Argosy Weekly*'s August 28, 1937, edition promoted its feature story, "Kingdom Come," by Martin McCall. *Argosy Weekly*, in its July 16, 1938, issue, premiered the first installment of a six-part serial, "The Invasion of America," by Frederick C. Painton, with the ominous descriptor: "This is the story of the second World War — the conflagration kindled by the world's unrest and fanned into flame by one man's ruthless ambition to become master of mankind. Beginning a powerful novel of Fascism tomorrow."[13] The narrator explains the international scene that neutral America faces in the story, an image that was not too divergent from the reality:

> Hitler was threatening Czechoslovakia, and demanding colonies on pain of drastic action. Mussolini was mobilizing troops on the Libyan border, threatening to invade Egypt. England was having another cabinet crisis and the anti–America prime minister, Joseph St. John, was castigating the United States bitterly for failing to back up England's protests to a new Japanese invasion of China. The Spanish Rebels had launched the final offensive against Valencia. Russia was purging itself of anti–Stalinites.[14]

In the story, despite continued negotiations between Secretary of State "Crull" and Japan, relations between the two nations remain tense. Unfortunately, all efforts at peace are shattered with the deaths of Japan's crown prince and princess, an act of assassination that receives sympathy from both Hitler and Mussolini, and is blamed on the United States. After days of silence on the part of the Japanese Emperor, the story's first installment ends with radio broadcasts reporting a Japanese attack on the Philippines and the taking of Manila. By the end of the story several issues later, the American republic had been toppled and reorganized into a totalitarian state.

The May 27, 1939, edition of *Argosy Weekly* contained the short novelette "Tomorrow," by pulp mainstay Arthur Leo Zagat. The cover illustration forecasts a foreboding world: a screaming Asiatic soldier, bearing a (seemingly) Japanese uniform and a bayoneted rifle, stands astride a burning continental United States, while a question, printed to the left of his head, asks "Will your children walk in chains as slaves of the Yellow Horde?" Similar in vein to Buck Roger's inaugural story, "Armageddon 2149 A.D.," "Tomorrow" paints a picture of a wild and backward America, destroyed by "yellow men" who "had come out of the East to make this world a Hell," and sparsely populated by the remnants of that bygone world — white Americans.[15] When compared to Buck Rogers' futuristic setting, it is not quite clear how long it has been since America had been conquered in the "Tomorrow" narrative; chil-

Japanese enemies began to replace Chinese enemies as war drew closer (*Argosy Weekly*, July 16, 1938, Argosy Communications).

dren are living in caves, speaking of "Old Ones" and "the yesterday," while airplanes and rifles are still in use by the enemy, which is composed of both "yellow" and "black" men. While America has been destroyed, it is prophesied that the white man will once again reclaim his own land from the "yellow horde." The story concludes with the protagonist Dikar's promise to lead the American revival. "I have to," Dikar explains, "because down there is the America of which the man spoke, an[d] this is the tomorrow he talked about, an[d] we are the children of yesterday who will re-conquer those green and pleasant fields for democracy, and liberty, and freedom."16

"Tomorrow" proved popular with audiences, and a sequel story, Zagat's "Children of Tomorrow" appeared in the

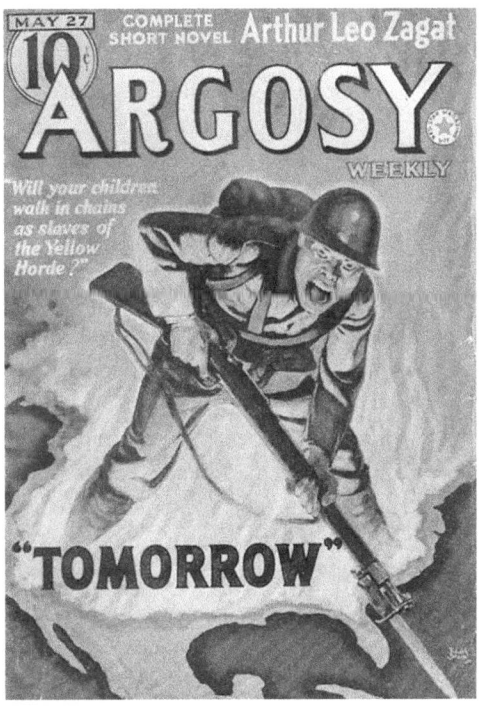

Shortly before America's involvement in the Second World War, stories such as Zagat's "Tomorrow" series projected the horrors of a Japanese invasion of America (*Argosy Weekly*, May 27, 1939, Argosy Communications).

June 17, 1939, issue of *Argosy*. "They are the hope and promise of America — these Lost Children who by a miracle survived the destruction of their generation," reads the sequel's tagline. "But before their Tomorrow can come they shall destroy the Barbarians who ravage their country's green fields and rolling hills — for the night cannot last forever."17 "Children" covers the battle between the surviving Americans and "Captain Li Logo," leader of the "hordes who came out of the East" and commander of the "yellow and black men," whom Dikar defeats by the end, bringing America one step closer to regaining her sovereignty. The story was expanded into four more installments, with the final chapter, "Long Road to Tomorrow," published over two years after the first, in the March 1, 1941, issue of *Argosy*, the entire epic eventually being collected and titled "The Tomorrow Trilogy" (with the six short stories being combined so as to create three larger installments).

Even the science fiction-centric magazines of the day were affected by the rumblings of belligerency across the oceans. The February 1939 issue of *Marvel Science Stories* featured Willy Ley's commentary "Atlantropa — the Improved Continent," which provided pseudo-scientific evidence as to how a damming of the Straits of Gibraltar could "raise" more land throughout the Mediterranean and appease the dictators of "land-grabbing, war-crazy Europe."[18] In an issue dated a month after Hitler's September invasion of Poland, the October 1939 edition of *Thrilling Wonder Stories*, billed as "The Magazine of Prophetic Fiction," offered Oscar J. Friend's "Experiment with Destiny," which provided a fantastical and idealistic solution to the belligerence of Europe. A recent German émigré and famous scientist, who believes in "the destiny of humanity, a great destiny which transcends national boundaries," creates both a device that can instantly transport individuals from one location to another, as well as a ray that is able to greatly extend the life of anyone it "zaps."[19] Using these two innovations, the scientist transports the "mad dictators of Europe" to his laboratory in America and offers them a choice: take advantage of his life-extending ray and continue the relative stability they had brought to their countries (despite their ruthless policies), or face execution before their ambitions can bring disaster to an already fragile Earth. The world leaders choose long life. It would seem that the ray also had a secondary effect of making those who it touched more sympathetic to the world-egalitarian views of its creator: "From all appearances these were fit men indeed to rule Europe for a period of a full one hundred years, molding their countrymen into such an inflexible pattern of peace and charity and good will for four or five more generations that hatreds and prejudices and wars would become things accursed."[20] The September 1940 issue of *Amazing Stories* contained stories that both spoke to America's fear of an Oriental invader and the ambitions of power-mad European dictators. Robert Moore William's "Fifth Column of Mars" combines the fear of foreign saboteurs plotting from within with an otherworldly, Asiatic menace appearing at the height of Japanese imperialism. The cover features a Martian of stereotypical Oriental design: a bald head, beset with gigantic ears, bushy eyebrows atop slanted eyes, and fangs protruding from a grimacing mouth. While tracking a ring of foreign spies, a Federal agent named Keenan is whisked away to Mars and encounters a grotesque and evil menace to America:

The creature looked a little like a man. There was one horrible exception — he had a fanged mouth! The fangs were like tiger teeth, curved, round and yellow. The face was malevolent, evil. The fangs made it more sinister.... Displaying fangs, their captor answered. His voice was high and sing-song. It vaguely resembled Chinese. But it was in no language known to Keenan [the Federal agent].[21]

Though describing a Martian, the author of the story not only employs traditional "yellow peril" imagery but does so in such a way that, given the period during which it appeared, creates a correlation with the fears concerning rising Japanese belligerence. The issue's second feature story was "Blitzkrieg—1950," by Frederic Arnold Kummer, Jr. The story's inspiration is apparent from its tagline: "Coale had the secret of U-235 in his grasp. Then out of the sky came the minions of a conqueror seeking atomic power."[22] The goal of every major world power by the beginning of the 1940s was to acquire atomic power. This objective, combined with the Nazis' use of fantastically modern methods of warfare, such as the blitzkrieg and their eventual mastery of the dreaded V-2, provided ample characterization for the story's antagonist — Grom, who, following the end of the "European War," had become ruler over a federated "United Europe." "In the old days," one of the story's protagonists recalls, "conquerors made

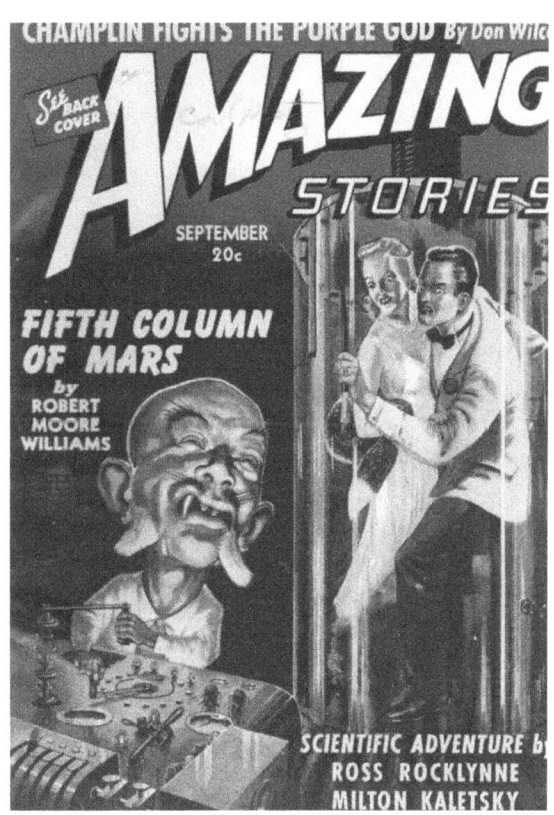

As was the case in preceding decades, science fiction often masked contemporary enemies in fanciful and alien disguises (*Amazing Stories*, September 1940).

slaves of the strong, put them to work. Grom's modern. He's made slaves of the world's best brains, using their genius to perfect the greatest of all war machines, and to deprive his future enemies of scientists."[23] The American hero eventually succeeds in preventing the secret of the volatile element from falling into the hands of the power-mad dictator, destroying the villain's enrichment plant (as well as the villain himself) in a terrific explosion that ensures that, with the secret of the unstable compound "in the hands of our government, America will remain inviolate!"[24] While both of these stories are based in the more fantastical realm of science fiction, they still relate the fears and hopes of the time. The fear of an alien invader (and from some nativists' perspectives, the "Orientals" were as alien as they come), and the hope that the ruthless warlords of Europe and Asia would eventually be stopped by American do-gooders, are both present even in narratives that are quite far from the "real" world of more general fiction.

The most popular pulp magazines were undergoing radical transformations by the beginning of the 1940s. Many genres, such as pulp hero and war titles, were still successful, but it was in the pages of pulp leader *Argosy* that one witnesses a profound change in both purpose and content. While other leading general fiction magazines, such as *Adventure* and *Short Stories* (which ran from 1890 to 1959, and was known for its slogan "Twenty-five stories for twenty-five cents!"), were able to retain their identities as primarily fiction-oriented periodicals, industry mainstay *Argosy* was undergoing something of an identity crisis. With the sales of pulps dropping and the popularity of "slicks" and comic books rising, *Argosy* was attempting to redefine itself in a new market. Seventeen years after the death of Frank A. Munsey, *Argosy* was sold to pulp rival Popular Publications in 1942, which also published *Adventure*. The years prior to, and immediately following, Popular's acquisition of the title saw the magazine shed its "all-fiction" persona and adopt more articles and "current event" pieces. (This was just one of the changes *Argosy* underwent until it completely converted years later into a "slick" magazine that just happened to contain some fiction.) In the months preceding Pearl Harbor, *Argosy* printed several "ripped from the headlines"–style pieces. These articles all generally followed a fairly similar formula: beginning with a fictitious account of warfare, wherein either Germany or Japan has attacked America, it offers details concerning the maimed and killed before finally returning to "reality" in order to posit several questions and possible answers concerning the prophesized attack. In its September 27, 194, issue, *Argosy Weekly* printed "We Bomb Tokyo!" by Jay Hamilton, which predicted a Japanese attack on the American naval forces in the Pacific, detailing how such an attack might be orchestrated and what the American response might be:

> We Bomb Tokyo! ... Who's afraid of the Little Yellow Wolf? Not your Uncle Sammy! Let the war lords of Japan beware: America is through with appeasement. The Panay bombed? So sorry! The Embassy damaged? So very sorry! The Tutuila? It won't happen again! ... Well, it had better not; and here are the reasons why.... The B-19's roared their answer, and a holocaust spread through flimsy paper houses!25

"We Bomb Tokyo!" was one of many articles of the time that predicted a possible Japanese attack in the Pacific and provided several options as to how America would retaliate. The October 4, 1941, issue of *Argosy* followed with "Nazi Terror Over New York," by Robinson MacLean, a rather ambitious attempt at predicting the when, how, and possible reasons for an attack on America by Nazi Germany. With illustrations depicting Nazi bombers bombarding New York City, the article's tagline reads: "Plummeting, screaming tearing at the Nation's vitals with parcels from Hell — oh, the Nazis can come: make no mistake about that. What every New Yorker — every American — wants to know is: What are the chances of being maimed, made homeless? *Argosy* tells the story."26 Answering his own question as to where the first attack will come from, Maclean responds:

> Of course, Germany, since we're talking about bombing of the continental United States. If we were to include Alaska, the Philippines, and Pacific wayports for the clippers, we'd have to consider Japan. But Japan has never distinguished herself as an adept operator of long-range motor aircraft.... If you want to bet that the first hostile bomb to burst on U.S. soil will come from any but a German airplane, you can get your money covered, at almost any odds, at almost any Army Air Corps field.27

After providing several reasons as to why Hitler may want to attack the United States, in addition to conveying the possible role of "incipient fifth columnists," the article ends with the prescient prediction that "if an attack on America is made, it is unlikely that a formal notice, or declaration of war, would precede it. That is the modern method of war."28

Japanese threats to America's mainland and territorial possessions featured heavily (and accurately, in a way) as the impetus for the coming war. In a 1941 piece ("Peril in the Pacific," E. Hoffmann Price), *Argosy* predicted war with Japan — not due to an attack on an American base directly, but rather through an invasion of the Philippines (which, according to legislation, were to be granted complete independence in 1946), an affront that would hit Uncle Sam too close to home:

The head-hunters are ready to sweep down from the hills for an orgy of murder; the Mikado's little men are ready with warships and wiles. Do the Philippine politicians really dare to face July 4, 1946? Do they really want freedom? The answers to these questions give every American something to think about.... Down in the valleys, the little brown men and their families make ready for the Mikado's equivalent of *der Tag*.[29]

Argosy continued to suggest that America would not be able to remain neutral for much longer with such pieces as "I Escaped the Nazis!" (November 1, 1941), "Destruction of the Panama Canal!" (November 15, 1941), "Veni, Vidi — Vichy" (November 29, 1941), and, eerily enough, a story that was likely in the last issue to be distributed before Pearl Harbor, "Peril in the Pacific" (December 13, 1941).[30] While pulps like *Argosy* struggled to stay relevant, a relatively new medium was growing in popularity.

The Comic Book Heroes Prepare for War

"Super-American — One Man Against the Mad Dogs of Europe!"—*Fight Comics No. 15* (October 1941)

The comic books were, in the words of comic historian Arie Kaplan, "one of the few commercial success stories" to originate during the Great Depression.[31] Comic books were originally distributed as promotional material in the early 1930s and contained only reprints of popular newspaper strips of the time. Harry I. Wildenberg and M.C. Gaines of the Eastern Color Printing Company saw the promise of releasing *Famous Funnies* (a collection of newspaper strips that had previously been used as newspaper and company premiums) in monthly, ten-cent installments. Almost as soon as the first issue hit newsstands (1934), the title — and the new medium itself— was a runaway hit.[32] Anthology titles such as Dell's *Popular Comics* (February 1936) continued publishing newspaper strips alongside new, original characters, and National Allied Publications (founded by pulp writer Malcolm Wheeler-Nicholson, and later renamed DC Comics) produced the first monthly comic book to feature all-original material, *New Fun* (also February 1936).[33] With the release of DC's *Action Comics* No. 1 (June 1938) and its introduction of Superman, the predominant mode of comic book storytelling was cemented — that of the superhero. The instant success of comic books created an industry almost overnight, with many periodical and pulp companies, such as Street & Smith and Fawcett, opening up comic divisions within their companies.

A host of new characters, and independent art studios drafting and selling their exploits to hungry publishers, rapidly emerged. They were one of the most ubiquitous forms of entertainment in the 1940s; millions sold out on newsstands across the nation, and, after December 1941, comic books were being sent to American soldiers on the front lines by the plane-load.[34]

Many of the early comic book creators had grown up on the action and adventure pulps that, by the time their own careers began, had existed for well over forty years. The influence of the pulps on the nascent comic industry cannot be overemphasized. The creators of Batman, artist Bob Kane and writer Bill Finger, were heavily influenced by the hero pulps, the Shadow in particular. Jerome Siegel and Joe Shuster, the creators of Superman, were avid readers of the science fiction pulps, such as *Amazing Stories*. Siegel is credited with creating the first fan-produced science fiction magazine, or fanzine, with the 1930 printing of his *Cosmic Stories*, featuring tales of his own and those of other contributors. After Siegel met Shuster, the duo, while still in high school, created a second, mimeographed fanzine, *Science Fiction* (October, 1932), the third issue (from a total of five) of which featured "Reign of the Superman"—about a being with extraordinary abilities who uses his powers not for good but for villainy.[35] Although no known connection has been found between the two, one would be hard-pressed to argue that the alien and mechanical illustrations of pulp artist Mark Marchioni did not perhaps lend some small amount of inspiration to the work of comics illustrator Jack Kirby, especially the intricate (and often mind-boggling) mechanics and spacecrafts he would created in later decades for titles such as *The Fantastic Four* (Marvel Comics) and *The New Gods* (DC Comics).[36] Other legends from the Golden and Silver Ages of Comics, such as Gardner Fox, Julius Schwartz, Mort Weisinger, and Mort Meskin were readers of pulp science fiction and were active members in its fan community. Many of these same individuals, and others, including Otto and Earl Binder, Will Eisner, and Alex Schomburg, got their start illustrating or writing for the pulp magazines.

The comic books also inherited from the pulps the idea of the foreign "other" and, particularly the yellow peril. Magicians, detectives, and superhuman heroes all battled Asiatic menaces. In the comic books, American heroes (usually of the superpatriot variety) were sent abroad to battle Axis powers, or their unnamed equivalents, long before America ever entered the conflicts raging in Europe and Asia. Many comic book historians, such as Les Daniels and Ron Goulart, write of the early comic creators as something akin to visionaries who foresaw that eventually it would be America's purpose to stop Axis aggression; a kind of comic book "manifest destiny" surrounds the pre–World War II Timely and DC titles. There were probably a few writers putting this much forethought into their stories; indeed, many of the "pre-war" war comics seem to be speaking of spreading American ideals of freedom rather than actually preventing war. It is safe to assume, however, that the comics, as with all published media, were created with what the public was buying in mind. If the sales of pre-war comics are any indication, the public wanted both characters that appealed to the nation's rising patriotism and stories that provided the hope that, in some fantastical way, American involvement could be averted. Comic book heroes took such preventative measures in both "real" settings, such as China or Europe, and fictionalized locales against fictionalized nations acting as proxies for the actual belligerent nations themselves. The villains of these stories featured traditional nativist imagery of foreigners transplanted onto America's (likely) enemies.

In December 1939 the first issue of *Top-Notch Comics* featured the introduction of a new superhero, the Wizard. *Top-Notch* was an early title published by M.L.J. Publications, which later would find decades-long success with its introduction of teenager Archie Andrews (after whom the company would rename itself in the mid–50s). In his inaugural story, the Wizard, the "Man with the Super-Brain," battles against an Asiatic enemy, the "Jatsonians," whose submarines are on their way to attack the American naval base at Pearl Harbor. Another M.L.J. hero, the Shield, was the first of the "superpatriots"— colorful characters clad in star-spangled costumes and fighting not only on the domestic front, but against all manner of foreign enemies. The Shield, a young scientist named Joe Higgins who, thanks to modern science, is transformed into a near-indestructible fighting machine, first appeared in the inaugural issue of *Pep Comics* (January 1940). In the third issue of *Pep Comics* (April 1940), the Shield, operating under orders directly from "Top Cop" J. Edgar Hoover, investigates the sinking of an Armed Forces vessel in New York Harbor (in the shadow of the Statue of Liberty, no less). The Shield discovers not only that the vessel was sunk using a new type of underwater mine, but also that the mines themselves are being laid by a fantastic new type of submarine that can both maneuver underwater and fly through the air. A combined international assault on America is revealed when the Shield stows away upon this craft and is taken to a large underground cavern and the giant subterranean city contained therein. Upon seeing the crew exit the ship, the Shield exclaims, "Men of all races and lands, but in one uniform! It looks like an international army!"[37] Indeed, the following panel depicts the crew as belonging to

African, Asian and Caucasian ethnicities, all garbed in the same militaristic uniforms. While ostensibly international, the enemy is obviously intended to invoke German imagery, with their uniforms greatly resembling *Wermacht* garb. Their leader, Count Zongarr, aside from the stereotypically German title of "Count," also wears a uniform of apparent Teutonic inspiration. The story is notable not only for its thinly-veiled reference to the Nazis, but also for the Count's reasons for forming his army in the first place. "We will drive America into the war," the Count proclaims. "In the end, when all countries are weakened, we shall rise to power!"

In the February 1941 issue of Dell's anthology series *Popular Comics* (No.

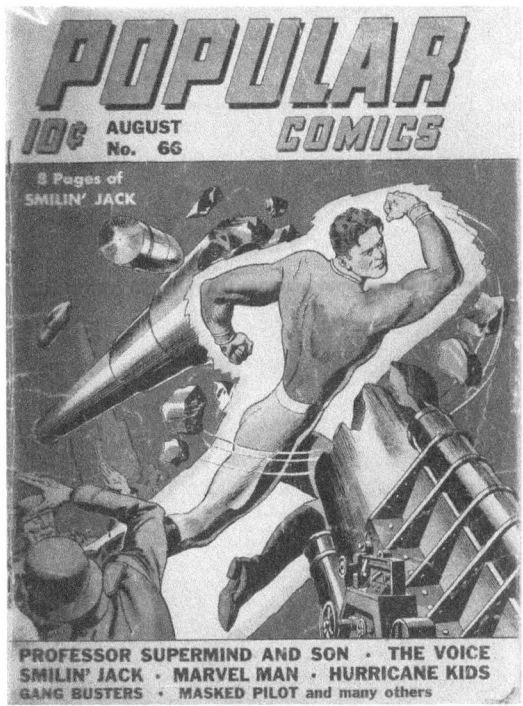

Every new superhero that debuted during the Golden Age of Comics at one point or another battled the Nazis; many, such as Professor Supermind and Son and the Super-American, did so long before war was even declared (*Popular Comics* No. 66, August 1941).

60), the team of Professor Supermind and Son first appeared. American Dan Warren, upon seeing images via one of his father's unbelievable inventions of "submarines of a foreign power" invading American harbors, volunteers to be the test subject in the elder Warren's greatest experiment: the harnessing of fantastic, otherworldly energies inside a living being.[38] Now capable of flight, telepathy and incredible strength, Dan sets out to battle America's enemies, both foreign and domestic. The duo battle on in later stories against death rays and tunneling, subterranean assault forces, all of foreign origin. In succeeding issues of *Popular Comics*, Professor Supermind and Son battle "invasion armies" and militaristic "parasites of the world," that, while speaking the German equivalent of Engrish ("ve" instead of "we," or "zee" as opposed to "the," etc.) and wearing obvious imitations of Nazi uniforms, are never identified as such.

Another superpatriot that arrived just in time (as superheroes often do) to fight a fictionalized (but obviously German) enemy was the Super-American, who appeared in Fiction House's *Fight Comics* No. 15 in October of 1941. In the Super-American's first appearance, war is raging overseas, and "even in America, totalitarian traitors destroy and murder for their power-mad masters." In the midst of this terrible chaos an American scientist constructs the "Chronopticon," a gigantic lens that allows him to see into the far future.[39] Contacting the president of "an amazing race of Future Americans" and pleading with them for help, a lone warrior from the future is sent back, an unnamed soldier who takes on the identity of the Super-American just as "fifth columnists are marching on the Capitol!" Surrounded by exclamations of near–Messianic praise on the part of thankful Americans ("Lead Us!!" "He's the one we've been waiting for!"), the Super-American, all in one story, prevents a dam from being bombed; fights off a battalion of invading tanks; thwarts assassination attempts on several American senators; and rescues President Roosevelt from the foreign usurper who is responsible for this chaos, the foreign despot Tyrannus. In the final panel of the story, Super-American

Fight Comics No. 15, October 1941.

reminds his readers that "Nobody can conquer America if we all stick together! Unity is the strength of democracy!" While the offending nation is never named, the German-styled uniforms (complete with armbands), the propensity on the part of dying enemies to yell "ACH!" and the Hitler lookalike that appears on both the cover and the story's splash page, point to the obvious nationality that is intended to correlate with the totalitarian forces of Tyrannus.

As the war drew ever closer to American shores, other comic book characters bypassed the national proxies, such as Zongarr and Tyrannus, and instead attacked the Nazis and Japanese themselves. Even the first costumed comic superhero took preemptive measures to keep America safe from named European belligerents. In a strip exclusively created for the February 27, 1940, edition of *Look* magazine, Superman flies first to Germany to take hold of Hitler, and then to Soviet Russia, grabbing Stalin. He carries them both to Geneva, where the League of Nations condemns the pair for "modern history's greatest crime — unprovoked aggression against defenseless countries!"[40] In his first appearance on a comic book cover, Namor the Sub-Mariner battled several enemies at once on the deck of a Nazi U-boat (*Marvel Mystery Comics* No. 4, February 1940). In *Shield-Wizard Comics* No. 1 (M.L.J. Publications, Summer 1940), it is revealed that the Shield held a grudge against the Nazis, even before assuming his superhero identity; the Shield, alias Joe Higgins, gained his superior strength and reflexes from drinking a chemical concoction created by his father, who was murdered by German spies during an attempt to steal the formula.

A newcomer to the comic industry was Timely Comics, founded in 1939 by Martin Goodman, a publisher who had specialized in pulps throughout a variety of genres, including westerns (*Complete Western Book*), science-fiction (*Marvel Science Stories, Uncanny Stories*), and crime fiction (*Star Detective*).[41] In October of 1939, Goodman, following the lead of Wheeler-Nicholson at National Allied, launched his first comic title, full of all-new original material. *Marvel Comics* No. 1 (renamed *Marvel Mystery Comics* with its second issue for reasons unknown) was an instant hit, selling out of its first printing. This inaugural edition not only launched what would become one of the most successful comic book companies in existence (Marvel Comics), but also provided the debut of characters that are still highly popular today — namely, the fiery Human Torch and the amphibian Atlantian prince Namor the Sub-Mariner. In the fall of 1941, several months before Pearl Harbor, the Sub-Mariner in the third issue of his own series travels to neutral Ireland in hopes of overturning the plans of "Mueller, evil genius of the Gestapo" and his intent to use a secret underwater society of druids as slaves for Germany's war machine. Namor, a half-human prince of Atlantis who hated the surface world ever since his 1939 debut, had allied himself with America and started battling Nazis by the time his own series began (Spring 1941). The Sub-Mariner and Human Torch actually participated in the first comic book hero crossover in March of 1941 by teaming up to thwart an underwater Nazi invasion of America (*Marvel Mystery Comics*, No. 17).[42] Even the jungle hero Ka-Zar, Timely Comic's answer to Burroughs's Tarzan, battled the Nazis when they invaded his jungle refuge in the August 1941 edition of *Marvel Mystery Comics* (No. 22). Aside from introducing the world to characters such as the amphibious Namor and the android Human Torch, Timely provided America with what is certainly one of the most iconic comic book images in the history of the medium. The cover of the March 1941 debut issue of *Captain America Comics* featured superpatriot Captain America smashing into Hitler's war room. With a television screen in the background showing saboteurs blowing up an American munitions factory, the cover depicts the Captain punching the Fuehrer squarely in the jaw amidst a hail of gunfire. Part of a secret "super-soldier" project authorized by President Roosevelt himself to combat a possible Nazi menace, scrawny "4-F" (rejected volunteer) Steve Rogers is given a serum that instantaneously transforms him into the super-powered, blond-haired and blue-eyed Captain America. Before any more "Captains" can be produced, however, a Nazi spy in the program murders the doctor who created the formula, ensuring that Rogers is the first and only "Captain" that America will ever have.[43] Later joined by his youthful friend, Bucky Barnes, Captain America battles the evil Red Skull (second in power only to Hitler himself) and other villains of the Nazi and Japanese strain in one of the era's most popular series, which ran from 1941 to 1949.

Like Captain America, both new and established heroes took the fight to the enemy, before the enemy could strike first. In July of 1941 the first issue of Lev Gleason Publications' *Daredevil Comics* featured the cover story "Daredevil Battles Hitler," in which the titular hero fights against the combined might of Adolf Hitler and the Claw, an Asiatic menace of yellow peril designs. Gleason also published the exploits of Captain Battle, who, in the debut issue of his self-titled comic, had already taken the fight to the Japanese (Summer 1941) on the battlefields of occupied China. By August of 1941, Centaur Publishing's superhero Amazing-Man was battling

Nazi spies and saboteurs threatening American sovereignty (*Amazing-Man Comics*, No. 23).

By the time the first superheroes appeared, Japan and the United States were on uncertain ground diplomatically. America's condemnation of Japanese atrocities in Nanjing and throughout China, and the oil embargo the U.S. levied against Japan in late 1941, placed the two powers in a precarious situation. America's Lend-Lease program with the Allied Nations similarly worsened the United States' relations with Nazi Germany. With the December 7, 1941, attack on the Pearl Harbor Naval Base and the declarations of war that flew in both directions across the Atlantic and Pacific Oceans, Japanese and Nazi belligerence changed from a mere literary device to a very real threat, one that the pulp and comic book writers were only too willing to make use of.

The German

> "Many more than a million, in high probability, is the number of those corrupted by propaganda, whose loyalty has been coaxed away from the United States, who themselves are channels for foreign propaganda and who would turn without qualm to any successful-looking movement for the overthrow of free American democracy."—*The Fifth Column Is Here* (1940)
>
> "Smashing through, Captain America came face to face with Hitler..."— *Captain America Comics No. 1* (1941)

American depictions of the bloodthirsty and brutish Hun of Germany reach back to the First World War; propaganda posters and stories of the time detailed the barbarism of the German hordes, with images ranging from German soldiers carrying off American women to Kaiser Wilhelm casually conversing with Satan over the bodies of murdered women and children. Imperial Germany was depicted as the vanguard of a barbaric invasion intent on wiping democracy and civilization from Europe. The imagery of a belligerent Europe stretches back to long before the advent of World War I; Allied propagandists at the time could relate German war-mongering to long-standing and ever-present fears concerning Marxist and radicalized European masses eager to bring anarchy to American shores.

There was never an anti–German sentiment in America, however, that reached the levels of anti–Catholicism, anti–Chinese, or anti–radical movements that have peppered American history. Germans, alongside Britons, were among the "preferred" stock when it came to questions of immigrants' national origins. Ideologically, American institutions owed a great deal to many German thinkers, and the teleological drive behind the "American experiment" is traceable to several German thinkers of the Enlightenment period of Western thought. German immigrants had always been among the easiest of new arrivals to assimilate into the larger American population. The simple fact that Germans did not differ a great deal physically from what was considered standard American racial stock at the time undoubtedly played a role as well. Suspicions of Germans in America did not appear in any significant capacity until World War I, although a desire for isolationism and a large number of pro–German groups throughout the States countered a great deal of any nativist hostility. Many periodical and newspaper editorials did not take sides, or in some cases actually sided with Germany rather than with Britain and her allies. The sinking of the *RMS Lusitania* by German U-boats in 1915, and the release of the Zimmerman Telegram, which proposed a joint Mexican-German war upon America, in the spring of 1917, soon changed the situation. Following the April 6, 1917, American declaration of war upon Imperial Germany, anti–German pamphlets, posters, songs and any number of paraphernalia streamed out of both the governmental and private sectors. President Wilson enforced the remnants of the Alien and Sedition Acts of 1798, which allowed the Commander in Chief to essentially do whatever he deemed necessary with foreigners of "questionable" loyalty residing in the country. And the new Sedition Act of 1918 permitted lengthy jail sentences for anyone seen or heard disrespecting America, its system of laws, or even its flag.[44] Federal agencies had their power to deal with "disloyal" citizens of German heritage greatly expanded, and near-official recognition was granted to many patriotic groups whose sole purpose was to roam about, discovering and apprehending anyone not displaying "100 percent Americanism." Even essentially racist ideas concerning the white race itself were amended to appeal to the new anti–German America; In 1918, Madison Grant, author of *The Passing of the Great Race*, issued a revised edition of his seminal work which utilized different racial terminology when referencing early Americans, amending the original version's reference to the Founding Fathers' contemporaries as "Teutonics."[45]

The pulp magazines of wartime America, not surprisingly, featured stories of wartorn Europe and of the American Expeditionary Force fighting to bring democracy to a beleaguered, ravaged continent. The long history of anti–Eastern European attitudes was easily shifted slightly to the west in order to encompass the mad and rampaging "Hun." *Argosy, Adventure, Short Stories, Blue Book,* and other general action/adventure titles featured stories of the war; war-centric titles did not, however, appear until well after the 1918 Armistice, interestingly enough. Following the end of hostilities and the Versailles Treaty of 1919 officially concluding the First World War, anti–German sentiments receded in large part, with both the ever-present anti–Oriental suspicions and anti-radical nativism returning to their former levels of predominance, especially after victory of the Bolsheviks during the Russian Revolution and ensuing Civil War.

As soon as World War I began, pulp narratives swiftly changed in content, featuring more war stories than the medium had previously carried (*Argosy*, April 15, 1942, Argosy Communications).

After World War I, a multitude of war pulps appeared in America, with stories telling of American heroism overseas. It was a popular genre, with many titles devoted solely to war stories and air combat enjoying long, successful runs. Fiction House's pulp *Aces* lasted a total of eight years (not including a small hiatus that occurred mid-run) and produced fifty-five issues of World War I aerial combat fiction. *Battle Stories,* a product of Minnesota-based Fawcett Publications, ran for nearly a decade, beginning in 1927.

The Germans in these stories predominantly fit into one of two categories. Either, the German was rather stupid and slow-witted, or he was a deadly enemy worthy of admiration, as well as fear. Physical exaggerations usually were not utilized, as they had been in the earlier war posters; a possible reason for this may have been predominantly-white America's reluctance to portray an ethnic group so very close to themselves in a "de-evolved" fashion — without the impetus of war, that is. *Action Stories*, in its May 1926 issue, contained the short novelette "Lady Luck," in which American doughboy Bud Nolan, after being separated from his regiment, finds himself in the company of a German soldier, also estranged from the rest of his detachment. Both the German (with the stereotypically German sounding name of Heinrich Hinkelhausen) and the American try to stare the other down, each trying to convince the other that it would be best to simply just accept the fact that he has been captured, and to come with him in search of his respective army. Eventually, Nolan is able to beat the dim-witted German through card games, eventually betting both his own freedom and the German's imprisonment, ending in Nolan's triumphal march back to his army's base with the German prisoner in tow. Another case of German stupidity in the pulps is found in a 1935 issue of *Spy Novels Magazine*, in the story "The Ace of Intrigue," by Dana R. Marsh. In this novelette, an American secret agent is able to dupe the Imperial High Command and members of the Prussian royal family itself into thinking that he is, in fact, a German soldier who had been captured and then escaped. Using the cover story that he was instrumental in the escape of one of the Kaiser's captured sons, the American ingratiates himself into the German hierarchy. Sitting at the same table as Kaiser Wilhelm himself and the "huge, ponderous von Hindenburg," the American (known only as Major–A, so that the hero of this "true" tale could retain his anonymity) learns of various plans and military arrange-

Argosy, March 7, 1942, Argosy Communications.

ments while fooling the majority of the Germans in his presence.[46] Such a narrative speaks to both a nativist understanding of foreigners' intelligence levels and to the tradition of making the enemy, whatever his ethnicity, relatively stupid when compared to the American hero.

If not dimwitted, the German soldier of the pulps was a very astute and much feared warrior whose abilities were often demonstrated through vicious aerial dogfights or stealthy submarine warfare. The September 1933 issue of *Lone Eagle* featured a tale describing the deadly menace of ace German pilot "Adolf Goering" (an obvious allusion to two cotemporary Nazis) and the devilish "black-crossed wings of the German Fokkers commanded by Baron Stieger von Littman."[47] The March 1930 edition of *Flying Aces* contained the menace of "the arrogant double-eagles of Austria," and the January 1934 issue of *Adventure*

The pulp heroes did their part, battling saboteurs and fifth columnists at home (illustration from "The Spider and Hell's Factory," *The Spider*, October 1943, Argosy Communications).

told the tale of "The Last Dispatch," in which the Allies had to contend with German U-Boats patrolling off the coast of Scotland.[48] As German aggression in Europe intensified, more belligerent and threatening images of the Germans (or, in some cases, unnamed European nationals) appeared. "Hunnish" interpretations of Germans from years past, as well as the "uncivilized" and "barbarous" nature of many Europeans that warranted the "Americanization" programs of previous decades, were utilized to separate Americans from this newest incarnation of the "other."

As soon as America entered the World War II, the pulps had new enemies to pit their characters against. General fiction, such as *The Argosy* and *Adventure*, featured stories telling of Nazi villainy and the American soldiers who battled them, and the hero pulps showcased their titular characters' battles against the new "Hun." G-8, star of the pulp magazine *G-8 and His Battle Aces*, fought a host of mad Teutonic villains in fantastical tales set during the First World War but intended to capitalize on contemporary anti–German sentiments:

> The Squadron of Death Flies High! Red are the skies over no Man's Land as G-8 and his Battles Aces stake their lives on the strangest mission a warbird ever faced. What lies behind the fatal enigma of the masked flying Hun and his squadron of Death, each of whom is ranked on the Allied list of honored dead — but who has risen from the dust of a hero's grave to strike back at the flag he once served?[49]

Herr Doktor Kreuger Stahlmaske (a grotesque German soldier who had had half his face blown apart thanks to G-8's sharp use of a firearm), Herr Doktor Wormer, Herr Feuer, and Baron von Todscmechker — all were villains of both the hideous and Hunnish varieties that returned again and again to plague G-8 during the war years.[50]

In October of 1943, "The Spider and Hells' Factory," by Grant Stockbridge, appeared, featuring the Spider, "the Master of Men," battling against Nazi spies and saboteurs: "For hell's own handyman, The Chief, had moved into America's greatest center of war industry, to organize a mass blood purge for all patriots!"[51] The Shadow opposed Nazis searching for precious jewels in "Clue for Clue" (*The Shadow*, October 15, 1942), and Doc Savage attempted to prevent the Nazis from acquiring doomsday weapons in "According to Plan of a One-Eyed Mystic" (*Doc Savage*, January 1944). While continuing the trend of war-themed fiction, pulp flagship *Argosy*'s strongest portrayal of Nazis as inhuman monsters came in the "real world" editorials that had begun to appear shortly before America's involvement in the war. The horrors of the Nazi regime were laid bare for the reader in such informational and documentary pieces as "Hitler Murders Nations" (January 10, 1942), "Blood Bath for Poland" (January 24, 1942), "Five Monsters of the Gestapo," (March 7, 1942), and others. These editorials, in addition to the fiction that had been a central part of *Argosy* for decades, aided in the demonizing of the Nazis and continued the imagery of the marauding Hun of wars past.

COMIC BOOKS VERSUS THE NAZIS

The most diverse group of Nazi villains, however, appeared in the pulps' contemporary (and, in some cases, competitor), the comics. Taking cues from both the earlier war propaganda and the pulps, comic books following America's entry into the Second World War depicted Nazis in two distinct ways—that of the Nazi spy (the dreaded "fifth columnist") and the Nazi mad scientist (or super-villain). The belief in the fifth columnist spoke to the nativist fears of a disloyal, subversive enemy from within, as well as to the xenophobia concerning the onslaught of foreign ideologies and un–Americanism from without. Both characterizations, but most commonly the mad scientist and super-villain, were depicted as abominable in physical appearance; rotund and muscular giants often sporting bald heads, fangs and a pig-like nose, as well as the stereotypical German monocle. Such imagery's relation to the earlier World War I depiction of "the Hun" is found less in such physical deformities and more in their depravity and disregard for human life. Such demonization was just as forceful as any visual depiction of physical malformation.

The saboteur, or fifth columnist, was the first Germanic terror to appear on America's (comic book) shores. The term fifth columnist actually dates to the Spanish Civil War and the year 1936. According to popular mythology surrounding the term, Spanish Nationalist commander Emilio Mola was supported by four columns of Nationalist troops ready to take Madrid, in addition to a secretive, clandestine "fifth column" he claimed was subverting the city from within and awaiting their commander's arrival.[52] Nazi Germany had allied itself, politically and militarily, with the Nationalist army and its understood leader, Francisco Franco. Such close ties with Franco's regime, when combined with rumors of traitorous organizations within France which were responsible for its rapid collapse following Hitler's passing of the Maginot Line in 1940, caused the term "fifth column" to be automatically connected to any suspicion of attempted treason or sabotage related to purported Nazi infiltrators. Many books, pamphlets and periodicals were produced in the years immediately preceding Pearl Harbor that spoke to fears of fifth columnist incursions. In many cases the claims made by fifth columnist agitators were outrageous, even by agitator standards. Newspaperman and lawyer George Britt, in his aptly named *The Fifth Column Is Here* (1940), made rather startling claims about the imminent threat posed by American fifth columnists. Like other works in a similar vein, *The Fifth Column is Here* had far more to do with sensationalism than any sort of attempt at disseminating hard evidence and facts:

> A Nazi Fifth Column one million strong now is strategically occupying vital points of United States territory and is dug in, camouflaged, sniping

vigorously at American interests and gathering strength by new recruits. It is ready for war against this country, and greater services may be confidently expected from it as they are required.... A million Fifth Columnists — and that is cold official estimate based on investigation — walk the streets and have the run of American homes, offices and shops, their hearts black with hostile intentions. Marching orders have not been issued yet, so they remain at their normal occupations, but on momentary call for treachery.[53]

Britt's fifth column agitation seemed to be more nativist than anti–Nazi in reasoning, as it lists a variety of ethnicities as confirmed co-conspirators of the secretive Nazi operation. Secret Italian fascists; those of French heritage fearful of further Nazi acts against their occupied homeland; and the perennial nativist target, the Irish, due to supposed hatred of Britain that transcends any loyalty to America or democracy — these and other groups contain "blood-strains responsive to old-country appeals."[54] Other authors wrote tracts denouncing the many pro–German or pro–Fascist groups found throughout the country as probable saboteurs; and, after the signing of the Nazi-Soviet Non-Aggression Pact in 1939, communist and socialist organizations were branded not only as radical agitators but as likely Nazi conspirators.

It was the spy, the saboteur, the fifth columnist that the early comic book heroes fought most often. Timely's Sub-Mariner, Human Torch, Captain America and others battled German spies both on land and at sea. Most superheroes spent more time fighting spies than enemies out on the battlefields of Europe. In fact, within the first few pages of the very first Captain America story, a fifth columnist appears and is quickly subdued by the Captain. Standard Comics' publication *Exciting Comics* was an anthology series that chronicled the exploits of several superheroes, such as the Black Terror, the Liberator, and the American Eagle. In *Exciting Comics* No. 23 (December 1942), the Black Terror, a timid pharmacist who, alongside his sidekick Tim, is given super-human abilities via a special "druggist's concoction," uncovers a plot by Nazi saboteurs to distribute throughout American homes a new type of coal that, once burned in one's fireplace, releases a toxic gas capable of spreading throughout entire city blocks. In the same issue the American Eagle foils a Nazi plot to blow up aircraft factories, and the Liberator breaks up a ring of saboteurs operating on the very grounds of the university campus where his alter-ego teaches. The combination of belligerence and depravity, as well as the inability to "fight a fair fight," all speak to World War II's imagery surrounding the uncultured "Hun."

Another superhero who battled German spies was Standard's flagship superpatriot, the Fighting Yank, a descendant of a Revolutionary War soldier who uses a mystical cloak which provides him with superhuman abilities. In many of the Yank's stories he is aided by both his girlfriend Joan and the helpful spirit of his Revolutionary ancestor. In the seventh issue of *The Fighting Yank* (August 1943), the Yank and Joan have been called on behalf of the government to aid in the investigation of a recent series of calamites striking at the heart of American defenses — the literal "breaking up" of American defense planes flying routine patrols throughout the country.

The belligerent, ogre-like Hun rampaging across Europe, for the most part dormant since Versailles, reappeared in American popular media in the early 1940s (illustration from *Headline Comics* No. 1, February 1943).

The Fighting Yank eventually uncovers the explanation behind the sudden disintegration of American defensive capabilities: sabotage on the part of Nazi master criminal Der Talon. Der Talon is depicted as a Neanderthal-like brute sporting a metal claw to replace the hand destroyed in the First World War. In the third story of the same issue, the Yank, while attending a Bond Drive, foils the plot of several German spies to dynamite the Hoover Dam. In the ninth issue of his eponymous title, the Yank battles a group of Nazi spies that have infiltrated West Point, and in a second story he fends off fifth columnist-arsonists using chemically-altered lottery raffle tickets in an attempt to incinerate American homes and infrastructure.

Many characters, such as The Fighting Yank's nemesis Der Talon, combined the role of saboteur and mad scientist to create the comics' most successful, antagonistic mainstay — the super-villain. Captain Battle foiled the schemes of Nazi mastermind Baron Doom, and *Super-Mystery Comics'* Magno the Magnetic Man thwarted saboteurs led by "the Clown," a Nazi genius who bore more than a passing resemblance to Batman's Joker.[55] Super-villain Agent Axis threatened DC Comics' team of all–American fighting youths, the Boy Commandos, in their self-titled series. The Hangman, a green-and-blue-clad masked American avenger, faced the evil Captain Swastika in the June 1942 issue of *Pep Comics* (No. 28). In an attempt to destabilize America's internal security, Captain Swastika (sporting a cape, swastikas covering both his chest and his face, and a rather fashionable dress-hat) plans to release all of the country's incarcerated criminals, setting them loose upon an unsuspecting nation:

With war underway, magazines such as *Argosy* devoted a large portion of their content to war-orientated fiction (*Argosy*, February 1943, Argosy Communications).

Once again the ominous figure of Capt. Swastika, with another plan of blood and strife. A plan so daring, so vast in scope as to appear impossible of achievement.... Impossible, you say? Our country is too unified! Nothing is impossible for Capt. Swastika [,] no stroke too bold to tear out the roots of our democracy. But there is still the Hangman to contend with.... Beware the Hangman's noose, Capt. Swastika![56]

Too late to prevent the success of the Captain's first phase of his devilish plot, the Hangman is able to infiltrate the Nazi's headquarters and send a signal to all the crooks to return to base for new orders, where a police contingent is ready to re-arrest them. Of course, Captain Swastika manages to outwit the Hangman and escapes to bring ruin to America another day.

The American Eagle, in *Exciting Comics* No. 23 (December 1942), fought against the "wildfire machine" (capable of destroying entire city blocks) and its creator, the nefarious Nazi villain the Bludgeon, whose ultimate goal is nothing less than to "wipe every living creature from the face of America — and assure a Nazi victory and a great empire for myself!"[57]

Often the villains of a franchise were as much of a draw as the heroes, such as Fawcett's

Illustration from *U.S.A. Comics* No. 4, May 1942, ™ and © Marvel Entertainment.

Captain Nazi, who first appeared in *Master Comics* No. 21, in December of 1941. Captain Nazi was not grotesque like many of his Nazi contemporaries. Rather, he resembled an Aryan Superman. Clad in a green, militaristic uniform with a cape and a giant swastika where Superman's "S" would normally be, Captain Nazi's "Hunnish" characteristics are found in his wickedness and unwavering devotion to the Nazi cause. He obeys the orders of Hitler to the letter, gladly murdering subordinates his Fuehrer no longer has use for, and regularly kills any American that gets in his way.[58] The character would appear in many of Fawcett's publications until the end of 1944. M.L.J.'s Steel Sterling, in the pages of *Zip Comics* (No. 31, November 1942), battled the Creeper, a Nazi supervillain and "arch saboteur" clad in a demonic green and purple costume. Bill Barnes and Sandy, the pride of American military aviation (and also pulp heroes that had transitioned to comics), battled "Dr. Berlin, Arch-Enemy of America" and his attempts to remake parts of Arizona into an airfield for Nazi bombers, in the first issue of *Air Ace*, published by Street & Smith Publications in January of 1944.

The comic book creators of the 1940s left no avenue of dehumanization unchecked, and were often able to combine imagery, such as the joining of Nazi science run amok with the physically disfigured Teutonic brute. Superpatriot Captain Terror, in *U.S.A. Comics* No. 4 (December 1941), faced "Dr. Gustave Leech, Nazi Scientist of Sudden Death," and his plan to prevent aid ships from reaching Britain, thus forcing the English to "think Der Fuehrer's way when they starve!"[59] The Doctor is monstrous in appearance, with a bald head (covered in Frankenstein Monster–like scars), rows of misshapen teeth, pointed ears and bushy eyebrows, under one of which sits the ever-present German monocle. As early as his first appearance, Timely's Captain America had to contend with the hideous visage of Nazi villain and saboteur-supreme the Red Skull; and *Zip Comics* featured both the evil Baron Gestapo, a monocle-wearing, fanged monstrosity with a blazing swastika across his chest, and the Nazi torture-master Captain Murder. In the summer of 1942, the eighth issue of *Human Torch Comics* pitted the titular character and his ally Namor against the evil of Herr Python, a Nazi scientist who is either a half-human, half reptilian abomination of nature, or perhaps a product of Nazi eugenics gone horribly wrong.

The World War II depictions of Germans drew upon anti–European imagery dating back to the propaganda of World War I — that of the brutish, uncultured descendent of Attila rampaging across the free world. Also evident is decades worth of anti-foreignism that identified particular groups as uncivilized savages. When combined with the comic book's inherent science-fiction elements, these stereotypes were augmented further to become the mad scientist or super-villain that bedeviled America's costumed defenders. It is important to note, however, another significant difference between the Hun of 1917 and the Hun of 1941: he was a Nazi first and a German second, showing further the growing link between nativist imagery and its focus on ideology, and race to a lessoned (but still influential) degree. As John Dower, in *War Without Mercy — Race and Power in the Pacific War*, points out, there were such things as good Germans and bad Germans during World War II. Such reasoning shows a shift in the nativist structure of thought that saturated the 1920s — that perhaps ideology mattered more, in some ways, than ethnicity. A good German was one who opposed the Nazis, such as Albert Einstein, who was represented in comics by Professor "Reinstein," the scientist who created Captain America's Super-Soldier serum. Put simply, not all Germans were Nazis. Unfortunately, in the case of the Pacific theater, there was no such demarcation. While the Chinese were now allies, the comic books followed Admiral William F. "Bull" Halsey's understanding in 1944 that "the only good Jap is a Jap who's been dead for six months."[60]

The Yellow Peril in the 1940s, and the Japanese

> "We shall never completely understand the Japanese mind; but then, they don't understand ours, either.... He and his brother soldiers are as much alike as photographic prints off the same negative."—*Know Your Enemy— Japan* (1945)

As the narrator from the government-produced film *Know Your Enemy—Japan* explains, the Japanese were seen as a race apart from that of Americans during World War II, just as much of the Orient was during the 1920s and 1930s. "Strange" religious practices and styles of dress, fanatical devotion to their sovereigns, and the willingness to commit suicide during battle rather than be captured—all of these promoted the "otherness" of the "new" Oriental, the "Jap." As summarized by the superhero Cat-Man's young sidekick Kitten's understanding of the Japanese mindset after having the "Nipponese" code of "Bushida [sic]" explained to her, "Gee, they must be nuts!"[61] Growing steadily as the 1940s approached, anti–Japanese imagery in popular literature remained diminutive, with the alleged Chinese threat remaining a mainstay of yellow peril narratives.

Unlike the depictions of the Hun, the yellow peril did not fade into desuetude during the heyday of the pulps in the '20s and '30s. Quite the contrary; it was one of the staples of the industry, and all of the pulps' highest selling titles featured a yellow menace story within their pages at least several times a year, or even several times a month in the case of a weekly title. The yellow peril also featured prominently in the early comic books. The first issue of DC Comics' *Detective Comics* (March 1937—the title from which the company would later derive its name) featured on its cover the threatening Oriental Ching Lung, and introduced hard-hitting sleuth Slam Bradley (created by Siegel and Schuster while they were trying to find a buyer for their newest creation, Superman) who in his first appearance is seen fighting with a group of swarthy Chinese hoodlums. DC's ninety-six-page special commemorating the 1939 World's Fair in New York City contained a feature starring super-hero/magician Zatara in a yellow peril adventure risking death from "the curse of Ti-Lo."[62] The eighth issue of *Detective Comics* featured "The Claws of the Red Dragon," a story of the yellow menace that could have been lifted straight from the pulps; it told the tale of physically and morally perfect American sleuth Bruce Nelson battling against the tong forces of the "Ruthless Chinese Lu Gong."[63] The nineteenth issue of the same title contained an early comic adaptation of Sax Rohmer's *Fu Manchu*. Superpatriot the Shield, before battling Nazis and Japanese, took the fight to sinister Chinese criminal tongs in *Pep Comics* No. 9 (1940). In June of 1941 (*Detective Comics* No. 52), superheroes Batman and Robin uncovered "The Secret of the Jade Box." The "secret" was actually the signet ring of Genghis Khan, an object of mystical power sought by a tong leader (and heir to Khan himself) in hopes of creating a new criminal empire.

The yellow peril was still prevalent in a number of other mediums. A popular comic strip and "Big Little Book," *Dan Dunn* dealt with the titular Anglo-American detective hot on the trail of the elusive Chinatown crime boss Wu Fang.[64] Sunday comic strips also continued Asiatic imagery of years past. *Terry and the Pirates*, a popular newspaper strip created by artist Milton Caniff in 1934, featured the character of Connie, a Chinese servant who acted as comic relief and spoke in broken English. Alex Raymond's *Flash Gordon* Sunday strip, beginning in 1934 as well, featured as its antag-

The Japanese enemy in one of his more zoomorphic forms (*The United States Marines Comics* No. 3, 1944).

onist Ming the Merciless, a kind of intergalactic Fu Manchu. Not surprisingly, stories featuring Sax Rohmer's yellow emperor were still enjoying profitable sales, with the original novels serialized in *Liberty* magazine in 1940, and the production of a film adaptation in the form of an episodic serial — *The Drums of Fu Manchu*. Starring Henry Brandon in yellow-face as the evil doctor, this 1940 serial was later edited, compiled and re-released in 1943 as a feature film. Director Josef von Sternberg's *The Shanghai Gesture*, released in December of 1941, played on a related stereotype — that of the "dragon lady," an evil and conniving Oriental woman who showed all of the depravity of her male tong counterparts. While not quite yellow peril, Charlie Chan and other similar characters in yellow-face continued to appear on cinema screens unabated throughout the years preceding Pearl Harbor.

The Japanese have somewhat of a divergent history regarding immigration when compared to the Chinese. For a significant amount of time, and throughout many parts of the United States, the Japanese were "preferred," in part due to the manner in which they emigrated. The earliest Japanese immigrants to arrive in significant numbers arrived with their spouses and children, with the obvious intent to settle — in contrast to many Chinese laborers (all men) who were more likely to stoke nativist fears of foreign immigrants coming to steal away their jobs without any vested interest in the nation's wellbeing.[65] In contrast to the Chinese, Japanese immigration did not occur until much later, near the end of the nineteenth century. Throughout a great deal of its history, Japan has gone through several cycles of isolation interspersed with brief periods of engagement and diplomacy with other nations. Such a sporadic system of diplomacy is responsible for Japan's unique culture. For example, ideas concerning government and Buddhist faith were brought to Japan during its contact with China in the Sui and Tang Dynasties of the seventh through tenth centuries A.D. The period of isolation that followed those centuries allowed for such imported concepts to gain distinctly Japanese identities. With short lapses in isolation over the centuries (including diplomatic voyages to Mexico in the early seventeenth century), such policies remained in effect until American Admiral Matthew C. Perry used a display of military might to open Japan to international trade and relations in 1854 (full diplomacy between the two nations would wait until 1860).[66] Since the late twelfth century and the rise of Minamoto no Yoritomo, supreme military and political power in Japan was held by a series of warlords called shoguns (of which Yoritomo was the first recognized), while the Emperor, whose legitimacy traditionally dated to the mid-sixth century B.C., was largely relegated to a ceremonial or figurehead status. Within fifteen years of Perry's arrival, the Shogunate was overthrown by a group of nationalists (many of whom were Western-educated) determined to abolish the feudal state and restore the Emperor (or Mikado, as he was often called in English) to authority.[67] During the thirty-seven-year period between the Meiji Restoration in 1868 and Russia's defeat in the Russo-Japanese War in 1905, Japan engaged in a rapid industrialization campaign that placed it far ahead of any of its Asian neighbors; while Qing China was crumbling largely due to Western encroachment, Meiji Japan was embracing Western science and technology, quickly reaching levels of modernization that had taken most of Europe two hundred years to achieve.

The anti–Japanese movement, prior to the Second World War, has often been overshadowed by the much larger Sinophobic imagery of the early twentieth century, but there were many outlets for this new fear following Japan's 1906 emergence as a major military power. William Randolph Hearst made it a personal task to spread warnings of the awakened Japanese leviathan, with many of his papers printing sensationalized (and blatantly untrue) stories of Japanese threats to American sovereignty. His *Examiner* carried, in 1907, an exposé warning of "recent arrivals of Japanese troops [in Hawaii] in the guise of coolies ... secretly preparing for hostilities."[68] Conversely, there were signs of positive relations between the two nations. Japan was an ally of America during both World War I and the international intervention in the Russian Civil War from 1918 to 1922 (when the U.S. left, the Japanese stayed on for several more years). Japan was a party to a naval disarmament conference in 1922 with other industrialized nations that posted a limit on the number of battleships each nation could possess. And Sessue Hayakawa, a silent film star of Japanese descent, became a sensation in America and appeared with starlet Mary Pickford in bond drives during World War I, rivaling Rudolph Valentino in terms of popularity.

Anti-Chinese sentiment was fostered in the nineteenth century by fears of cheap immigrant labor supplanting American workers; anti–Japanese feelings, on the other hand, were nourished by American reaction to international situations in the early twentieth century. As stated earlier, native-born Americans' reaction to the Japanese differed a great deal when compared to the Chinese; attempts at discriminatory actions and legislation were largely isolated to the Western states — California in particular, where many Japanese were beginning to settle and purchase large tracts of farmland. The most significant effort at curbing Japanese immigration was the "Gentlemen's Agreements" of 1907 and 1908 between the United States and Japan in which Japan promised to hinder Japanese laborers from immigrating to America in return for the U.S.'s assurance that it would try to restrain any anti-Japanese sentiments at home.[69] Following the Russo-Japanese War, and as suspicion and outright antagonism towards Japan grew, fueled in part by its aggressive stances in Korea (the annexation of the nation in 1910), China (repeated attempts, and successes, at colonization in mainland China and Formosa), and throughout the Pacific, the pulps found a

Adventure (at this point a sister publication to *Argosy*) also provided war-themed literature (*Adventure*, May, 1942, Argosy Communications).

new vehicle in which to buoy the stereotype of the Asiatic menaces — that of the militaristic Japanese soldier, as evidenced by Zagat's "Tomorrow" series of stories. Since the end of the Russo-Japanese War, which thrust Japan onto a stage reserved for world powers, and the contemporaneous rapid modernization of nearly all aspects of Japanese life, "Nippon" (a Japanese name for the nation that was often used in the American press) was seen by many fearful Westerners as a technologically-advanced "other," one far more dangerous than the fragmented and lethargic Qing Empire. Just as reports of attacks upon Westerners (and, indirectly, white Christendom) during the Taiping and Boxer Rebellions helped encourage the yellow peril sentiment of the early twentieth century, the stories out of Asia concerning Japanese actions in China aided in the creation of a new yellow peril in American popular literature. Following the attacks on Pearl Harbor and other American holdings in the Pacific (and later by events such as the Bataan Death March), negative depictions of the Japanese were given more "fuel for the fire," as it were.

The pulp magazines of the day began to feature stories containing Japanese (or Japanese-like) antagonists long before Pearl Harbor, as described previously. The general fiction titles (*Adventure, Argosy, Blue Book*, etc.), as well as the new war-themed titles, all began to feature "realistic" war novelettes and serials as soon as the war began, in addition to non-fiction editorial-like pieces that covered the war and promoted patriotic sentiments. The dead, yellowed soldiers on the cover of *Adventure*'s May 1942 issue, or the sneaking, saffron soldier about to plunge his knife into the back of an American G.I. in *Complete War Novel*'s March 1943 edition, or any of the other multitude of wartime pulp images — they all served to demonize the Japanese along "yellow peril" lines. *Argosy* and other magazines began featuring more "real-life stories," many of which dealt with past, and suspected, acts of Japanese devilishness and treachery. "The deadly dagger blow thrust in our backs while Japan's diplomats bowed and grimaced at us in Washington was such a piece of treachery as the world has seldom seen," argued the author of "The Secret Behind the Stab in the Back by Japan," Robert Carse, in *Argosy*, April 1, 1942.[70] While the pulps were

While many war titles existed in the '20s and '30s, these were mostly concerned with past conflicts — the First World War, specifically. With declarations of war flying back and forth across the Atlantic, many war titles with contemporary themes quickly appeared (*Complete War Novels*, September 1942).

not lacking in their depiction of Japanese as the "revised Oriental," they did so in a way that helps elucidate a change in American nativist attitudes occurring at the time—this is deserving of further examination in the next section. For now, our focus will be primarily on comic books.

After America's entry into World War II (and, in some cases, several months prior), the use of the yellow peril motif shifted from generic "Asiatic hordes" to the Japanese specifically. The dehumanizing terms and descriptors examined in the previous chapter as part of a nativism that existed in-between the two World Wars were all carried over to be used in relation to the Japanese. The imagery depicting Japanese during the war was often harsher than that of the earlier pulps, fueled by both a wartime mentality and the stream of reports in the press relating to Japanese atrocities committed against both Americans and their allies.[71] Japanese speech, supposed ideas of morality, and basic physical differences were all used in the depictions of the "Nipponese" enemy, just as they had been years prior in the pulps and early comics. Japanese villains either spoke in "Engrish" or spoke in ways that reduced the entirety of the race to a single collective will, existing only to serve the Emperor. Everything is "honorable" ("Honorable Emperor!" "Honorable Suggestion!" "Honorable soldier," and the like), or if not honorable, then "Honolable." Archaic language is frequently used by the "Japs" to add a tinge of ancient evil to an already evil nemesis, and broken English is often utilized to portray the Japanese as stupid and childlike. "That is all I want know! You no longer chief! All finish for you now! Banzai!" screams a Japanese officer after killing a native chief of an unnamed Pacific Island in an issue of *National Comics* (January 1944). Asking if his men thought the murder was "a good joke," a soldier replies, "Ha-Ha! Wonderful Joke, Honorable Colonel, Yesss!"[72]

Following their Fu Manchu predecessors, the Japanese villains of the comics showed a lack of the inherent morality and humanity assumed to be an innate trait of the West, as shown by their depictions as lovers of torture and violence purely for the sake of torture and violence. As was the case with the depictions of Nazis, Japanese officers were depicted as ruthless, miniature warlords, willing to kill underlings and innocent bystanders who do not obey their slightest whim. The unique military culture that, in many Western minds, defined the Japanese also factored into the imagery of the time. Often the Japanese were depicted as near-mindless drones gladly willing to die as long as the honor of the Emperor was maintained. Such an irrational and thoroughly undemocratic (and therefore un–American) mode of thought further alienated the Japanese villain from his all–American enemies. A copious amount of superhero comic books printed during World War II featured scenes of Japanese brutality and torture, both within its pages and more often on the covers, such as the September 1942 cover of Holyoke Publishing's *Cat-Man Comics* (No. 13), featuring fanged Orientals about to thrust a twisted dagger into the head of Cat-Man's adolescent sidekick, the Kitten. From M.L.J. superheroes the Web and Steel Sterling saving a group of blindfolded American nurses from a Japanese firing squad on the cover of *Zip Comics* No. 33 (January 1943), to the cover of *Captain America Comics* No. 24 (March 1943), with sidekick Bucky moments away from having his fingers ripped out of his hand by yellow, fanged monstrosities, the Japanese were not only depicted as brutal torturers, but nearly every such scene had, in one form or another, distinct "Oriental" trappings (kimonos, dragon statues, Buddha statues, etc.) that appeared previously in tales of Chinese and tong torture. The Japanese placed pacifist monks on the rack in order to gain information (*Headline Comics* No. 2, March 1943) and dripped burning candle wax onto captured Allied soldiers (*Zip Comics* No. 36, April 1943). In *The Fighting Yank* No. 7 (1943) the Yank, upon discovering that a traveling troupe of faux–Japanese performers are actually "Japs," is subsequently captured and tortured; tied to a searing coal furnace, the Yank's clothes and flesh begin to melt, his reprieve coming only in the form of his ever-present ghostly ancestor.

A predilection towards cruelty and torture was not the only defining factor of the comic's newly re-imagined yellow peril. Depicting Asians (now primarily Japanese) as subhuman by exaggerating or inventing physical differences

Headline Comics No. 11, Winter 1944.

was a staple of the 1940s comics; as it had been with the pulps, physicality was the chief demarcation between "Americans" and the "other." It is safe to say that the mood and propaganda of wartime pushed such depictions farther, as much of the imagery goes beyond anything that was seen in the pulps. Many pulp stories displayed the "Oriental" as human, subhuman, or at least something approaching human; the wartime comics showcased an entity, more often than not, more bestial in depravity and physicality. Unarguably the most infamous and sensationalized caricature of supposed "oriental monstrosity" is that of the Claw, who first appeared several years before Pearl Harbor, in *Silver Streak Comics* No. 1 (December 1939) but would continue to appear as a foil for publisher Lev Gleason's superheroes throughout the entirety of World War II. The Claw was a monstrous giant, a "God of Hate" who ruled his minions from "Tibet, land of strange religions and mysterious customs.... High on the pinnacle of a mountain far removed from prying eyes is poised the skull-like castle of The Claw!!"[73] A yellow goliath of Asiatic evil, with pointed ears, serrated fangs protruding from a sinister mouth, slanted eyes, and long, knife-like eyelashes, the Claw orders his saffron minions, with inhumanly long fingers and nails, to do his bidding:

> While Europe boils over with war, America has been stupid enough to think itself safe from invasion! It is the most unfortified country in the world!! It is ripe for attack! Yes Attack!! We, the forces of the Claw, are better equipped for war then was Hitler! But we must strike quickly! As America is beginning to arm and soon she will not be so easily overcome![74]

Originally conceived as a traditional (if outlandish, even by its own standards) yellow peril villain, the Claw, in subsequent battles with superheroes Steel Sterling and Daredevil, would take on a more Japanese identity and officially ally himself with the Nazis. Villains of similar grotesqueness could be found in a multitude of World War II comics, predominately in those of the superpatriot variety.

On the splash page of *The Fighting Yank* No. 9 (1944) there is a striking image of the hero choking a fanged, saffron abomination. As the issue's first story opens, Bruce (the Yank's alter ego) and Joan are driving through downtown San Francisco, just about to cross the Golden Gate Bridge, when, without warning, an airplane flies overhead, dropping a small round cylinder in front of the Yank's car. The canister suddenly pops open, and out march a group of (as Joan announces) "Tiny Japs!" who speak of destroying "the bridge for Honorable Emperor!"[75] Growing to full size (which usually in the case of Japanese soldiers was never quite as tall as their Anglo-American enemies), they are quickly beaten by the Yank, with the lone survivor of the attack committing ritual suicide, preferring death to interrogation. The scene then shifts to a Japanese base where a monstrous Japanese soldier named Mojo is shrunk down to the same size as his lilliputian predecessors, able to regain his normal stature by an exposure to oxygen. Mojo's plans to invade America with minuscule battalions are foiled by the Yank, and the Japanese shrinking gas is destroyed. In this story, Mojo is a horrendous beast, demonized much more than any other Japanese he appears alongside. As with many depictions of Japanese in the comics of World War II, exaggerated simian features are attributed to the villain. Mojo's head is sloped forward, and large slanted eyes are set above an extremely wide nose. He possesses a monstrously large maw full of razor-sharp canines. Even when his mouth is closed the bottom and lower canines still protrude from his mouth. He wears not the standard uniform of the Imperial Army but rather a green t-shirt and briefs, with a gigantic rising sun emblazoned across his chest.

The notion of ritual suicide was one of the many cultural differences that helped separate Americans from the "new" yellow peril, the Japanese (*Daredevil Comics* No. 10, May 1942).

A similar character, in both fashion sense and hideous physicality, appeared a few years earlier in the twenty-ninth issue of *Pep Comics*, wherein ultra-patriot the Shield and star-spangled sidekick Dusty battle the forces of "the Fang," a murderous "Jap" agent who stowed away on an American transport and was "dispatched here by the Emperor himself!" The Fang, yellow in complexion and with giant, razor-like fingernails, bellows at his henchman from a mouth resembling that of a shark, serrated teeth running the length of his massive gum line.

Master Comics No. 29 (August 1942) pitted super-patriot Minute Man against the horrible experiments conducted by Japanese mad scientist and spy Dr. I.M. Fear. "In a west coast hospital laboratory" Dr. Fear finally achieves his goal — the creation of an airborne toxin that makes those who inhale it hallucinate and become tormented by imaginary horrors.[76] The Doctor is apparently undercover, working in full view of the nearby army base, even providing medical services to the officers there. His appearance is so monstrous, that one wonders how the soldiers did not recognize him as an enemy. He has bright yellow skin, enormous buck-teeth that nearly encompass the entirety of his mouth, and protruding, monkey-like ears. He wears stereotypical Japanese round glasses and works with long, protruding nails that one would think might hinder his ability to conduct experiments. Regardless, the Doctor tests his creation on one of the base commanders, and a personal friend of the Minute Man in his alter-ego as Private Westin. Minute Man, summoned by the pitiful cries of his superior officer, arrives just in time to witness

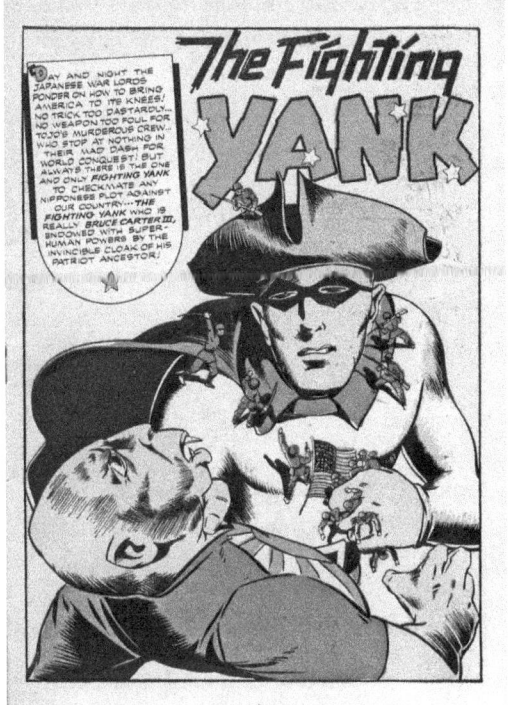

All manner of stereotypes were allowed in wartime comics; if the Japanese soldier was not diminutive, with large round glasses and buck teeth, he was a war-mongering, inhuman monstrosity (illustration from *The Fighting Yank* No. 9, August, 1944).

the Doctor's victim hurl himself out a window to his death. After escaping the Minute Man's retribution, Fear travels to what the narrator calls "the Oriental section of town" and "within, Doctor Fear worships a strange Shinto idol." "I return to the race of my forefathers, oh mighty. With fumes of fear," Fear prays. "I will defeat this nation of democratic upstarts." After ordering his all–Asian henchmen to steal a plan of the city in order to more effectively distribute the hallucinogenic fumes, Fear is attacked by the Minute Man. The hero dons a gas mask, force feeds Fear his own concoction, and realizes, before hauling him away to the authorities, that "Why.... He's a Jap!"— only after the villain's spectacles fall away to reveal his "deceitfully" slanted eyes.

"Dragon ladies" also make their appearance in the comic books. The term actually originates in the comics; the Dragon Lady was a character in the newspaper strip series *Terry and the Pirates*, by Milton Caniff. This character, however, is more akin to the mysterious women of past stories than to the virulent anti–American "Jap" that appeared in the wartime comic books. Originally a foil for the title characters (and possible love interest), Caniff's Dragon Lady became something of an anti-hero during World War II, battling to save her homeland from Japanese intrusions. While the early comic books featured many traditional dragon ladies, such as "Ah Ku, Crime Queen of Chinatown," who battled against Bob Phantom in the pages of *Top Notch Comics*, over the course of the Second World War dragon ladies underwent a transference of ethnicity — from Chinese (or generic Oriental) to Japanese specifically. The female Japanese soldier in "U.S. Rangers" (*Rangers Comics* No. 16, April 1943) embodies the wartime "Jap" dragon lady; she poses as a helpless civilian under the yoke of militaristic Japanese soldiers (even going so far as to have her own subordinates whip her), only to call to the other, hidden "Daughters of Nippon!" to turn on and capture their would-be liberators. Unlike her male counterparts, there are no attempts to make her (physically, at least) into a vile or repulsive creature; she is shown in a short peasant-woman's dress as part of her ploy, to be followed only by undergarments before finally changing into her "best uniform," which, of course, fits rather close to her frame.[77]

The Blue Beetle and partner Sparky foiled the plans of the nefarious "Madam Fang" and her band of Japanese saboteurs intent on destroying America's supply of clean drinking water. Feline superhero Cat-Man battled a Japanese operative who was passing information to her fellow spies via messages hidden in her dress (that the Cat-Man, with his feline-like eyesight, could easily detect).[78] Characters that evoked the "exotic love interest" of previous years still existed, such as Princess Aura of Mongo of the *Flash Gordon* comic strips, and the numerous oppressed Asian women that American soldiers and superheroes liberated from Japanese domination. The war with Japan had refashioned an old stereotype and given it more prominence (at least as far as the comic books were concerned) in the form of the Japanese dragon lady.

Reformed China and Transplanted Heroes

> "History has proven that whenever Liberty is smothered and men lie crushed beneath oppression; there rises a man to defend the helpless ... liberate the enslaved and crush the tyrant ... such a man is BLACK-HAWK." — *Military Comics No. 1* (1941)

The comic books of the 1930s and 1940s show not only a shift in discriminatory imagery from Germans to Nazis, and from "Orientals" to Japanese, but also a broadening of what Americanism can encompass. In both the pulps and the comics one can find instances of an internationalist attitude that simply would not have been found in the popular literature of the 1920s. A "re-envisioning" of China, coupled with the inclusion of what can be called "international" or "transplanted" heroes, provides us with evidence that the nativist notions that appeared in the pulps had begun to fade in the popular consciousness. Just as decades-old notions concerning "the other" were being dismantled academically, they were replaced with a popular international understanding of America's place in the world, a redefinition that would continue into the later Cold War. It was still "us against them"; now, however, "us" meant a great deal more than it had previously. The enemy was becoming defined less by ethnicity (although that continued to play a large role) and more by ideology — by what he did, or did not, believe in.

An excellent example of this trend from outside the pulps and comic books comes in the form of Monogram Pictures' *Mr. Wong* series of films, the sixth in particular — *The Phantom of Chinatown* (1940). The change in lead actor from "yellow-face" Boris Karloff to Chinese-American Keye Luke was only one of the modifications brought to the franchise with the sixth installment. Placing an Asian-American male in such a positive, leading role almost twenty years after nativism forced silent-film star Sessue Hayakawa to leave Hollywood was revolutionary in and of itself.[79] The character was remade from a stereotypical "Charlie Chan" type of figure into a young, suave and sophisticated Chinese-American detective who spoke perfect English. There are scenes wherein Wong makes it a point to emphasize that his loyalties lay not with China but rather with "my country," the U.S. "Naturally my sympathies follow my heritage," Detective James Lee Wong tells a Republican Chinese operative (Hawaiian-American actress Lotus Long) as he attempts to gain information from her concerning an international criminal plot; "but, after all, I am an American." The hunched, bespectacled, dragon tunic–wearing Wong as portrayed by Karloff provides a stark contrast to the polished, energetic Keye Luke. Several stereotypes still exist in the film, such as Wong's man-servant Foo and the notion that many Chinese speak in riddles and have some connection with secret societies. The transformation of the central character from "Charlie Chan" copycat to an American character in his own right is noteworthy in a study of American cinema and nativist imagery. Released a year before Pearl Harbor, the film precedes a trend found in the pulps and comic books of the war years—a transference of the yellow peril from China to Japan, as well as the elevation of China as a partner in an international crusade against Japanese belligerence. While the simple economic reality that movies starring Asian-American leads still fared poorly in comparison with the yellow-face antics of Warner Oland and Peter Lorre should be remembered, the fact that studios were willing to try such tactics still speaks volumes.

Similar changes were demonstrated in cinema through the work of film star Anna May Wong. Previously relegated to roles as dragon ladies or exotic beauties, during World War II Anna May Wong was given top billing as a Republican Chinese freedom-fighter in such films as *The Lady from Chungking* (1942) and *Bombs Over Burma* (1943). While there was obviously a propaganda-based reasoning behind the production of such films, it is nonetheless important to take note that an actress who did not require yellowface was chosen for such roles.

Perhaps a good place to begin a dialogue of transplanted heroes is with the first hero: the Man of Steel himself, Superman. Superman's unique place in the comic book/nativism discussion should not be overlooked. Coming from an alien planet, Superman is the "ultimate other." However, Superman can also be seen as the "ideal immigrant" in the eyes of many 1930s (and certainly World War II–era) Americans. He is different but has assimilated, and has accepted American culture and values. He comes from a working-class background in Kansas, has come to Metropolis, and, in both of his identities, fights for truth and the righting of societal wrongs. Far from being an outsider, Superman became an American through assimilation, thus reducing any nativist sentiments that could be brought against him. Whether as Clark Kent reporting on the ills of society or as Superman using brute force to right them, the Man of Steel embodies the most traditional of American values — the righting of wrongs, and the mental and physical determination to get things done. While there are obvious discrepancies between a fictional locale like the planet Krypton and the war-torn battlefields of Japanese occupied China (and the fact that he was White probably did not hurt, either), Superman's success in America provides a suitable frame of reference for discussing the transplanted heroes and reformed Asians of World War II pulps and comic books. What was once alien and different now (through adoption of similar values or the sharing of a common enemy) becomes a member of America, and a larger, anti-fascist world community.

Aside from the typical Asiatic stereotypes to be expected at this point, the pulps hit upon an interesting way of dehumanizing the Japanese — taking the side of the occupied nations (usually China) and denouncing any attack on them as an attack against America as well. *Argosy* (at this point more of a "slick" than a "pulp"), in its February 7, 1942, issue, carried the article "How Japan Debauches Chinese Girls," by Earl H. Leaf. China is an ally of America in its fight against Japan, and the article stresses that the fortunes of China are intertwined with those of the United States, and vice-versa. Leaf's exposé describes the effects of the opium trade in China as a cash crop of extreme importance for Japanese occupiers, both as a supplier of wealth and as a means of control over an occupied populace. An example is made of Hsiang-li, a young girl in the Hopei province of occupied China. The young girl is brutalized and sexually assaulted by the invading Japanese troops, who force her into prostitution and opium addiction, a fate that is worsened by the author's emphasis of the fact that she "attended the mission school" and "prayed to the great Foreign [Christian] God."[80] Not only was this girl a member of an Allied nation, but she was also Christian — she was like *us*. The author continues, demonstrating how the Japanese traffic in opium undermines not only the integrity of America's partner in the Far East, but also the United States itself:

> While opium is grown and prepared in most sections under Japanese domination, heroin and opium derivatives are manufactured mostly in North China. The Japanese Concession at Tientsin has long been known as the

"heroin capital of the world." Tientsin is also the source of eighty percent of the heroin that illegally enters the United States in a steady, deadly stream.[81]

Thus, non–Japanese Asians are depicted as victims of a horrendous onslaught that not only threatens world peace but American security as well. More importantly, the Japanese treatment of women is used to demonstrate the enemy's inhumanity. A 1942 issue of pulp *Detective Fiction* ran an article entitled "Japs Making Sex Slaves of Women." The cover of an April 1943 issue of *Argosy* depicted two Japanese soldiers lustfully prying a Chinese woman from fiction anthology to a mix of her home. The sale of *Argosy*, and other Munsey titles, to Popular Publications in 1942, bringing a change from fiction anthology to a mix of fiction and shock stories, allowed for more sensationalized and graphic articles.

Many covers (and related stories) helped support the American vision of the nation's role in the war in two ways; not only did they demonize the Japanese, but they also transformed other Asian nationalities (previous victims of the yellow peril stereotype) into either empathetic fellow victims or stalwart allies against Japanese aggression (*Argosy*, April 1, 1942, Argosy Communications).

Pulp fiction operated in much the same fashion as the preceding "real-life articles"— demonizing the Japanese by elevating their enemies, our allies. The May 1942 edition of *Adventure* featured "Black Pigeons," by Walter C. Brown, which told of a village of Chinese warriors, known throughout the ages for their success against all manner of invaders. The Chinese guerrilla leader, General Mong, has grown weary of Confucian priests who insist that their ancient deities will protect them:

> Yo Fei [the local deity] has slept these thousand years, and he will still be sleeping when the Brown Devils

come pouring down over your precious hills, with their sky-dragons and iron cavalry. If Wan-teh falls to them, the rice that is young and green in your fields will be harvested by the Brown Men. Aye, and they will harvest your wives and your daughters as well! Have I not told you in plain words of the slaughter at Shanghai and the horrors at Nanking? I have seen these things with my own eyes![82]

General Mong's fears concerning the inactivity of the ancient gods in the face of the Japanese onslaught are unfounded, as the black pigeons of Yo Fei's temple do indeed leave when the village is directly threatened (just as the prophecies predicted would be the case), and his men rally behind him to repel the invaders.

In the *Argosy* issue dated March 7, 1942, "The Streamlined Dragon," by Louis C. Goldsmith, began its serialization. The story chronicled the exploits of the crew of the *Dragon*, an American ship serving Republican China on a mission to liberate Chinese soldiers who had been taken prisoner by the invading Japanese shortly before Pearl Harbor:

Spring, 1941 ... Japan was Uncle Sam's so very good friend, yes, and she dearly loved peace. But two veteran American flyers had seen the treachery and the savage brutality of Nippon; they knew these yellow men for enemies. So they headed their giant plane toward beleaguered China — and toward flaming battle.[83]

One of the central players in "The Streamlined Dragon" is Mi, a young Chinese girl who is depicted as a sympathetic character in opposition to the lustful and marauding Japanese antagonists that fill the serial. In the comics the Orient was no longer strictly a haven for "Fu Manchus" and "Mr. Changs." Rather, Allied Asian nations were depicted in much the same manner as any other Allied nation — as a partner against fascist aggression.

A change in attitude towards the East, and China in particular, can be seen even before America's involvement in the war. The premiere issue of *Military Comics* (August 1941) featured "Loops and Banks," two American aviators fighting on behalf of China against the Japanese. *Top-Notch Comics* featured the adventures of the ace American pilot Dick Storm who, when asked to serve the Chinese government against an invading (but obviously Japanese) army, replies, "I am always at the disposal of the forces for law and order!"[84] Captain Battle, first appearing in Lev Gleason's *Silver Streak Comics* No. 10 (April 1941), was a veteran of the First World War who fought alongside the Chinese in the early 1940s. In the first issue of his self-titled series (1941), Captain Battle, labeled as "the Savior of

Chungking," aids in the rescue of a Chinese diplomat from the clutches of an invading Japanese army. The Captain eventually returns the diplomat to the headquarters of Generalissimo "Mao Tung" (a likely amalgamation of Nationalist Generalissimo Chiang Kai-shek, whom the character is depicted as resembling, and of Communist enclave commander Mao Zedong). After revealing a Japanese spy within the ranks of the Chinese high command, Captain Battle tells the Generalissimo that he is always at the ready to aid China against foreign invasion.

After America's entry into the war, the stories that had previously featured Americans helping poor, beleaguered nationalities (albeit with superheroes instead of soldiers) changed into that of Americans (super or not) fighting side-by-side with an ally deserving of our friendship. In the third issue of *The United States Marines—Authentic U.S. Marine Corps Picture Stories*, published by Magazine Enterprises in cooperation with the U.S. Marines Corps in Spring 1944, "Japan's First Victim" informs the reader that "there is a captive nation in the East, a nation owning the dubious distinction of being Japan's *first* victim…. This is the Jap-ruled country of Korea, described by realistic sons of Heaven as 'a sword pointed at the heart of Nippon!'"[85] Korea's status as Japan's "first victim" implies a sense of camaraderie and solidarity with American, as well as a shared hatred for the enemy. Considering itself the prey of unprovoked aggression, America now reaches out to the "first" such victim. The narrative begins by providing a fairly brief history of Japanese-Korean relations, with the attempted invasion of Korea's Joseon kingdom in the late sixteenth century by Japan, and its eventual failure due to the Koreans' use of armored battleships. The narrative skips ahead three centuries to Japan's taking of the entire Korean peninsula following the Russo-Japanese War of 1905 (annexation occurring in 1910), and the Japanese murder and incineration of the remnants of Korea's royal family (with the exception of its Emperor, who was soon forced to abdicate). Scenes of Japanese soldiers finding a great deal of enjoyment in torturing Korean civilians follows. Men are burned alive; fleeing civilians are ensnared with meat-hooks by Japanese on horseback; and children are shot down in the streets. Christian Koreans are crucified, and women are set ablaze in their own homes. Finally, a Japanese building is seen exploding in the last panel, with the caption:

> This, then, is the background…. Today, in Chungking [in the Republic of China], Korea has a Provisional Government, its President that same Kim Ku [Gu] who strangled the Jap Tsuchida [a retaliation for the assassination of Korean Empress Myeongseong by the Japanese Army] . And it is the

burning desire of President Kim Ku and his followers to establish the Korean Declaration of Independence as a living document of freedom![86]

This short, four-page story is significant for its depictions of Japanese barbarism, but more so for the detour it takes from the traditional yellow peril tale of decades earlier. The Koreans are "patriots"; Provisional President Kim Ku desires only "freedom" for his country; and a Korean Declaration of Independence has been drafted. All of these terms speak to American history. The application of American qualities in reference to the inhabitants of the "East" would have been (and was) quite rare in the decades prior to the Second World War. However, the times had obviously changed, and as this and other stories illustrate, the "other" was coming to be defined more by ideologies than by race or ethnicity.

As was the case before the war, Americans (in the comics and in reality) volunteered their aviation skills to serve in the routing of Axis invaders after America entered the fray. Many tales were set in occupied Europe, such as in the fourth issue of Street & Smith's *Pioneer Picture Stories* (September 1942). The Legless Ace (so-named due to his damaged legs being replaced by nigh-invulnerable prosthesis) does battle with Luftwaffe fighters in the skies over occupied France, determined to beat back "the enemies of the world!"[87] The majority of wartime "America to the rescue" comics, however, focused on either China or Korea, or

International brotherhood, banding together to confront fascism — and, if gathered in America at the time, possibly violating several quota laws (*Air Ace* Vol. 2, No. 3, May 1944).

any number of fictionalized South Pacific islands threatened by the "sons of Nippon." The Flying Tigers (based on a group of actual American aviators) appeared in a series of stories in *Air Ace Comics* (1944), with an early edition proclaiming: "China's fight to exterminate the Jap disease invading her country is the fight of a peace-loving people aroused to hate-fervor, determined to sacrifice ALL rather than give up the freedom they cherish.... From the Western world came the Flying Tigers, in their hour of greatest need, to help defend this freedom."[88] Costumed superheroes were involved in the fight to aid occupied nations and protect the sovereignty of fellow democratic republics. In the thirteenth issue of *Captain America Comics* (April 1942), the titular hero and his sidekick battle "the League of the Unicorn." The Unicorn is a monstrous "Jap" with a single metal horn protruding from his forehead, who is determined to sour relations between the United States and China by killing a member of the Chinese nobility.[89] Under threats from the Unicorn, a Chinese princess (despite China's having been a republic for the previous thirty years) responds that, though she is not afraid to die, she is saddened that it may cause a rift in the "friendship between East and West."[90] The plot is foiled by Cap, and China and America remain allies, pledging to battle Japan to the very end. The thirty-eighth issue of *National Comics* (January 1944) featured the story of the oddly-named superhero "The Unknown," who liberates a small, unnamed Pacific Island from the "diminutive warriors of the Son of Heaven."[91] After murdering the island's (strangely enough, white) chief, the Japanese go about torturing, raping and murdering the inhabitants until the Unknown arrives, planting bombs and inciting the natives to revolt. The Japanese are all driven off (or killed), and the island is returned to peace, with a contingent of U.S. Marines stationed there "to keep it that way!"

Transplanted Heroes

The transplanted hero-character is not of the traditional Anglo-American stock, as is the case with Captain America, Batman, the Fighting Yank, and a host of others. He (or she) comes from somewhere other than America, yet is given a central role in narratives through earned "Americanness." These "honorary Americans" are given all of the attributes of their Anglo-American counterparts but come from many nations that in the past were regarded as inferior, politically or biologically. A number of ethnicities, European and Asian, that were denied immigration and/or citizenship by acts of Federal law in years past were now welcomed as wartime allies, with past accusations of inferiority conveniently and suddenly swept

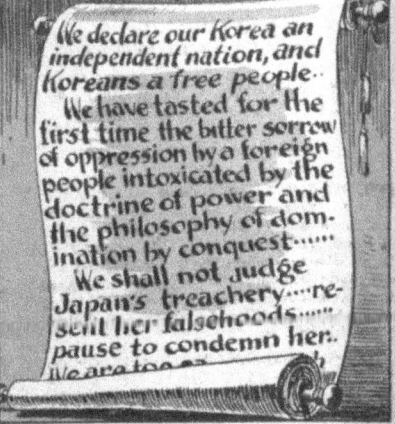

Formerly depicted as just another member of a larger, homogenous "Asia," here Korea is portrayed as yet another victim of Japanese aggression, and following in America's footsteps towards democracy with its own Declaration of Independence, no less (illustration from *The United States Marines Comics* No. 3, 1944).

aside. Often such a character was secondary, in relation to the American hero, and appeared in the form of heroic locals battling Axis domination. Fawcett's Captain Marvel, Jr. travels undercover to occupied Europe in order to free tortured resistance leaders in "Captain Marvel, Jr. and the Iron Heel of the Huns!" (*Master Comics* No. 29, August 1942). In the seventh issue of *The Fighting Yank* (1943) American superhero The Grim Reaper finds "The Heart of a Patriot," not in a fellow American, but in Anton Gyssen, a native of Belgium and prisoner of a concentration camp, who the Reaper liberates and then recruits as his partner in an operation to destroy Nazi operations throughout the country. In the second issue of *Headline Comics* (March 1943), "Uncle Sam's Battling Nephews," the Junior Rangers (a group of adolescent boys whose leader's family was murdered by Nazis) are joined in their mission by Chin Lee, a Chinese boy who becomes a full-fledged member and appears in subsequent adventures.[92] The Spring 1944 issue of DC's *Boy Commandos* finds the adolescent adventurers aiding resistance fighters in Belgium, and later fighting alongside Indian nationalists against Nazi invaders.

In other cases the feature character of a story was one of these "honorary Americans." The best example of this "transplanted hero" or "international American" is the character Blackhawk, who first appeared in Quality's *Military Comics* No. 1 (August 1941). Blackhawk's origin opens with Nazi planes bombarding the Polish countryside during Hitler's invasion in 1939. A lone figure stumbles through the rubble of a shelled farmhouse, carrying the body of his younger brother, searching in vain for the corpse of his kid sister. After burying his siblings, the unnamed figure wanders off into the darkness:

> Months pass by.... Like a huge steamroller the Nazi war machine crushes all of Europe.... One day a new name appears on the horizon.... A name that strikes terror in the hearts of men.... Blackhawk.... Like an angel of vengeance, Blackhawk and his men swoop down out of nowhere, their guns belching death, and on their lips the dreaded song of the Blackhawks.[93]

The prologue continues with the shadow of a mysterious, uniformed man overpowering Nazis all over Europe, from the craters of Poland to the cities of Vichy France. At a concentration camp in collaborationist Vichy, a prisoner is sentenced to execution, when suddenly a shadow appears, looming over the firing squad. Blackhawk finally emerges — a tall, robust figure, wearing a blue military uniform and a large, yellow-and-black hawk motif across his chest. He is soon joined by members of the Blackhawk team, all wearing similar uniforms but each one of a different nationality. Blackhawk defeats the camp commander (incidently, the same Nazi responsible for his family's death), and he, along with his team of international freedom-fighters, go forth to battle the Nazi menace wherever it appears.

The character was an instant hit, with *Blackhawk Comics* beginning publication soon after his initial appearance, a series that would last into the mid–1980s. Blackhawk's Polish ancestry is worthy of note, as this was one of the "undesirable" groups that numerous immigration acts sought to prevent from immigrating to America in large numbers following the First World War. Eastern Europeans, such as the Poles, were among the nationalities to receive the lowest "quotas" in the immigration laws of the 1920s. Eastern Europeans were also more readily suspected as being radicals and anarchists during the century's earlier Red Scare. Leon Czolgosz, President McKinley's assassin, was of Polish ancestry, and his (assumed) relationship with anarchist (and fellow Eastern European) Emma Goldman furthered the popular imagery of the European "socialist." Nearly twenty years after the drafting of the Quota Laws, Poland was no longer a place from where the atheistic hordes of Eastern Europe sprang. With the spread of World War II, Eastern Europe became the home of allies in the battle against Nazism, an ideology more threatening than any ethnicity. The Blackhawk series of comics may seem a contradiction in this regard due to the inclusion of Chop-Chop, Blackhawk's sidekick and cook, who is a stereotypical Chinese "coolie" character; Chop-Chop has tawny yellow skin and is rotund, with buck teeth and slanted eyes. While Chop-Chop's presence does, in fact, show that the previous decades' worth of Oriental imagery had not fully receded, it nonetheless does not devalue Blackhawk as a significant detour from the standard Anglo-American heroism that populated most comic books and pulps in the previous years.

South and Central Americans, Russians, Chinese and other ethnicities, long proclaimed as inferior in nativist circles, were given "center stage" treatment in the comics as allies of the United States in the struggle against Nazi domination. Senorita Rio, South American spy extraordinaire and former Hollywood glam girl, appeared in the pages of *Fight Comics*, battling Nazis that threatened the security of both her homeland and her American allies. Senorita Rio's appearances continued long after the war, as she appeared in *Fight Comics* through 1951 (first appearing in 1942), a testament to both her popularity and the lasting influence of her probable inspiration, silver screen star of the 1920s and '30s, Dolores Del Rio.

Bob Reed, an American who grew up in China, used the mystic arts he had learned in his adopted home against the invading Japanese following the murder of his parents by Imperial officers. In the guise of the supernatural hero the Red Dragon, Reed, and his sidekick Ching Foo, battled on behalf of the victimized Chinese in the pages of Street & Smith's *Red Dragon Comics* and *Super-Magician*, beginning in March of 1943.[94]

The Four Musketeers, first appearing in the third issue of *Air Ace Comics* (Vol. 2, May 1944), served as a symbol of Allied cooperation across ideological and ethnic lines. The Musketeer's Creed reads:

> Through faith, understanding, co-operation, blood, sweat and tears, our nations have crushed the enemies of freedom.... Only through those priceless qualities can our United Nations maintain the peace and freedom for which our united forces gave their blood. Therefore, we have this day pledged ourselves, our fortunes and our lives to the cause of world brotherhood, freedom and peace![95]

As their splash-page introduction suggests, the Four Musketeers are a group of Allied soldiers who come together to fight the Axis menace, despite their varied international backgrounds. Bill Bright (America), Tommy Atkins (Great Britain), Ivan Igoroff (Soviet Russia) and Lee Chung (China) band together through a series of adventures spanning successive issues to battle the Japanese and Nazis — not in the name of American liberty, but rather in the name of freedom from militant aggression for all the nations of the Earth.

The shift in the imagery regarding China and Korea — from sanctuaries of Yellow Emperors to friendly, democratic, and modern nations — represents an important transformation occurring at the time. The popularity of "international" heroes such as Blackhawk speaks to this change as well. Did the fact that Blackhawk, despite being Polish, looked more or less just like Superman come into play? Certainly — just as Senorita Rio's dual role as both spy and "eye candy" for adolescent males cannot be ignored. However, a popular character arising from an ethnicity that years earlier had been labeled inferior by both popular American sentiment and federal law is something notable. The need for popular culture to portray Allied nations in a positive light for propaganda purposes is, of course, obvious, but such portrayals, when combined with the shrinking public support for scientific racism, belies a change in popular American thinking that could have vanished just as easily as it had in years past. But this time it did not. As the idea of a "master race" was being attacked academically and linked to Nazism in the greater public sphere, the stereotypes and imagery concerning the previously "unassimilable" alien were beginning to lose ground. Friendships and partnerships between varieties of ethnicities that would not have been found in the majority of pulp stories of the inter-war years were now being promoted wholeheartedly in the pulps and comics of World War II.

As the Second World War drew to a close, the United Nations had been established, and there was hope for greater international security and checks on nationalistic belligerency. The yellow peril villains of Sax Rohmer and the pulps had been re-envisioned as the emissaries of Imperial Japan, and the Hohenzollern Hun had been recast as "Schicklgruber's" henchman. These changes were both patriotic and propagandist in nature. They were also a result of the era's adjusted attitudes regarding race. In the case of the Japanese, the yellow peril had come to mean less the threat posed by a gigantic, unintelligible rabble of tong-men and cheap labor, and more so the threat posed by those of an entirely un–American ideology who (conveniently) happened to be Asian. As for the Germans, the World War I propaganda posters had painted them as the Hun; during the Second World War, the notion of the German people being evil was downplayed, replaced with that of the Nazi, his identity determined not by race but, again, by ideology. The lurching, drooling "Kultar" Gorilla storming across America's coastline was done away with in favor of imagery that downplayed ethnic distinctions and emphasized the role of Nazi ideology. The "white domination" views of Madison Grant and Harry Hamilton Laughlin had been overturned in academia, and the public consciousness was slowly following suit. While their wholesale end as a respected worldview would not come for several decades, the change that took place in popular fiction between Versailles and Yalta cannot be overlooked. The portrayal of one or two Asians as allies of America would not have been out of the question in the pulps of the 1920s and 1930s. The notion that appeared in the comics of the 1940s, however—that nations like China and Korea were equal allies in a battle against something as "un–American" as fascism—was something that would have been hard to find in the earlier pulps (but not impossible, as "A Daughter of the White Star" demonstrates). Such a drastic departure from nativist rhetoric is of significant import. But this change, this shift of emphasis from race to ideology, was not complete by the conclusion of the Second World War. It would continue into the Cold War, during which ideological antagonisms threatened to obliterate mankind itself.

III

RUSSIAN COMMUNISTS, RED CHINESE AND NUCLEAR ANNIHILATION

The American Pulps and Comic Books of the Early Cold War, 1946–1956

1946. During his speech at Missouri's Westminster College, former (and future) British prime minister Winston Churchill evoked an image that would come to define the following decades: "From Stettin in the Baltic to Trieste in the Adriatic an 'iron curtain' has descended across the Continent."[1] Churchill's description of the precarious post-war balance between the West and the Soviet Union foreshadowed how American escapist literature would depict the emerging Cold War.

By its very nature, Communism has no indigenous ethnicity or cultural traits, and therefore a shift from the more nativist and racial imagery prevalent in the 1920s through the early 1940s would be expected. Unlike in the past, one could not point to a person, judge his appearance, and automatically know whether he was "one of them." The threat was hidden and elusive, adding an even more sinister nature to its character. Such an enemy at this juncture of internationalism and nativism is rather fitting for the times. With a rise in America's standing in the international community during and following the Second World War, the enemy invariably could no longer maintain the ethnocentric nature it had previously. The Fu Manchus and Koshingas of the 1920s and 1930s pulps, devilish simply by their nature and "un–Americanness," had been supplanted by the wily minions of Hideaki Tojo and Hirohito in the pulps and comic books of the late 1930s and early 1940s. In the 1950s a shift in the nature of racial imagery occurred once again; the Cold War was a war of ideologies, and the confrontations found in popular literature mirrored such an alteration. Communism, while being a product of German intellectual thought, could comfortably be placed in the ever-foreign "East" thanks to its ascendency in Russia. With such a traditional backdrop seemingly ready-made, other established imagery was utilized. The Nazis of World War II were replaced, in their savagery and ruthless determination to extinguish democracy, by the Soviets. Similarly, the fanged, clawed grotesqueness given to the Japanese soldier was, following the events of 1949 (the fall of China to Communism) and 1950 (the outbreak of the Korean War), transferred to the Chinese and North

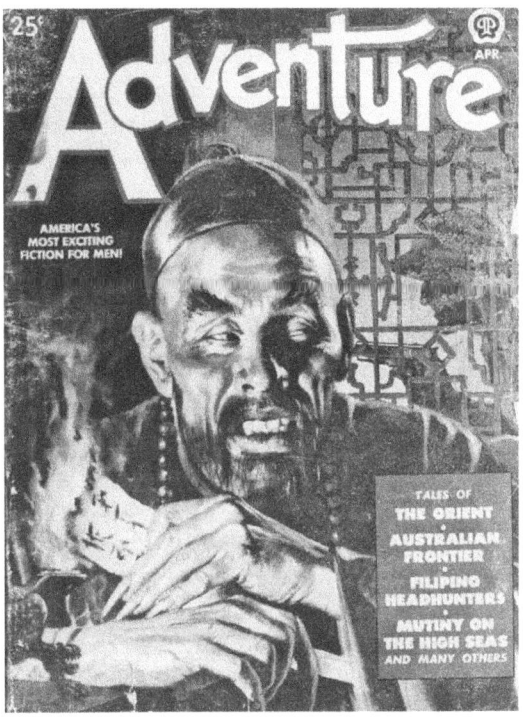

For some time after the war's end, pulp magazines returned to "tried and true" genres, including the yellow peril (*Adventure*, April 1949, Argosy Communications).

Korean soldier. The disgust that many Americans felt at the "loss" of their Chinese "brothers" to Maoism, and the vehement anger it generated throughout the country and against President Harry Truman, is visible in the political rhetoric of the time.[2] Obviously, the continuation of nativist imagery underlies a parallel continuation of racially-biased views on the part of many Americans of the time. On the other hand, it can also be understood as a changing feature of what was considered "American" and what was not. With America taking up arms, both ideologically and militarily, around the world to defend its values (and the values of nations it considered worth defending), an understanding of physical differences as the basis for identifying an enemy no longer seemed relevant. Pure racism was not the sole motivation for nativist imagery in the '20s, '30s, and '40s, when other factors concerning the fear of a loss of traditional, supposedly-homogenous American values are taken into account, as has been demonstrated. These factors proved even stronger during the Cold War, when (although racial intolerance still played a role in America domestically) it was ideology in a much more pronounced manner that defined the "other" in inexpensive escapism. Just as mainstream, Caucasian America had feared the dissolution of what it considered its culture at the hands of immigrants (not taking into account those immigrants' contribution to the American character itself) after the First World War, so too was this disintegration feared in the 1950s — the only difference was that the enemy was harder to detect than ever before, and now had support from a world superpower.

What the Red Spectre of Communism allowed popular fiction was an arena in which traditional imagery of the "other" could still be used, imagery that had been selling out on the newsstands for decades yet would still fit with the internationalist message America was broadcasting to the free world. As was the case during World War II, "good Asians" were not depicted as monsters, but rather as normal people and often in a heroic light. "Good Russians" were depicted as equally human as well, often as rural peasants suffering under the yoke of Stalinism. If a Russian or an Asian appeared as a physical or mentally-depraved abomination, it was because he was a Communist. The 1950s also gave rise to a new manner of demonization that, while not necessarily racial, certainly invoked past imagery concerning the savagery and inhumanity of the "un–American"—that of the ever-present threat of subversion, and of worldwide nuclear holocaust. Such anti–Communist and apocalyptic imagery, as well as "leftovers" from the yellow peril days of the medium's heyday, can be found in the pulp magazines that continued publication after World War II.

By the late 1940s and early 1950s the pulp magazines had begun to recede in popularity and in circulation. Motion pictures and comic books were now joined by television and inexpensive paperbacks as siphons that drained away the interest of those who previously would have read the pulps on a regular basis. While comic books are often considered the successor to the pulps in terms of cheap literature, paperback novels more appropriately fill that position, as much of the action, adventure and nativism that existed in the pulps transitioned to paperbacks. Cold War–era tales of Communist spies and Red saboteurs appeared alongside new reprintings of Sax Rohmer's Fu Manchu titles on paperback shelves. Several pulp stalwarts, such as *Argosy* and *Adventure*, managed to endure, but in forms closer to the more popular "slicks" than to the purely fictional periodicals they were during their zenith. The brainchildren of Frank

Munsey and Trumbull White, respectively, experimented with several genres in post–World War II America, alternating between general-interest periodicals, men's magazines, and some sort of combination of the two. This dabbling in "male-only" magazines would set the stage for later publications such as *Men, Man's Action* and *Man's Illustrated*. Such titles, with lurid covers of torture, bloody warzones, and half-naked women, that are usually (erroneously) referred to as pulp fiction, started to appear in the late 1950s and provided the sleaze that is usually (again, in error) applied to the pulps. *The Blue Book Magazine*, one of the most popular of the

Following the Chinese Communist revolution in 1949, and the Korean War (1950–1953), Nazi storm troopers and Japanese imperial officers on the covers of pulp titles were replaced by Red Chinese or North Korean soldiers (*Adventure*, January 1952, Argosy Communications).

pulps, also went the route of men's magazine, changing its title to *Bluebook for Men* for a number of years beginning in the early '60s. A number of magazines did survive, and new ones appeared, but those were primarily in smaller niche markets, the largest being the science-fiction genre. *Astounding Stories*, which began in 1930, survived as the re-titled *Astounding Science-Fiction* (later renamed *Analog Science Fact and Fiction* in 1960, and then *Analog Science Fiction and Fact*, as it is still known today), and new titles, such as *Venture* and *Fantastic Story Magazine*, debuted to cater to a growing readership, one made possible by both a robust economy and a growing fandom dedicated to science fiction and fantasy. Other genres, such as westerns and detective stories, continued on during the '50s, albeit not at the level of circulation they once enjoyed. Some pulp purists may (understandably) disapprove of placing Korean War–era *Argosy* alongside *Astounding Science-Fiction* in the same medium; the only significant tie such titles had in the past, aside from the science fiction that *Argosy* ran from time to time, was their printing on pulpwood, which even by the early '50s was no longer the case. This discussion, however, concerns continuity, and a dialogue relating to nativism in pulps must undoubtedly continue into whatever forms these magazines took over the years.

The pulps, in attempting to keep with the times, did their part to warn of the Marxist menace. *Argosy*'s March 1951 issue offered "I Survived the Korean Death March," chronicling one American's harrowing experiences at the hands of North Korean captors.[3] *Argosy*, now sporting the subtitle "The Complete Men's Magazine," featured many such pieces, fiction and non-fiction alike, that spoke to the barbarism of international Communism. In March of 1952, *Adventure* published the novelette "Gift of Mourning," by George C. Appell, detailing the bitter struggle between the Nationalist and Chinese Communist forces that had ended several years prior.

In March 1952 the science-fiction pulp *Fantastic Adventures* published an anti–Communist tract in the form of "He Fell Among Thieves," by Milton Lesser. In Lesser's tale, a visitor from another world falls prey to Communist brainwashing and almost destroys America due to his Russian-influenced belief that the West is belligerent and harboring plans for world domination. The alien, upon meeting a captured American spy, learns that he has been deceived and journeys to the West:

> But in the end the man from space would see the truth. With his cultural heritage telling him he must fight evil wherever he saw it, he would place undreamed of science at the disposal of the United Nations. Because the Commies had seen samples of that science for themselves, it would be a big stick they would be able to understand. It might — it just might — negate the necessity for war. But, if it didn't, no bookie in the world would place his money on the Commies.[4]

Much in the same way that comic book heroes had served as idealistic avenues of preventing war over a decade prior, so too does the creature in "He Fell Among Thieves." The October 1954 issue of *Astounding Science-Fiction* also printed an editorial about the horrors of "Red-brainwashers," and titles from *Amazing Stories* to *Astounding* and beyond all featured, from time to time, images of mushroom clouds and nuclear apocalypse on their covers.

Argosy did not remain as a men's magazine for as long as some of its competitors, and existed for much of its post-pulp life as a general interest title, carrying much less material that could be considered nativist mainly due to its need to appeal to as wide an audience as possible. Some pulp magazines continued to promote racial stereotypes, many of which reflected the nativism rampant in earlier eras. The first issue of *Mammoth Adventure* (July 1946) featured the "Manchu Terror," by William P. McGivern, showcasing on its cover a sickly-yellow/green Asian with thin slits for eyes and a treacherous smile, pointing a pistol at the reader. The pulp medium's reluctance to separate itself from its past

Yellow peril fiction from the '20s and '30s continued to be reprinted in pulp magazines decades after their first appearance (*Famous Fantastic Mysteries*, December 1951, Argosy Communications).

can be seen in its continuing to print yellow peril type stories ("The Hands of Han," by George C Appell, *Adventure*, November 1950), narratives that literally belonged to a different era. In July 1950, *Adventure* published "The Wrath of Genghis Khan — A Tale of the Mongol Horde," by Malcolm Wheeler-Nicholson, the founder of DC Comics who had seen his most prolific work appear during the inter-war years of the 1920s and '30s. The science fiction pulps, usually the more forward-thinking of pulp literature, also had a somewhat difficult time in relinquishing old stereotyping habits. The creature on the cover of *Fantastic Adventures*' October 1950 edition is the antagonist of L. Ron Hubbard's "The Masters of Sleep," an alien with slanted eyes, an elongated nose, and a bristling Oriental mustache. *Fantastic*

Adventures, in January of 1953, presented "A Call for Mephisto," by Frank McGivern; the titular demon appeared on the magazine's cover with the slanted eyes and elongated mustache reminiscent of the yellow devil Fu Manchu. The July 1953 issue of *Astounding Science-Fiction* featured "Enough Rope," by Poul Anderson, starring an intergalactic dictator with a Mongol-sounding name (Hurulta, Arkazhik of Unzuvan) as well as a rather "Asiatic" appearance, albeit with blue as opposed to yellow skin.

The heyday of the pulp was long over, and aside from newspapers and periodicals, newsstand space belonged to comic books. Comics continued to be a popular form of printed escapism, produced for an audience that included more adolescents within its ranks than did the pulps of the '20s and '30s. Following the end of the Second World War, an explosion of differing genres occurred within the comics industry, eclipsing and eventually overtaking the superhero books so popular during the war. Anthologies that had given rise to the superheroes shifted focus, leaving the costumed crusaders behind: *Marvel Mystery Comics* became the horror title *Marvel Tales*; *All-American Comics* (birthplace of the Green Lantern and other heroes) eventually changed to *All-American Men of War*; and Wonder Woman's debut title of *All-Star Comics* became *All-Star Western*. Crime, mystery, horror, romance, humor, sports, and war — numerous genres appeared and supplanted the superheroes. DC Comics heroes like Green Lantern and the Flash had to make room for comedy series such as *The Adventures of Dean Martin and Jerry Lewis* (which ran from 1952 to 1971, focusing solely on Jerry Lewis after the comedy duo's break-up), and romance comics such as *Girls' Love* and *Girls' Romance* (beginning in 1949 and 1950, respectively). Timely's superheroes retired in favor of horror and mystery comics, such as *Adventures into Terror* (1950), *Mystic Tales* (1951), and *Journey into Mystery* (1952). It was also during these years that Entertaining Comics, better known as EC Comics (and founded by one of the creators of the first modern comic book, M.C. Gaines), began producing the science fiction and terror titles that would come to define the company — *Tales from the Crypt* (1950), *The Vault of Horror* (1950), *Weird Science-Fantasy* (1954), and others. The boom was cut short with the 1954 publication of Dr. Frederic Wertham's *Seduction of the Innocent*, in which the psychologist and juvenile delinquency expert proclaimed that comic books were the cause of all of American youths' troubles, from promiscuity to juvenile crime.[5] *Seduction of the Innocent*, in addition to the Congressional hearings and public comic book burnings that followed its publication, almost destroyed the industry. Within a decade, however, the comic book had rebounded and reached new heights of popularity thanks to the revival of the superheroes, starting with DC's "revamp" of the Flash and Green Lantern in 1956 and 1959 respectively, and Marvel (formerly Timely) Comics' introduction of the Fantastic Four in 1961. In a bit of irony, the one genre that Wertham singled out as most harmful helped keep the medium alive, and flourishing for the rest of the century.

Anti-Radical/Eastern Europeanism Before the Cold War

> "New and strange conditions have arisen in the countries over there [Europe and Asia]; new and strange doctrines are being taught. The Governments of the Orient are being overturned and destroyed, and anarchy and bolshevism are threatening the very foundation of many of them."— *Lucian Walton Parrish* (1921, in Congress)

The anti-radicalism of the 1950s was the latest in a long line of related nativist sympathies that stretched to the country's origins and to the earliest misgivings Americans held concerning European threats to the new republic. Historian M.J. Heale points out that anti–European sentiment was an intricate part of the early republic; during the Revolution and beyond, the "American experiment" in republicanism was promoted as teetering on the verge of failure due to the imperialistic interests of European monarchs and despots. In time, this fragility relating to a lone republic in an otherwise autocratic world was joined by the nineteenth century's rapid advancement in industrialization — and the highly capitalistic society it produced.[6] The uncertainties that are intrinsic to a capitalist system of economics (such as the minor collapses that seem to happen every few years or so) added an additional layer of vulnerability to American institutions and civil society. As with other forms of nativism, anti-radicalism's influence waxed and waned over the years, depending on domestic, international and ideological circumstances. Owing to America's history as a home for revolutionaries and the downtrodden, there were times when radicals were tolerated if not outright welcomed by the native population. There were many collectivist movements (mostly religious in nature) throughout the country in the early part of the nineteenth century, and during the series of liberal revolutions that wracked Europe in 1848, many Americans saw heroes within these revolutionary movements, chiefly Hungarian freedom-fighter and temporary president Lajos (or Louis) Kossuth, who enjoyed great fanfare upon his visits to the United States and the United Kingdom.[7]

While fears of communist subversion had been promulgated ever since Marx and Engel's publication of *The Communist Manifesto* in 1848, a solidifying and strengthening of anti-radicalism that lasted for decades can be traced to the events of the Paris Commune in Spring, 1871. Owed in part to devastating losses and a humiliating surrender in the wake of the Franco-Prussian War, the Commune consisted of leftist revolutionaries transforming the anger of starving and suffering Parisian workers into action, resulting in the formation of a communistic state that lasted several months before being overrun and destroyed by government troops. Much like the French Revolution eighty-two years prior, the violence and bloodshed that accompanied the birth, life, and death of the Paris Commune shocked many Americans and became points of argument for anyone advocating vigilance against the importation of European-born leftist ideologies. Memories of 1848, merged with the violence of 1871 and the economic depression that struck America in 1873, created an atmosphere ripe for the flourishing of anti-foreignism. Labor unions became particular targets for "red-baiters" of the latter half of the century; industry leaders fearing challenges to their control could label even the most innocuous worker organization as Communist or anarchist in nature, betting on an age-old American fear of foreign infiltration. It did not help matters that, in all actuality, many of the most prominent radical orators and instigators were in fact either European immigrants or members of families that had arrived in America within the last several decades — either way, they did not constitute the long, Anglo-Saxon American heritage that nativists revered.

Fear of communists by name was a product of later decades; during the late nineteenth and early twentieth century, anarchists were the preferred foreign monster, although it is safe to argue that a majority of Americans more than likely did not fully understand the difference between the two. German immigrant Johann Most and Russian émigré Emma Goldman became symbols of the anarchist movement, generating great popularity among many foreign-born laborers and resentment from native-born workers and members of the "respectable classes." The number, and ethnic composition, of immigrants entering the country also stoked nativist fears; in 1882, only thirteen percent of the 708,922 documented arrivals into the United States that year were from the "undesirable" regions of Europe — the eastern and southern countries. By 1907, that number had risen to over eighty percent of that year's total newly-arrived immigrant

In popular literature at the turn of the century, if the enemy was not a heathen Asiatic, then often enough he was a follower of European radicalism (*Secret Service* No. 1283, August 24, 1923).

population of 1.285 million.[8] Domestic incidents, such as the Haymarket Affair in 1886 and the Homestead Strike of 1892 (and the resulting assassination attempt on Henry Frick), solidified the Eastern European communist/anarchist/socialist as one of the most popular bogeymen of late nineteenth and early twentieth century popular literature. Most of the earliest imagery to be found in American periodicals depicted the Eastern European radical in ways that did not differ a great deal from the standard nativist interpretation of foreigners in general at the time. He was a subhuman (often bearded) menace whose only goal was chaos and the overthrow of the American government. It is important to stress that in many nativist minds (and popular media helped spread such a notion) there was no difference between a European immigrant and the radical insurgent and socialist — the two identities were inseparable. By the turn of the century, the image of the wild-eyed, crazed European anarchist was firmly entrenched in the public consciousness, if not long before.

The super sleuths of the story paper *Secret Service*, when not battling tong lords and opium fiends in Chinatown, also occasionally ran afoul of the many radical, subversive organizations that apparently existed in America at the turn of the century. In "The Bradys After the Bomb Throwers; or, Smashing the Anarchist League," published in 1909 (and later reprinted in 1923), Old and Young King Brady are sent to Chicago to unravel the plans of a sinister group known as the Anarchist League. The fact that the duo are sent to Chicago, site of the Haymarket event nearly twenty years prior, is telling — "the place [was] crowded with a wild bunch of foreigners ... [a] typical Chicago anarchists' hold-out."[9] And what of the foreign-born denizens of such establishments? "For the door flew back, revealing a gigantic foreigner, dark and dirty, with an immense mass of hair standing up all over his head, with a tangled beard, which appeared never to have known a comb, down almost to his waist."

In 1911, Congress' Dillingham Commission published the findings (forty-one volumes, total) of a three-year investigation into the question of immigration's relation to the (perceived) rise in radical activity in America. Consistent with the nativism of the time, the report found that the presence of eastern Europeans led inarguably to acts of subversion, and concluded that immigration quotas were needed to stem the tide of such individuals.[10] In the dime novel *Jeff Clayton's Red Mystery; or, the Nihilist Conspiracy*, published the same year the Dillingham Report was released, the titular detective battles a group of Russian radicals determined to kill the Czar and (even worse) infiltrate the American government. The radical ideas of Eastern Europe (in this case, the teachings of the Russian Nihilist movement) threaten the idea of "Americanism," acting as a poison upon the government of Russia and, much to Clayton's horror, threatening to infect the United States as well:

> The man who holds the most menial post of the Russian Ambassador at Washington is one of Us. The man who in his household is his closest friend is one of Us. We bear tidings, in hovel and palace. Ours is the propaganda of education. Nihilism must be taught everywhere until all Russia rings with it. It must be taught to the Russian Ambassador to the United States as well as to the Czar in Russia.[11]

As evidence of how "memories" of past atrocities played into popular literature, an earlier act of terrorism is invoked in the story. The Nihilist mission? "To remove the Czar of Russia, as Alexander, his forebear, was removed."[12] The 1881 assassination of Czar Alexander II (grandfather of Czar Nicholas II) by the radical, left-wing organization *Narodnaya Volya* ("The People's Will") appears here in the same context as the Taiping Rebellion or the Boxer Uprising in other publications — to both conjure fears of foreign infiltration and barbarism, and to bring a sense of justification to the nativist imagery that permeated such characters. It screams at the reader "Look what *they* are capable of."

The Russian Revolution and the ultimate success of Lenin's Bolsheviks seemed to only vindicate the barbarous and sub-human nature of the Eastern Europeans that *Jeff Clayton's Red Mystery* suggested. What was called "the Bolshevik experiment" equated in many Americans' minds with pestilence, poverty, and unceasing warfare. There were some Western voices that offered calm, such as the University of Edinburgh's Charles Sarolea, who suggested, in *Impressions of Soviet Russia* (1924), that the West had nothing to fear, and that the Bolshevik regime was only a temporary phase on Russia's path to joining the more democratic nations of Europe and America.[13] Such a reassuring voice seemed to fall only upon a minority of readers in the United States. During the 1920s the Communist was lumped together with all manner of socialists, anarchists, syndicalists, and radicals to create an amalgamation of various nationalities (usually German or Russian) that stood for a foreign "other." The nativist aversion to Eastern Europen immigrants (immigrants who were among the primary targets of Quota Laws and "Americanization") provided ample grounds for demonizing socialists, and vice-versa. Condemnation of foreigners as radicals appeared throughout the press and in political rhetoric. President Woodrow Wilson, during the last years of World War I, supported (and succeeding in passing) the Sedition Act of 1918, which aided in the deportation of immigrants considered possible dangers to national security. And a young J. Edgar Hoover joined the Justice Department's new Radical Division, tasked with finding and deporting suspected communists, socialists and other "political threats."[14] The first "Red Scare" in American history occurred in the 1920s. Prompted in part by an assassination attempt on Attorney General A. Mitchell Palmer, J. Edgar Hoover helped manage wave after wave of raids, arrests and deportations of hundreds of suspected anarchists and radicals, including famed anarchists Emma Goldman and Alexander Berkman. The recent events in Eastern Europe, compounded with past instances of radical violence (such as President McKinley's assassination in 1900 by Leon Czolgosz, and the sensationalized show-trials of Ferdinando Sacco and Bartolomeo Vanzetti), provided "legitimate" grounds for such a scare.

Jeff Clayton's Red Mystery; or, the Nihilist Conspiracy (1911).

Throughout the Great Depression and the 1930s, as in decades past, Communism was continuously labeled an enemy of all things American, with the depictions of Communists shifting from that of subhuman, disorganized monsters on the prowl, to systemized and organized vanguards of an underground army bent on both world domination and the destruction of all Christian nations. In years past, labor unions had often led nativist attacks, especially against the Chinese in the Southwest; alternatively, labor unions themselves were often accused of being conveyers of socialist and communist aggression against all–American institutions and democracy. During the early 1920s, several instances of labor violence, such as the Battle of Blair Mountain in 1921 and the Herrin Massacre in 1922, demonstrated the delicate balance between labor unions, as organs of workers' rights, and the state's role in quelling unrest. In the 1930s, mass-produced pamphlets such as *Unmasking the C.I.O.* (1934) and *Communism's Iron Grip on the CIO* (1937) delineated the labor union as a tool for Bolshevik subversion of America.[15] This continued one of the oldest strains of American nativism — that of the anti-radical. Whether during the Homestead Strike of 1892 or labor unrest in the 1930s, anti-radical nativist rhetoric always found a waiting target in the form of unions and union organizers. Now with a looming power present in

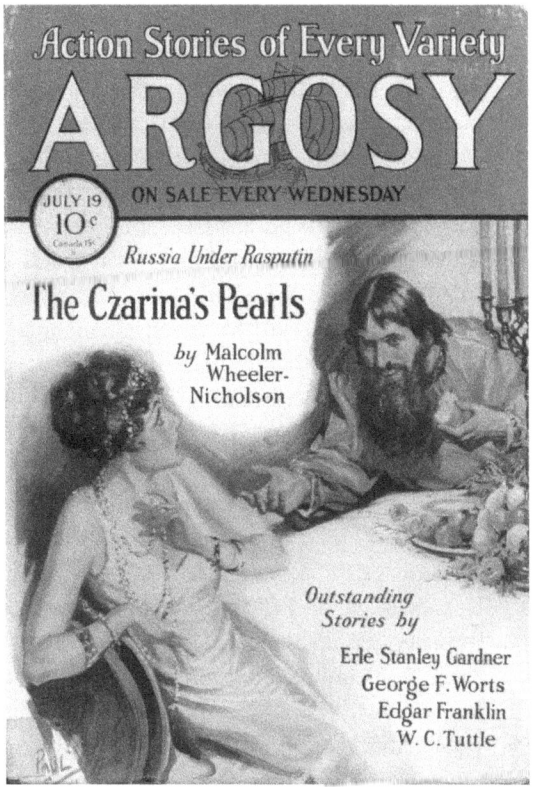

During the inter-war years, pulp narratives of the barbaric Eastern European and bloodthirsty Russian Communist appeared, much as they had for most of the twentieth century prior (*Argosy*, July 19, 1930, Argosy Communications).

the form of the Soviet Union, nativists had even greater tools with which to spread fears of a radical European seizure of American institutions.

Socialist agitators and swarthy Europeans appeared throughout the pulps' peak years in a variety of genres, but it is safe to say that Asiatic tong men, coolies, and yellow emperors far outweighed them in page presence. The pulp magazines featured the same type of Eastern European "degenerates" as magazines and newspapers from decades past, such as the lustful and barbaric Rasputin that leered sinfully at the terrified Czarina Alexandria on the cover of *Argosy*'s first installment of Malcolm Wheeler-

Nicholson's serial "The Czarina's Pearls" (*Argosy*, July 19, 1930). In some cases, atheism was used as the demonizing factor, as opposed to political doctrine — as with Kosloff the Russian, "an agent of the Soviet, spreading his curse of atheism — the Red Scourge of Russia," who, in the 1930 pulp story "White Man," was recruiting Chinese for a proposed Communist revolution throughout the Orient. Street & Smith's pulp hero sensation The Shadow battled Russian Communist agents determined to locate the whereabouts of the late Czar's royal jewels in the fourth issue of his self-titled magazine ("The Red Menace," November 1, 1931). Bolshevik villains also appeared in Fred MacIssac's "Sabotage," which began its serialization in *Argosy Weekly* in late 1933; the issue's cover featured a Neanderthal-like Russian holding a bomb, alongside a woman in Russian dress preparing to thrust a knife into the protagonist's head.

Going against the stereotype of the generic Eastern European barbarian, and separating faceless Bolshevik agents from the general Russian population, there were pulp writers who found heroes in Soviet Russia. In 1933 and 1934, S. Andrew Wood chronicled the adventures of a young Russian vagabond named Sasha the Frog, a thorn in the side of the Soviet secret police. In the serialized stories "Red Terror" (*Blue Book Magazine*, April 1933) and its follow-up, "The Frog of Moscow" (*Blue Book Magazine*, June, 1934), Sasha's exploits include aiding Americans on the run from Russian authorities, and destroying secret Soviet weapons. Sasha, and the underground group to which he belongs, are enemies of the state who seek an egalitarian lifestyle free from Stalinist oversight: "The Freebooters must have no dealings with the State. We are our own proletarian revolution. We are our own State. This is the classless socialist society."[16]

The history of science fiction and the history of Communism in America crossed paths in the early 1930s. While many authors wrote to the predominant anti-communistic theme, the SF community also provided writers who sympathized with the "Soviet experiment" for one reason or another. Philip Jacques Bartel (a pseudonym of Philip Barshofsky) wrote "When Time Stood Still" and its sequel, "The Time Control" (*Amazing Stories*, February 1935; *Amazing Stories*, December 1936), two science fiction tales that featured American and Soviet scientists working side-by-side to conquer the barriers of time and fight off counterrevolutionaries. The stories even starred members of the G.P.U., or the State Political Directorate (a secret police force that existed until 1934, the precursor to the K.G.B.), as protagonists.[17] Some authors believed that the utopia communism offered was, in actuality, the logical endpoint of all science-fictional wanderings. Following such thought, the young SF fandom community splintered with the founding of a group called the Futurians, who believed SF needed to be more political (with an emphasis on communism) in its message and purpose than had been the case previously.[18] For the most part, however, a majority of SF narratives carried the traditional American scrutiny of Marxism and communism. In the back-story to Nowlan's "Armageddon 2419 A.D." (*Amazing Stories*, August 1928) and its sequel, "The Airlords of Han" (*Amazing Stories*, March 1929), it was the Soviet Union who, following a war between America and a United Europe, joined forces with the Chinese to wage a war against democratic civilization before they in turn were overpowered by the "Han."[19] While Hugo Gernsback had created the first SF-only titles in the mid-to-late '20s (*Amazing Stories* and *Wonder Stories*), within a few years other titles had appeared on the market to challenge *Amazing*'s dominance of the field, one of the most successful being *Astounding Stories*. *Astounding Stories* first appeared in 1930; published by Clayton Publishing, it was one of, if not the, most successful science fiction magazines to appear, after Gernsback's *Amazing Stories*. Beginning with stock pulp stories that were simply wrapped in fantastical environs, *Astounding*'s later editors, such as F. Orlin Tremaine and John W. Campbell Jr., were able to incorporate Gernsbackian desires for scientific extrapolation in fiction into narratives filled with situations and scenarios as interesting as anything found in the action pulps. Campbell, who held *Astounding*'s editorship from 1938 to 1972, was responsible for discovering such SF mainstays as Isaac Asimov, L. Ron Hubbard, Clifford Simak, Lester del Rey, and a host of others.[20]

"Redmask of the Outlands," by Nat Schachner (published in the January 1934 edition of *Astounding Stories*), posited a dark A.D. 5000 wherein a secure world government had fractured several decades prior. What was once America is now a hodge-podge of rival city-states with varying ideologies; monarchy, fascism, communism, oligarchy and others — all vying for supremacy over the others. Representing the precarious nature of 1930s international stability, the city-states are on the verge of war, protected from one another via varying technological constructs. Threats come not only from other states, but also from the dreaded Outlands where strange customs and nomadic bandits roam freely. The barren Outlands contain the last vestiges of American democracy, and a visitor to one of the communist enclaves clarifies the author's opinion regarding the regimented Soviet lifestyle: "He watched the well-fed bodies of the Pisbor men, saddened at the memory of famine in his own city of Washeen. Yet none of its citizens," the visitor asserted proudly, "would yield one jot of their free, independent life, even with death the result, for this bestial, degraded, bodily comfort; not even for the regimented birth-to-the-grave ordered life of the communes."[21]

RUSSIANS AND COMMUNISTS DURING THE SECOND WORLD WAR

The years immediately preceding the Second World War brought a need for the American government to have more congenial dialogue with Stalin's regime. President Roosevelt was the first American President to recognize the Soviet Union, with the United States resuming official relations that had remained severed since 1919. While many saw Stalin and Hitler as men of equally devilish ambition, and despite Stalin's signing of a non-aggression pact with Hitler on the eve of the war in Europe, Soviet Russia was becoming, in many eyes, a probable ally against the fascist aggression of Nazi Germany. Former American ambassador to the Soviet Union (1936–1938) Joseph E. Davies' account of his time in Russia, published in 1941 as *Mission to Moscow*, paints a glowing picture of a friendly, fatherly Stalin. He depicts the Stalinist purges of the 1930s as nothing more than a "cleaning house" of poisonous German fifth columnists.[22] Despite America's long-standing animosity towards communism and radical socialism, there was a surfeit of popular media in the vein of Davies' memoir that praised the Soviets following America's entry into the European Theater. American films such as *Miss V from Moscow* (1942), *Mission to Moscow* (a dramatization of Davies' memoirs, 1943), *The North Star* (1943), *The Boy from Stalingrad* (1943), and imported Soviet films, including *Our Russian Front* (1942) and *The City That Stopped Hitler— Heroic Stalingrad* (1943), fed American propagandists' need to lend moral support to its new ally. Hollywood star Edward G. Robinson narrated a collection of documentary footage chronicling the Russian counterattack to Nazi invasion entitled *Moscow Strikes Back* in 1942. The government-sponsored *Why We Fight* series of films, in its *The Battle for Russia* installment, quoted Secretary of War Henry L. Stimson's assertion that "history knows no greater display of courage than that shown by the people of Soviet Russia." The film went as far back as the thirteenth century to show that Russia had always been battling for national freedom against belligerent invaders. Hollywood was not alone in this dramatic, yet temporary "rehabilitation" of Eastern Europeans, socialist or not. Magazines, pulps, and "slicks" did their part. *Argosy* chronicled the struggle of Yugoslav partisans in November

1942's "Guerilla Chief of the Balkans." In March of 1943, *Adventure* featured the novelette "The Way of a Cossack," by Joe Abrams. The story invoked the belief that Russia was an ally that had a proven history of fending off belligerent (often Hunnish) invaders: "Five feet of concentrated fury. That was Igor the Bug [so named for his small stature], in whose veins flowed the same blood that had congealed to stem the tide of invasion on another winter battle line four generations ago."[23] Igor Schinkowsky is part of a small resistance group that forms when German officers seize the collectivized farm on which he works. Chafing under the proud ancestry of his Cossack forebears who had fought off Napoleon a century prior, Igor finally gets his chance to do his part, first by destroying a prized shipment of Russian grain being sent to feed German troops, and later by cleverly convincing the Fuehrer himself (on a visit to his new "Russian provinces") that one of his most trusted generals in the area is actually a traitor to the Reich.

There also appears in the same issue of *Adventure* the short story "Patrols Are Everywhere," by R.W. Daly, which details the exploits of a young Yugoslav partisan starting what he hopes will be a long fight against the Nazis who recently attacked his village and murdered his loved ones:

> When a man finds his Maria, a gentle girl of sixteen, sprawled on her innocent face, quite dead because of two holes in her back, a man cannot overlook her death. A man asks questions. "Who did it?" Alexei demanded of Maria's father, who had only lost an arm in the raid. "They did it," the old man answered sadly.[24]

Young Alexei begins his trek across his homeland, killing as many Germans as possible along the way. He hopes to enter into the partisan-controlled "Mihailovitch's domain" and join more of his countrymen in their struggles. However, Alexei becomes a martyr for his people; felled by several bullets from an advancing German column, he does not die until after wiping out the invading Germans and leaving behind an impressive arsenal for forces loyal to partisan fighter Mihailovitch. The character of "Mihailovitch" is based on, or in some cases directly referred to as, Draža Mihailović, a Yugoslav royalist who fought against both the Nazi and Communist partisan leader Josip Broz Tito. Characters bearing the Mihailovitch name must have been popular, as they appear in stories chronicling the war in the Balkans in both *Argosy* and *Adventure*. Joseph Stalin himself was often portrayed as a heroic and, more importantly, human figure, such as in the June 27, 1944, issue of the popular *Look* magazine, which featured a cover story about Stalin that praised both his friendliness among children as well as his fashion sense.[25]

Moving from the pulps to the comics, in the thirty-second issue of M.L.J.'s *Zip Comics* (December 1942), "Zip's Hall of Fame" presented the story of Maria Baida, a young peasant girl from the Crimea who was awarded the Order of Lenin for helping to fight back a German incursion several months prior. *Zip*'s March 1943 Hall of Fame entry spot-lighted the accomplishments of Marshal Semyon Timoshenko, Soviet officer and member of the Bolshevik Party since its inception: "A man who belongs more to the world fighting for freedom than to the proud, courageous country of his own birth."[26] Similar to Ambassador Davies' opinion of Stalin, Marshal Timoshenko's entry in *Zip Comics* at times seems to sound like Russian, as opposed to American, propaganda. Following his arrest for striking a superior offi-cer. "Standing before the firing squad, Semyon awaits the final word when ... REVOLUTION.... The infuriated people, aroused at last, pour into the prison.... The Czar is overthrown! Semyon is made a cavalry comman-der in the new Red Army which has broken the shackles of oppression." The piece also goes so far as to alter the historical account concerning the early history of Soviet Russia itself, speak-ing of how Timoshenko battled "the white guard supporter of the Czar and their German

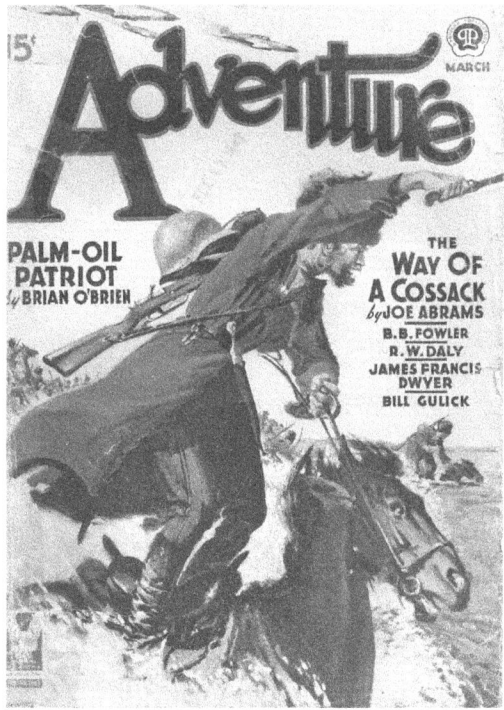

With the joining of American and Soviet forces during World War II, the Eastern European, long a target of quota laws and discrimination, was re-imagined as a valiant freedom-fighter, fighting to rid his homeland of Nazi oppression (*Adventure*, March 1943, Argosy Communications).

allies." The writer seemed to disregard that the Kaiser actually aided in the rise of the Bolsheviks by secreting Lenin back to Russia in order to destabilize the Czarist forces on Germany's Eastern Front, and that it was the Americans, not the Germans, who were counted among the White Russians' allies during the Civil War. Other comics simply pressed the cause of international brotherhood and unity between democracy and communism. A member of *Air Ace Comics'* heroic quartet the Four Musketeers was Russian, and many superheroes of the war years found allies in nations that were either Soviet satellites or soon would be.

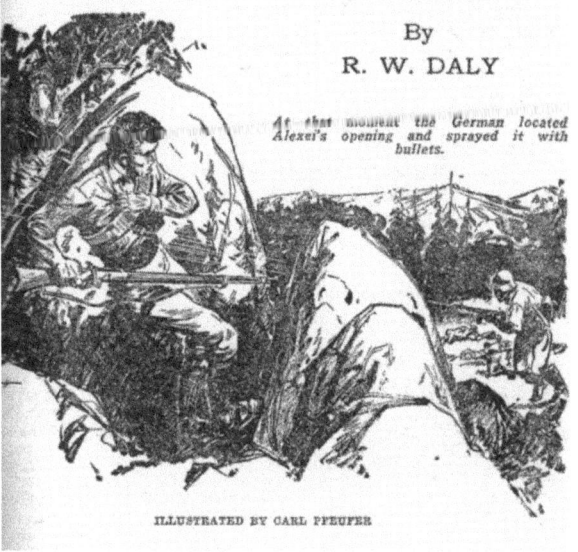

Illustration from "Patrols Are Everywhere" (*Adventure*, March 1943, Argosy Communications).

Not long after Japan's surrender, Stalin and communism were once again understood to be enemies of America. The dawning of the atomic age only adumbrated the fears of the first Red Scare. There were some voices that spoke for tolerance and understanding between the two ideologies, such as the first chairman of the American Civil Liberties Union, Harry F. Ward, in his pro–Stalinist pamphlet *Soviet Democracy* (1947). The booklet showers praise on both Stalin and the Soviet system of governance. The Soviet bureaucratic machinery, wherein the populace (it is claimed) has the power to recall unproductive representatives, is lauded as closer to a truly democratic structure than anything to be found in the United States.[27] To Ward's probable dismay, such idealism was not reaching the majority of Americans. The era's new enemy was quickly emerging in the form of Russian Communists now buffered by a bloc of puppet states, and the popular literature of the time would make use of such distrust. The imagery pertaining to Russian Communists, with a few exceptions, was not as "monstrous" physically as had been the case with the Germans and the Nazis previously.

U.S./U.S.S.R. Antagonisms

"Captain America and Bucky — they fought and battled all through World War II, these valiant and courageous patriots! But, with the coming of peace, there was still no rest for them. Communism was spreading its ugly, grasping tentacles all over the world!"—*Captain America No. 76* (May, 1954)

By the early 1950s, many superheroes had begun battling Communist infiltrators rather than the Nazi saboteurs of the previous decade (*Captain America Comics* No. 77, July 1954, ™ and © Marvel Entertainment).

With Russian Communists being the most frequent enemy in American comic books during the early years of the Cold War, the "Ruskies" inherited characteristics used to define the previous European enemy of America, the Nazis. Such continuity, nonetheless, was not fluid. In the case of Nazis, their ideology was to be demonized, not necessarily their ethnicity; owing to the history of nativism directed at Eastern Europeans, ethnicity played something of a larger role in 1950s anti–Communism. The main avenue of characterization, ideologically speaking, lay in resurrecting the Nazi's depravity and transferring it to the Communists. The Communists' path to such wickedness lay in both their resorting to espionage and trickery to undermine the

West, and in their determination to conquer America and the rest of the free world, made possible by the use of modern technology and weapons. Communist villains were often teamed up with criminal, underworld gangs, imagery that further served to project the degenerate nature of Communism in the comics.

Aside from any relation to the Nazis, anti–Communism in the 1950s was, of course, an extension of general anti-socialist/radical nativism that had existed for years. The outspoken dislike of immigrants may not have been as prevalent as in years past, but the same distrust of Europeans, those from the East particularly, as barbarians and uncivilized brutes bent on violence is still clearly discernible. The quota system of immigration restrictions was still in effect, and a poll conducted as early as 1946 showed that seventy-two percent of Americans questioned did not want any change in the amount of European (and Jewish refugee) immigrants that the quota system allowed.[28] As an indicator of America's new international standing, a large part of American immigration policy changes during the late 1940s and early 1950s dealt with the refugee situation that existed throughout Europe following the end of the Second World War. Despite several government agencies, and President Truman himself, attempting to amend or circumvent the quota laws, any large-scale immigration of refugees from either formerly-occupied Nazi Europe or newly-acquired Soviet satellite states proved an uphill battle in the face of entrenched anti–European nativism. Over time, and after much wrangling in Washington, immigration policies were amended to allow more refugees fleeing the spread of the Soviet Union throughout Eastern Europe.

Many pulp and comic narratives featured the same physical and psychological stereotypes assigned to Bolsheviks and anarchists in 1900s-era newspaper illustrations, story papers, and dime novels. As in years past, nativism did not die away entirely; instead, it changed to survive in a new situation, ferreting out xenophobic sentiments wherever they could be found.

Traditional forms of dehumanizing the enemy were still used from time to time, such as the Neanderthal-like Communist commander who uses killer whales to attack America's shipping lanes in a Sub-Mariner tale from the early 1950s ("Killer Whales," *Men's Adventures* No. 28, July 1954). Likewise, the gluttonous and lecherous espionage master Mr. Sarano battled Treasury agent Pete Trask (*T-Man* No. 2, November 1952). Instances of physical grotesqueness still factored into many depictions of the Eastern European Communist, many of which were based on imagery from decades prior, such as the swarthy, bearded brute in "Assault on Target UR-238"

(*Atom-Age Combat* No. 3, November 1952), or the grimacing, dynamite-wielding Soviets on the cover of the February–March 1955 issue of *Phantom Lady* (No. 2). Communists could also take the form of hideous abominations of nature, such as the green-skinned behemoth Electro, a product of Soviet bio-engineering created for the sole purpose of destroying Captain America ("His Touch Is Death!" *Captain America Comics* No. 78, September 1954).

By and large, however, European Communists, from the lowliest of lackeys and saboteurs to the highest echelons of the Comintern, visually appeared no different from other characters. A shift away from the stereotypical image of the wild-eyed, Rasputin-like Russian savage, combined with the 1950's ever-present warning that Soviet agents could blend in and look "just like us," were probably responsible for this. Even more so than the Nazis prior, the evil and nefarious nature of the Communists depended more on their motives and actions than on any sort of physical grotesqueness.

Some titles sought to return the Nazi to the forefront of world terror, despite the fall of the Third Reich. Fawcett Comics released in 1947 *Comics Novel* No. 1, which featured "Anarcho, Dictator of Death," an American-turned-Nazi who, after the war, had rounded up a group of similarly-minded traitors to destroy the new sense of international camaraderie and create a fascist, one-world government. In the first, and only, issue of Fawcett's *Comics Novel*, Anarcho's team of worldwide fascists is opposed only by Radar, the International Policeman, and his team of global crimefighters based in Geneva, Switzerland. While the enemy is still Nazism, more or less, the sense of internationalism that appeared in American comic books in the early 1950s can be seen as early as 1947, in both the ethnic make-up of the protagonists and the shared ideology of the multi-racial villains. Nonetheless, such enemies had become passé. Savagery, brutality, criminality, sneakiness, and sabotage, were increasingly being reserved not for the Nazis, now relegated to bogeymen that would reappear to haunt the free world from time to time, but the current (perceived) threat to Western Civilization — the Communists.

While superheroes had receded in popularity for the most part, with the exception of DC's "Big Three" of Superman, Batman, and Wonder Woman, a few new superheroes appeared in the early 1950s. Many only lasted several issues, such as Atlas' *Marvel Boy*, Farrell Publication's *Black Cobra* and Magazine Enterprises' *The Avenger*. One of the most literal instances of the Nazi-turned-Commie menace was present in the popular

Captain America series. In the December 1953 issue of *Young Men*, all three premier Golden Age heroes of Atlas Comics (known during the 1940s as Timely Comics)— Captain America, the Human Torch and the Sub-Mariner were recalled into active service, each with his own explanation as to what had transpired during the inter-war years. Namor, the monarch of Atlantis who swore vengeance against all mankind in his first appearance, first changed his stance regarding the surface world in order to battle the Nazis during World War II. In *Young Men* No. 24 he throws his lot in with America once again, this time in the face of growing Soviet domination of the oceans. In the case of Captain America, he and his sidekick Bucky had retired from "costumed" life, with the

Socialist radicals returned as international bogeymen following the end of World War II (*Comics Novel* No. 1— Anarcho, Dictator of Death, 1947).

Captain's alter ego assuming the position of a history professor, satisfied that America's need for Captain America had ended with Japan's surrender. Many had come to believe that Captain America never existed, or, if he did, he was long dead, killed in the last days of the war. "Gangsters tremble! Spies hide in fear!" opens Captain America's first 1950s story. "Out of a glorious past comes the greatest crime-fighter of them all! The enemy of crooks and dictators, foe of injustice and friend of the downtrodden! Is it only the Red Skull's awful nightmare or is Captain America really 'Back from the Dead!'"[29] The Red Skull has returned and thrown aside his previous allegiance to the Reich in order to form "an international syndicate of crime ... bigger than Murder Inc., working with the Reds in murder ... sabotage."

Meanwhile, Professor Steve Rogers is retelling the origin of Captain America to his somewhat doubtful classroom, prompting Bucky to ask his teacher if he thinks the heroic duo will ever be needed again. At just that moment a radio bulletin interrupts the duo's conversation: "Here's terrible news, folks! The worst criminal mind of all has come back to plague humanity! This time he's joined our Red enemies to fight against America! Yes ... THE RED SKULL IS BACK!... He and his gang have crashed the United Nations building ... and they're holding the delegates prisoners!" Upon hearing this news, Steve and Bucky decide their country is now threatened by a new enemy, one just as dangerous as the Nazis (if not more so). They don their costumes and proceed to the United Nations building, freeing the hostages and receiving the praise and adulation of their countrymen once again.

The same issue of *Young Men* also featured "The Return of the Human Torch." Opening with the Human Torch, Atlas' fiery hero that first appeared in 1939, making short work of a group of criminals, the story explains what happened following the Second World War. The Torch and his partner Toro were attacked by a criminal syndicate and doused with a chemical compound that extinguished their flames. The Torch was buried in the desert for years, and Toro was taken to an undisclosed location. After relating this back-story (which also informs the reader that it was, in fact, the Human Torch that killed Hitler, burning him alive in the depths of the *Führerbunker*), the Torch, now freed from his desert prison thanks to the testing of a nuclear device which reignited his flame, discovers that Toro had been given "to a country behind the Iron Curtain." Upon hearing reports of a "fireball" threatening American troops in Korea, the Torch finds that Toro is indeed still alive and has been brainwashed by the Communists to hinder American movements in the area. After the brainwashing process has been reversed, The Human Torch and Toro both vow to work together to fight tyranny and injustice in this new era. Once again, as was the case with the Red Skull, the literal criminal nature of the Communist mindset is shown, with organized crime and Communism working in partnership to cripple America. Also, the abhorrent practice of brainwashing, the only way to turn a true, red-blooded American into an ardent Marxist, has been used on one of the nation's most beloved defenders.

The Communists' dependence on brainwashing is seen in other stories from the era, such as "Captain America Turns Traitor!" (*Young Men* No. 26, March 1954), in which a drug is secretly administered to the Captain in order to turn him against his country. This practice is also seen in

"Come to the Commies!" (*Captain America* No. 76, May 1954), which finds Captain America in Korea attempting to understand why a group of captured American soldiers are broadcasting messages to their country urging the nation to give up the fight against Communism.

The communist's ability to subvert America from within using treachery, trickery and sabotage, much like their Teutonic forbearers during the previous world conflict, was also a staple of many Cold War stories. In "The Hour of Doom" (*Captain America* No. 78, September 1954), such sabotage takes the form of a popular media personality. An all-star athlete and intellectual whiz named Chuck Blayne has taken America by storm, with every boy in the country hanging on his every word. His popularity prompts a suspicious Captain America to remark that such a sway over public consciences reminds him of "someone." After a successful broadcast, the reader is shown Blayne's true colors. He is, in actuality, a servant of International Communists, who has done his best to endear himself to the hearts and minds of loyal Americans — all for the purposes of "destroying the faith of the youth in world cooperation as exemplified in the United Nations!"[30] At a meeting of the United Nations General Assembly, an enraged Blayne exclaims to the attending delegates, as well as the millions of viewers watching the assemblage via television:

> Boys of America! Listen to me! You know I always speak the truth! Now I tell you that world cooperation is a falsehood! Friendship among nations is not possible! I have placed a bomb in this building! A bomb that will blow up the U.N. and part of New York! I want you to realize that the U.N. is powerless against a stronger power.... World brotherhood is a farce! You boys must allow one stronger than you to lead you!

Quickly arriving on the scene, Captain America and Bucky race into action and defuse the bomb, capturing the Communist agent. Upon Bucky's inquiry as to who Blayne reminded him of, Cap replies, "Hitler! Same words 'Strong minds in strong bodies' and 'Play to win!' Americans play not to win, necessarily, but for the sake of sportsmanship and fair play ... which Nazis AND Reds know nothing about at all!"

Quality Comics' Pete Trask also enjoyed popularity during the early 1950s, with every issue chronicling the wily Treasury Agent's battle against Stalinist subversion, both in America and abroad. In "The Deserters to Red Doom" (*T-Man* No. 26, June 1955), Trask is sent abroad to answer the splash page's question: "Why should American G.I.'s suddenly desert and go over to the Reds? Why should decent American kids write letters to their grieving parents.... Letters spouting Commie party-line lies?

Why?"[31] Upon his arrival in Berlin, the "T-Man" attempts to save a young woman from mugging, only to find himself knocked unconscious in the melee, awakening later with strange burns etched into his skin. Later that evening Trask is unable to control himself and runs like those before him over to the Soviet-side of Berlin. Later he comes to his senses but is thrown into a prison full of the previous "deserters." In speaking to the other captives, he ascertains that they are all part of a Red brainwashing scheme used by Soviet propagandists to weaken American morale. Eventually escaping with the aid of the other soldiers, Trask returns to the free side of the divided city, to the soldiers' exclamations of "The Commies keep trying to hypnotize the free world with propaganda ... but, we're wise to them, Trask.... We're wise to them!"

New Aspects of Eastern European Barbarism

> "Success is ours, Comrade! The whole of Manhattan is a shambles! The A-Bomb hit the Midtown area, flattened it completely! ... Da! The once great American republic is ruined! Their back is broken — and their will!" — *World War III* (1952)

Many depictions of Russian Communists contained characteristics of Nazi imagery, such as inhuman belligerency and the use of spies, saboteurs and other "underhanded" methods of attack. The wild-eyed European radical who had existed in the minds of anti-immigrant agitators and jingoistic rhetoricians, with torch in hand ready to burn America to the ground, was reformatted into an envoy of Stalinist aggression. This new variant of anti-radical/Eastern European nativism did not rely only upon the old steadfast of stereotyping, but also created new avenues of demonization to suit the escalating Cold War. Whereas the radical in decades past had been part of a small group of infiltrators and saboteurs, they now encompassed an entire nation-state — the largest in landmass, no less. Such strength allowed the Communists of popular literature entirely new avenues through which to destroy democracy and American constitutionalism.

The 1951 promotional comic book *How Stalin Hopes We Will Destroy America* explains how it has been the goal, since the earliest days of the Bolshevik government, to use monetary inflation as a weapon against the United States. The narrator, a kindly old grandfather, explains to his family how "We're weakening our money — lowering its value. And that's just what the Communists want us to do!"[32] Explaining how "Nikolai"

Lenin had demanded the new Soviet state begin a program that would "force the United States to spend itself into destruction!" the grandfather extols to his family the devastation inflation can bring. Going as far back as the Roman emperor Valentinian, the narrator elucidates how inflation can devastate even the mightiest of nations. He explains why it exists in America today (increased spending thanks to the fear of a Soviet attack) and what can be done to end it.

In addition to sabotage, brainwashing and financial espionage, a new type of characterization appeared that further demonized the Soviets along ideological lines: the threat of Communist hegemony over the Earth and of nuclear Armageddon. Whether through atomic bombs, undercover invasions, or manipulation of American and world financial markets, the Russian Communists of the 1950s were exponentially trickier than any of their Bolshevik or Nihilist brethren in literature past. While not directly referencing the negative opinions reserved for Eastern Europeans during earlier decades, such portrayals were based largely on stereotypes historically associated with these groups. "Red Scare" media, such as the popular 1952 film *Invasion U.S.A.*, depicted a Communist takeover of America. Related comic book stories warned America against complacency and promoted vigilance against the threat of Soviet infiltration. In such stories the Communists' use of the Nazis' ruthlessness approached levels that the latter had not the means to achieve. Communism had enveloped almost all of Eastern Europe and was making inroads

"Uncle Joe," once a friend of the Allies, had replaced Hitler as the greatest threat to American civilization (*How Stalin Hopes We Will Destroy America*, 1951).

in Asia. These circumstances, combined with the threefold threat of successful tests of Soviet nuclear weapons in 1949, the possible domination of one government over the Earth, and the potential annihilation of the human race, created an environment reminiscent of the 1920s' Red Scare, only ratcheted up in intensity.

The Soviet domination of the United States was the subject of the 1947 comic *Is This Tomorrow*, released by the Catechetical Guild, a Catholic organization. In the story, the Marxist revolution in America takes place during an agricultural crisis, when the nation is considered most vulnerable. The comic, in its opening pages, presented its reasons for publication:

> IS THIS TOMORROW is published for one purpose — TO MAKE YOU THINK! To make you more alert to the menace of Communism. Today, there are approximately 85,000 official members of the Communist Party in the United States. There are hundreds of additional members whose names are not carried on the Party roles because acting as disciplined fifth columnists of the Kremlin, they have wormed their way into key positions in government offices, trade unions, and other positions of public trust.... These people are working day and night — laying the groundwork to overthrow YOUR GOVERNMENT! The average American is prone to say, "It Can't Happen Here." Millions of people in other countries used to say the same thing. Today, they are dead — or living in Communist slavery. IT MUST NOT HAPPEN HERE![33]

The perceived Communist assault on Christianity is among the most virulent themes in this and other similar works of the time. The "godless commies" of *Is This Tomorrow* seem more concerned with wiping out religion than with territorial or political gains. A young boy who has turned over his parents to the new KGB-inspired authorities, after learning in school that listening to foreign broadcasts and harboring religious icons is outlawed, is seized by occupying KGB. "Take my son with you," the father tells the invading Red policemen, "You've got his soul — now take his body, too."[34]

The threat of nuclear exchanges between the two superpowers proved to be the most common depiction of the possible end-result of the new West-East antagonism. In 1952 the four-issue series *Atomic War!* debuted from Ace-Junior Books, Inc. At the top of each issue's splash page a reason for the title's publication was offered to the reader:

> This book is designed to shock America in vigilance — and to help keep the horrors of atomic war from our shores. IT CAN happen here, unless friend and foe alike can be made to realize the awful devastation that another war will bring to all. So as you read these pages, pray that what you see here will never happen. And it won't — if we keep America strong![35]

The series follows the hypothetical confrontations between the Western and Eastern hemispheres following the Soviet Union's nuclear attack on the United States in the year 1960. It also documents the various battlefields — on the land, under the sea, and in the air — that such wars, now in the Atomic Age, would occupy.

Another comic that approached the possibility of a future war with Russia was the aptly-named *World War III*, first published by Ace-Junior in March 1952. Like *Atomic War!* its purpose was to rouse America from its complacency and rally its citizens to preparedness in the face of possible Communist aggression. It warned that nuclear war could erupt within the next decade:

> This is the summer of 1960. We have for so long been saying "the Russians don't dare attack"— we have come to believe it. On this hot summer afternoon Americans' main concerns are The Giants' pennant chances, vacation plans, Junior's new tooth. All the small and pleasant bits of business that make everyday life as we know it in blessed peace time. But at this same fateful moment in the secret Kremlin headquarters of Russia's military rulers....[36]

Thus, around a table located in a secretive war-room, a Russian leader (who looks a great deal like Joseph Stalin) directs his minions to launch a surprise attack against the United States. By the third page, atomic bombs have decimated numerous American cities, including Washington, D.C.

Scenes of horrendous destruction follow, with dozens of cities annihilated by Soviet atomic bombs, in the midst of Americans boasting as to the invincibility of their country moments before their deaths. In every American city the threat of atomic warfare is realized: "Radiant heat, deadly aftermath of an A-Bomb blast, is only one of the ghastly secondary results of atomic warfare. Frequently, all that is left of a victim is a shadow-etching burned into the wall of a bomb-wrecked building!" By the end of the issue's first story, the President has gone on the airwaves to assure his fellow Americans that retaliation will be swift and soon. One member of the assembled audience exclaims, "Well, one thing's for sure! The Russkys'll never get surrender out of that tough old guy! I wouldn't want to be in their shoes, now!" The remainder of the series' two-issue run depicts individual stories and battles within the larger narrative of this Third World War. Ground forces of NATO and Soviet Russia engage on the battlefields of a divided Germany, and American and Soviet frogmen battle deep underwater off Allied coastlines.

Atlas Comics' Marvel Boy, one of the few new superheroes to appear during these years, battled alien weapons coming from the sky to wreak havoc on the communist's favorite target, Washington, D.C., in the second issue of his own title (January 1951). In Marvel Boy's origin story (*Marvel Boy* No. 1, December 1950), in an interesting reversal of Superman's arrival on Earth, it is revealed that the boy's father was a scientist in Europe who, following his wife's death at the hands of the Nazis, built a rocket ship with the hope of taking him and his infant son far away from the Earth. Eventually the two are drawn by gravity to Uranus, where the inhabitants no longer indulge in war or strife, and young Bob Grayson learns many fantastic abilities that he will use later upon his return to Earth under the guise of Marvel Boy. This origin story is telling in that it shows yet another link to the Nazis found in Cold War–era comic books — having fled the Earth due to Nazi belligerence, Marvel Boy must return to face of the "new Nazis" (international Communists) and prevent a reoccurrence of the types of horrors that led to his father's own self-imposed exile from Earth.

EC Comics' *Weird Fantasy* No. 14 (July 1950) featured the threat of "cosmic ray bombs," which produced Hiroshima-like clouds enveloping the Earth. Atlas Comics' mystery-horror series *Astonishing*, in its seventh issue (December 1951) offered "Out of the Darkness!" which depicted the underground world man inhabited two-thousand years after the atomic wars ended in 1999.

Much like many films of the time, such as *The Thing from Another World* (1951), *The War of the Worlds* (1953), *Them!* (1954), and *The Invasion of the Body Snatchers* (1956), popular youth literature of the early Cold War often incorporated science fiction, with aliens and other creatures as proxies for the Communist menace. For *Strange Adventures* No. 3 (December 1950), Gardner Fox (who would later oversee the Silver Age resurrection of the superhero genre) wrote "The Stranger from the Stars" about a shape-shifting alien who assumes the identities of several highly-placed American officials. The creature plants "Super-hydrogen bombs" throughout the major cities of the United States, waiting to set them off until the arrival of the rest of his invading compatriots. The story ends with an ominous threat that could have been attached to any number of Communist-themed plots:

> When I receive word from them, the bombs go off! In the resultant confusion, it will be easy to conquer the entire planet!" That is why this appeal is being made to you! To every man, woman and child in this nation! Be on your guard! Warn the authorities if you see this Alien! Remember — he can change his body to make it look like anyone — even like — YOU![37]

The Soviets, as the closest thing to Anglo-Saxon white enemies the Cold War provided, inherited the characteristics previously attributed to the Teutonic Nazis in popular printed media. The decades' long tradition of the Eastern European savage, bent on socialist upheaval and anarchic destruction, helped fill the void left by the Nazis as the obvious enemy of America and her democratic allies in the comics. Brutality, depraved indifference to human life, and at times monstrous physical characteristics combined with the new Cold War–era threat of global domination and/or nuclear annihilation to create the most common villain to appear in American comic books during the 1950s.

The People's Republic of China and the Democratic People's Republic of Korea

So he's talkin' the truth, eh, Fritz? The Claw IS workin' for the Commies! And when I hand over this briefcase, I'M workin' for the Commies, too!—
The Yellow Claw (October 1956)

On October 1, 1949, the People's Republic of China was founded, with Mao Zedong, Zhou Enlai, and other leaders of the Chinese Communist Party standing atop the rostrum erected at the Forbidden Palace in Tiananmen Square. The defeated Chinese Nationalists, led by Kuomintang Generalissimo Chiang Kai-shek, fled to the island of Formosa and established a rival capital in Taipei. The defeat of the Republican Chinese came after decades of civil war and broken truces between the two. The Maoist forces gained the support of the countryside in their efforts to fight off the invading Japanese during World War II, while the Kuomintang chose to fight their own countrymen rather than the foreign aggressor. The "loss" of China to Communism was significant for the United States, which had been backing the Nationalist forces for years. Although support for Chiang had begun to dwindle in the late 1940s in the face of rampant corruption on the part of the Kuomintang, the U.S. had seemingly lost an important buffer to the further spread of Communism. The fact that the Soviet Union had also backed the Nationalists, and that the Communism of Mao differed strongly from that of Lenin, did not seem to matter to America; Communism was spreading, and with it a new enemy had emerged — Red China.[38] One year prior, the Democratic People's Republic of Korea, presided over by Kim Il-sung, was established in the northern

(Soviet-occupied) portion of the Korean peninsula after disagreements between the U.S. and the U.S.S.R. had made any unification between north and south unattainable. The outbreak of the Korean War in the summer of 1950 cemented Asian communists as a staple of popular media villainy alongside the Stalinists of Russia.[39] It would be rather unrealistic to believe that nativist imagery such as that of the yellow peril or the Fu-Manchu archetype would fade away after Japan's defeat; unfortunately, systems of "oriental" characterization continued.

Whereas the portrayal of European Communists relied heavily upon demonization of the actual Marxist ideology, as opposed to physical abnormalities or deformities, imagery depicting Communist Asians often relied on bodily characteristics. These were the same characteristics that the pulps of the 1920s and 1930s utilized, and the war-time comic books of the 1940s. Also, as was the case during World War II, distinctions were drawn between the "good" Asian and the "bad" Asian. The "good" inherited traditional American values and ideologies, and the "bad" was demonized using standard depictions attributed to Asians in the past. A major difference now, however, was that such grotesqueness was not a result of their ethnicity, but rather the notion that only subhuman monsters would accept and obey the doctrines and orders of the Comintern. The majority of comic book depictions of Asians during the early years of the Cold War, it should be noted, were not as demonic as their counterparts from World War II. Certainly the characters were often depicted as monstrous or sinister looking, but the overly-exaggerated features (such as claws and fangs) were not as prevalent after the Second World War. All of the blood thirstiness and underhanded tactics attributed to European Communists were also credited to their Asian counterparts; but it was their physical appearances that separated the Red Chinese or Korean from their Soviet contemporaries.

Consistent with the growing connection between American foreign policy and immigration policies that resulted from the intensification of the Cold War, issues of immigration and citizenship were intertwined with the mounting number of refugees fleeing both European and Asian totalitarianism. This was the era of McCarthyism and the second Red Scare, and much of the country's immigration policies reflected as such. As immigration historian Roger Daniels points out, however, the notion that such policies were simple reinforcements of the nativist laws of the 1920s is rather erroneous. "The 1924 [National Origins] act was essentially nativist and there were strong nativist elements in its 1952 successor. But," Daniels asserts, "there were also liberalizing elements in the 1952 [Immigration and Nationality] act that helped lay the demographic basis for the multiculturalism that emerged in the United States at the end of the twentieth century."[40] The Immigration and Nationality Act of 1952 (INA), also known as the McCarran-Walter Act after its two central proponents, is often cited as a return to legalized nativism — and, to some degree, understandably. On the other hand, the bill did a great deal to dismantle many of the nativist bulwarks of post–World War, isolationist America. It provided more avenues for deportation of suspected "subversives," but it also eliminated the "aliens ineligible to citizenship" statute that had prevented many Asians from attaining citizenship for decades.[41] Quotas for other nationalities were altered but still existed, while quotas were introduced for ethnicities that previously had been excluded altogether. Many Asians, Chinese and Koreans in particular, were granted immigration rights under special provisions that allowed unique treatment for those fleeing the Communist regimes in the Far East.[42] Language used in defense of the bill was certainly nativist, and the continued use of (and new uses for) the quota system undeniably speak to the INA's nativist influences; the fact that it also repealed a number of nativist policies, nonetheless, should not be overlooked. The Refuge Relief Act of 1953, championed by President Eisenhower, provided further assistance to escapees of all ethnicities from Communist regimes across the globe.[43] Again, while this represents another sign that nativism was slowly being separated from American immigration policies, it should also be remembered that such acts represent the Cold War, anti–Soviet sentiments of the time, and it was becoming apparent that anything bolstering the image of America as a welcome home for anyone fleeing European Communism was an ideological "win" for capitalism and Western democracy.

One of the casualties of World War II was the superhero that had proven so popular during the 1940s. Almost as soon as the war ended, superhero titles began to falter in sales, in favor of other genres, such as romance, horror, crime, and humor. The few heroes that did survive — namely, DC's Superman, Batman and Wonder Woman — stopped dealing with "realistic" issues and instead became more "science fiction" in their nature, leaving behind the societal issues of the 1930s and the nationalism of the 1940s. Superman fought his evil twin Bizarro. Batman and Robin became intergalactic policemen, or were sent back in time to the Stone Age. Wonder Woman contended with villains from lost or parallel worlds. These heroes had seemingly left the more "grounded" basis they had

In the early 1950s, DC superheroes such as Batman and Superman battled racial prejudice and anti-foreign sentiments in the pages of their respective titles (Batman Public Service Announcement, reprinted in Mark Cotta Vaz, *Tales of the Dark Knight—Batman's First Fifty Years: 1939–1989* [New York: Ballantine Books, 1989], 50, ™ and © DC Comics).

enjoyed earlier, with few issues speaking to contemporary topics. To be fair, Superman and Batman did their part in promoting America's burgeoning multiculturalism via public service announcements found in the pages of their titles, encouraging diversity, understanding, and internationalism. These PSAs however are some of the few instances of the "Big Three" superheroes venturing into territory remotely related to the real world.

Of the many genres that replaced superheroes as a top-seller, war stories were among the most popular. The number of war-related titles was staggering: *Navy Combat, Battlefield, Battle Cry, G.I. Joe, Combat Casey, Two-Fisted Tales, Man Comics, G.I. Combat, Joe Yank, Battle Front, Combat Kelly, Battle Action, Battle, All-American Men of War, War Combat, War Adventures, War Comics, War Heroes, Wartime Romances* and more. The sheer number of titles dedicated to war rivaled the number of superhero books that flourished in the decade prior. Within the pages of the war comics the hero was the American soldier. At times he fought in past wars, such as the America Revolution or World War II, but typically he was involved in more contemporary battles—namely, Korea. The enemy was regularly Asian, employing traditional "Asian" imagery that, once again, was attributed more to Communism than to ethnic origins. As was the case in World War II, depiction of Asian women during wartime changed to fit the ideological climate of the new age. Now there were three types of "exotic" females: the Asian-American (ostensibly assimilated into white culture, but still bearing a bit of the "exotic"); the victimized women of Republican China or South Korea; and the new "Dragon Ladies," now agents of Red China and North Korea. In many cases the war comics featured their own recurring characters, such as Tripoli Shores, found in *Fightin' Marines*, and the title characters in Atlas' *Combat Kelly* and *Combat Casey*, Ziff Davis' *G.I. Joe*, and Standard Comics' *Joe Yank*. For the most part (with the exception of EC Comics at times), the American soldier "character" was not a great deal more realistic than his costumed predecessors who had fought the Nazis. In these stories the American soldier is often wise-cracking ("laughing in the face of danger" as it were) and taking chances that it is doubtful any soldier in his right mind would take. Nonetheless, the American soldier in the 1950s war comics provided the type of characterization the comic readers wanted from their heroes. Indeed, their longevity in comics published decades later (with World War II remaining the most popular setting) attests to that.

"Evil Chinese" were appearing in the comics as early as the late 1940s,

Superman Public Service Announcement from *Action Comics* No. 162 (November 1951, ™ and © DC Comics).

such as the August 1947 issue of *Wings Comics*, which portrayed the American Captain Wing's tribulations in bringing much-needed supplies to the Nationalist government through lands teeming with guerrilla fighters. The guerillas that get in the way of the aviator's mission are typical Asian stock characters — yellow skin, with eyes so slanted they appear to be mere slits as opposed to orbs, and a dependence on sabotage and trickery. The first issue of *Battle Cry* (November 1952) featured the story "Gunfire!" about an otherwise heroic American soldier on the Korean front whose only weakness was his fear of gunfire. The Koreans found therein are depicted as yellow, with sinister smiles, slanted eyes, and long, angular noses. The villain of "Plan of Attack!" in *Battle Cry*'s fifth issue (January 1953) appears in the form of a captured North Korean commander who is apparently modeled after Chairman Mao yet sports the stereotypical "Fu-Manchu" mustache.

The July 1953 issue of Fawcett Comics' *Battle Stories* pitted an American G.I. hero against "the Ape of Pung-Noi!" a North Korean soldier of abominable appearance as well as intolerable cruelty. "They dubbed him the Ape because he looked like one, and because up around the Pung-Noi sector he acted like one of the crazed brutes," Bill explains to his soldiers upon hearing that the Ape may be in the vicinity. "Rending, tearing, mangling all who crossed his path.... Koreans, yanks, men, women, children! It didn't matter! The Ape bathed in blood!"[44] "The Ape" is indeed simian in nature, a low brow melding with a large, primate-like nose between two small eyes, and a gaping mouth filled with serrated teeth. His "Oriental" tendency towards torture is shown through his favorite pastime — using live American soldiers for bayonet practice, being sure to keep the captive alive for as long as possible before he succumbs to his wounds.

It is interesting to note that the most exaggerated Asiatic villains still appeared in the pages of superhero comics, those few that survived the late 1940s, facing the Atlas (previously Timely) characters (Captain America, the Human Torch, and the Sub-Mariner), who enjoyed a brief revival between 1953 and 1955. While the resurrected Namor and Torch were battling both European and Asian Communists, as well as fifth columnists in America (in addition to the occasional monster or robot), it was Captain America who mostly battled the forces of Red Asia. This may be partly due to Private Steve Rogers (as was the situation in World War II) being posted near the front lines (in this case, Korea). The nature of the character himself may also have a played part in his constant antagonism with the Reds of Asia. Even in a time where internationalism was on the rise and nativism had declined to some degree, the editors at Atlas may have figured that the living, breathing symbol of America should be fighting the most "alien" variant of the Communist threat. In "Kill Captain America!" (*Men's Adventures* No. 28, July 1954), "Cap" and Bucky are captured by a contingent of Red Guerrillas after attempting to save the life of an American soldier who had been drugged into accepting Communist ideals. The soldier eventually regains his "Americanness" once the drugs wear off, and he aids the two heroes in killing all of the "Commies" and escaping. The two villains of the story are Korean Communists who would have fit very well into any Captain America story from the early 1940s. Commissar Kee-Sai favors depictions from years past of Hideaki Tojo, complete with bespectacled, slanted eyes, crooked teeth, "Fu Manchu" mustache, and a sickly yellow shade of skin. His partner in crime, Kag the Guerrilla, is a rotund Korean with all of the same features (sans the glasses) as Kee-Sai. Other Asiatic villains that appear in the Captain America stories from the 1950s, such as "Come to the Commies!" (*Captain America* No. 76, May 1954) and "The Green Dragon" (Captain America No. 78, September 1954) feature the same exaggerated portrayals. In one of their own excursions to attack the "Redskis," the Human Torch and Toro dispose of several battalions of yellow-skinned, slant-eyed Communists in "Playing with Fire!" (*Captain America* No. 78). This story retains much of the mockery of Asian "Engrish" that had been used years earlier. "Now you never gonna get peekie at Pontu where we have many 'Melican prisoners not reported to U.N. peoples!" yells one North Korean soldier to the Torch after dousing his flame. Another Red boasts, "And without flames you cannot melt bullets which honorable captain will now fill your bodies with!"[45]

One of the few titles to retain the more monstrous imagery of Asians was Fawcett Comics' *Captain Marvel Adventures*, which ran from 1941 to 1953. The stories found in the Captain Marvel series not only demonized Communists but also invoked the old yellow peril fear of the Mongol; of the Asiatic hordes descending in waves of destruction upon civilized societies. Captain Marvel, first appearing in *Whiz Comics* No. 2 (February 1940), was actually a young radio reporter named Billy Batson who, upon uttering the magic word "Shazam!" was instantly transformed into "the World's Mightiest Mortal," Captain Marvel. The character was immensely popular in the early 1940s, receiving his own film serial (still considered one of the best of the era) and actually out-selling other characters such as Superman and Batman.[46] Fawcett Comics folded in the mid–1950s, with the character laying dormant for several years until DC Comics licensed the character in 1972 and began printing new adventures, doing away with the racially-charged imagery that had appeared previously. During the 1940s, Fawcett's Captain Marvel titles featured overly-exaggerated depictions of Japanese soldiers and villains; this trend continued unabated into the Cold War, with Asian Communists depicted just as hideously as their Japanese predecessors. *Captain Marvel Adventures* No. 139 (December 1952) featured the menace of the Red Crusher, "A monster feared and hated all along the allied front in Korea!" The Red Crusher was a hideous, giant yellow monster with slanted eyes and

Oriental monstrosities, more associated with the color red than yellow, featured prominently in comic books during the early Cold War (*Captain Marvel Adventures* No. 139, December 1952, ™ and © DC Comics).

large teeth, clad in a red guerilla's uniform and wielding a giant mace and chain. This "Mongolian Menace" would appear in other Captain Marvel stories before the series' cancellation.[47] Issue number 140 (January 1953) of the same title featured an even more monstrous depiction of Asians than that of the Red Crusher, in the story "Captain Marvel Fights the Mongol Blood-Drinkers." After delivering a supply of blood to a badly-depleted Army outpost on the Korean front, Captain Marvel learns why a blood shortage has taken place. "A tribe of vampires has lived in Mongolia for centuries!" a nurse explains. "The Communists made a deal with them —

186 Anti-Foreign Imagery in American Pulps and Comic Books

Illustration from *Captain Marvel Adventures* No. 140 (January 1953, ™ and © DC Comics).

all the American blood they could drink if they'd join the red forces!"[48] Just as a thousand-strong force of vampires are about to descend on American troops, Captain Marvel races into outer space and returns with a "blob of blazing sun," the light from which weakens the vampires, rendering them defenseless against the giant wooden stakes he plunges into their hearts. The vampires themselves could have easily been pulled from the pages of a 1920s-era weird fiction pulp — bright yellow faces, with bushy eyebrows, elongated ears, flat pushed-up noses, slanted eyes, a Fu Manchu–like mustache, and extremely long canines, long even by *dhampir* standards.

Another Fawcett title that featured "the World's Mightiest Mortal" was *The Marvel Family*, which premiered in 1945. The series detailed the adventures of Captain Marvel, his younger sister Mary Marvel, and their friend Captain Marvel, Jr. (sworn enemy of the afore mentioned Captain Nazi), as well as other secondary characters, such as Tall Marvel and Hillbilly Marvel. In the eighty-first issue of *The Marvel Family* (March 1953), the Marvel trio contends with the villainy of "the Mightiest Mongol," a yellow, slant-eyed, buck-toothed giant named "Mong the Giant," who is capable of growing hundreds of feet tall, with battle ships and tanks being as toys before him.[49] Upon infiltrating the Commie base, the Marvels realize that Mong the Giant is actually a solider named "Red Runt" who, through the use of growing and shrinking pills, is able to reach any height he wishes. The trio eventually escapes imprisonment at the hands of the Reds, destroying all of the Giant's growing pills and even saving a decorated American soldier in the process.

Similar to previous yellow peril depictions, the dispatching of Red Chinese and Koreans was usually more brutal (especially in the war comics) than in the case of European Communists, as demonstrated by the North Korean soldiers being burned alive on the cover of *The United States Marines* No. 8 (Magazine Enterprises, 1952), or the American G.I.s crushing yellow-skinned North Korean soldiers under a bulldozer on the cover of *Exciting War* No. 8 (May, 1953). "Afraid of death? Can't Stand the Sight of Blood? Then Have ... An Extra Helping of Guts!!" reads the cover of Harvey Comics' *True War Experiences* No. 2 (September 1952), complimented by two American soldiers viciously running over two North Korean soldiers with their Jeep.

Exotic Females of the Early Cold War

After the end of World War II the character that had given a stereotype its name, Milton Caniff's Dragon Lady from *Terry and the Pirates*, returned to her chief role as a pirate, albeit changed a great deal due to her antiheroine status as a fighter against Japanese invaders in China. In this new guise she continued to appear in the *Terry and the Pirates* comic strips, as well as its derivative comic books, serials and television shows. In most cases, however, dragon ladies did not receive such a rehabilitation and continued to act as evil emissaries of a foreign land, beguiling Americans via their Oriental deviousness and exotic seductiveness. The central antagonist of the late 1940s' "evil Chinese" story "Captain Wings" mentioned earlier (*Wings Comics* No. 84, August, 1947) is Sin-Fe, a dragon lady/guerrilla leader who apparently believes that combat does not require much clothing, and is obviously meant to entice rather than anger adolescent male readers.

By the early 1950s and the beginning of the Korean War, the dragon lady had undergone yet another change, becoming military or political leaders in the North Korean Army, such as Colonel Yoo, a North Korean officer sporting a form-fitting uniform and using a quellazaire (as many dragon ladies tended to) in May 1953's "Red Trap" (*G.I. in Battle* No. 8). The fact that Colonel Yoo is later revealed to be a man in disguise not only confirms the supposed deceitfulness of North Korean soldiers, but also speaks to the feminizing of Asian males that had been appearing for decades — the idea that men could easily pass for women, and vice versa.

Clothed in a revealing red dress and seductively reclining on a sofa, surrounded by cobras is "the slinky, venomous Madame Cobra" on the cover of the second issue of Tobey Press's *Tell It to the Marines* (May 1952). As part of a plan to help free a captured intelligence officer, American soldiers Spike and Bat arrange for themselves to be taken prisoner by the enemy and taken to the prison camp of Madame Cobra, who is "notorious for her methods of extracting information by torture." Upon successful capture, the two are introduced to the infamous prison commandant and threatened with death at the fangs of her cobras, whom she treats as pets writhing around her neck and body. Rescued at the last minute by an air raid intended to facilitate their escape, the two (and the captured intelligence officer) flee Madame Cobra's lair and successfully return to American lines. Madame Cobra features all the characteristics of the stereotypical dragon lady — a domineering and egocentric attitude combined with a slender form and limited clothing. She also continues the yellow peril tradition of associations with animals, and reptiles in particular, as do many other North Korean *femme fatales*, such as the enemy of Atlas Comics' soldier-hero Combat Casey in "The Snake Lady of Sinyong" (*Combat Casey* No. 18, October 1954).

During the 1940s, exotic romantic interests for the protagonist often appeared in the form of natives fighting against foreign invaders; this would carry over into 1950s as well. While usually not given as much characterization (which is not a great deal to begin with) as the dragon ladies, the exotic beauties of early Cold War comics still "fit the mold" of such stock characters from years before. Most were demure and submissive (or at least willing to serve American soldiers and interests), yet still avidly patriotic and dedicated to what was now a world cause (against Communism) rather than merely opposing a singular foreign government. Joe Yank, in the ninth issue of his self-titled series (December 1952), is enticed into saving the life of a beautiful Korean villager named Su San, who has been sentenced to a most terrible fate. She tells him, "I hate the Communists and all they stand for! My father has promised me to Colonel Blood.... But I'd rather die than marry that loathsome beast!"[50] Su San aids in the escape of Joe Yank and his pals after they had been captured. The bestial Colonel Blood is murdered at the hands of Yank after he shoots Su San, "the bravest girl" Yank had ever known. It is later revealed that Su San was only grazed, and she gratefully returns with the Americans to their camp.

While war comics carried on from World War II, Nazis and Imperial Japanese soldiers were replaced with Red Chinese and North Korean combatants (*Joe Yank* No. 9, December 1952).

The brave Korean (or Chinese) woman, smitten by both the handsome and daring American soldiers, as well as with American ideals, was a common staple of the war comics. Many heroes (super, soldier, and otherwise) would team up with similar characters, and in some cases such heroines were given major supporting roles in titles, as is the case with the character of Suwan in *The Yellow Claw*, to be examined later.

Towards Internationalism

"The hillside was alive with sudden death! And trapped atop the summit of Kushi Hill the Free Chinese forces stood shoulder to shoulder with American troops against a common foe!"— *G.I. Combat No. 19* (December 1954)

In the pages of Atlas Comics' *Captain America* No. 77 (July 1954) the Human Torch and Toro encounter a hideous monster that has been terrorizing a small town in America. Upon finding the creature, they find him to be a friendly alien stranded on Earth and innocent of any wrongdoings (even going so far as to save Toro's life after a fall off a ledge). The townsfolk, judging him solely by his appearance, form a murderous mob and hunt down the visitor, who barely escapes with his life. In retrospect, the Human Torch hopes that the creature does not return "until the human race grows out of its infancy!" This Human Torch story obviously falls into the realm of science fiction, but its message against attacking anything based solely on its physical differences can be seen as a parallel to issues regarding race occurring in the comic books of the same era. While the exaggerated imagery of Asians from the 1930s and 1940s was not as rampant in the comic books of the 1950s, and depictions were more "tame" than in the past, the characterization of "good" and "bad" Asians begun in the war years did continue into the Cold War era.

Such an understanding of race relations began to appear in illustrated media during the late 1940s. "They Got the Blame," printed in the December 1943 issue of *True Comics*, explains the history of scapegoating and documents what groups have suffered under such a practice in years past, extolling the internationalism found in the form of the Allied Nations. A 1944 issue of the same title contained the short piece "There Are No Master Races" (later re-issued as its own promotional pamphlet), which argues against the Nazi ideology concerning the existence of an Aryan race. The 1946 animated film *The Brotherhood of Man* explains that the international interconnectivity following World War II demands that people put aside racial beliefs and stereotypes, and understand that all people, regardless of skin or cultural experiences, are fundamentally the same. The film even goes so far as to point out in one scene the many instances in the past in which both the Asiatic races and those of the Middle East surpassed Europe's White culture in technological and artistic achievements.

In 1950s comics, the "good" Asians often lacked the more sinister features given to their Socialist brethren and, as was the case in World War II, are portrayed as either friends to any U.S. forces they come into contact with or as heroes in their own right. In many stories, Koreans and Americans join forces to battle the Communist hordes, both sides contributing equally to the war effort. At times, the non–Communist citizens of China are represented as innocent victims in desperate need of American intervention, such as when Captain America witnesses a supernatural creature bringing doom to "the true enemies of China" (the Maoist leadership) and helps liberate the nation's oppressed peasants in *Captain America* No. 78 (September 1954). By and large, however, the "rehabilitated" Asians of the early Cold War were the South Koreans battling a Communistic onslaught from the north, and the "Free Chinese" (albeit under a dictatorship that lasted into the 1980s) living on Taiwan.

"'Gook' is a nasty word.... A word too often applied to our friends and allies in the Far East" opens "Kid Hero," from *War Battles* No. 2 (April 1952).[51] An American soldier who constantly berates a small Korean child following his squad, persistently referring to him as "gook" or "gookie," is forced to reevaluate his mindset (and choice of words) when the child aids him in discovering nearby spies, and even participates in a fire fight. Mortally wounded in the final battle, the solider tells the child he's a "good gook." The child's insistence regarding the slur ("Please Joe ... Don't call me gook") meets with the dying G.I.'s reply, "You're right ... *Soldier*! I know better now..."

The December 1952 issue of Atlas' *Battlefield* (No. 6) featured "Massacre at Manghowon!" in which the titular village is the scene of a battle between U.S. and North Korean forces, with "good" Koreans caught in the middle. The peaceful village of Manghowon is roused from its slumber by the advance of a column of Red troops fleeing a U.S. assault. Once in control of the village, the Communists embark on a terror campaign, attacking men, women and children, with only a handful of villagers escaping the massacre. With the aid of American soldiers, the villagers are able to retake their village, killing all of the Communist invaders. In this story,

Americans are seen as both friends and benefactors of the "good" Koreans, who do not show the traditional "Asiatic" characteristics, aside from a yellowish hue to their skin. An American soldier supplied them with the tools needed for their liberation, and, during the battle that led to the communist invasion of the village, a farmer remarks, "Let us hope it is the Americans who win the battle, Ku Li!"[52] The Japanese enemy of years past is invoked, in that "the Reds rushed out of the woods in a Banzai charge against the village" and a North Korean soldier refers to his commander as "his Excellency" and other such titles regularly used (along with "honorable") in the highly-stratified hierarchy of the Japanese in World War II comics.

In "Village of Sealed Lips" (*Battle Stories* No. 10, July 1953), distrustful villagers and prejudiced Americans both realize the folly of their ways under the threat of their common foe. The "tug-of-war" between North Korea and the U.N. over the South has taken its toll, and many in the village of Yong-Chee are suspicious of the newly-arrived American troops. Their reservations seem correct when an American soldier is heard complaining about having to fight "their" war, even as his fellow yanks deride him for such negative views of the Koreans. The village's opinion of the Americans is elevated after they witness the troops supplying food and medical care to all the inhabitants of Yong-Chee, and asking for nothing in return. A young boy who speaks English, named Kum, had never harbored any doubts about the Americans and considers them saviors; he is eventually attached as a scout to the unit, much to the dismay of one soldier. "So they did give you a suit and a gun, after all, eh? Well that don't change the slant of your eyes or the shape of your skull!" yells the soldier, who is once again chided for his opinions.[53] Ironically, it is this same American who is the lone survivor of a Communist ambush; healed by the villagers, who refuse to tell the North Koreans where the survivor is hidden, the soldier promptly realizes his error in disliking the South Koreans. He admits he "has been a heel!" and asks for the honor of a handshake from Kum and the village elders.

In *Tell It to the Marines* No. 10 (November 1954), an American soldier is aided by a Korean civilian — not on the battlefield, but on more psychological and emotional grounds. In "The Gunner and the Kid!" Sgt. "Howitzer Howie" Burns is recovering in a Marine hospital from wounds inflicted during a recent skirmish. Despite his physician's assurance that his leg is almost fully healed and ambulation will soon be within his grasp once more, Burns is hopelessly depressed. He refuses to believe he will walk and exclaims over and over again, "I'm no murderer!" His doctor can provide no explanation for the Sergeant's behavior. On a whim, the doctor introduces Burns to Ram Wo, a young Korean boy also staying in the hospital, and the two connect almost immediately. After a few hours of jovial conversation and card games, Burns inquires as to why Ran is in the hospital. Ran explains that his family was killed when the Red forces made his village march across a bridge as human shields, a bridge that American forces were shelling. It is then revealed that this is the same battle during which Howie was injured. After hysterically pleading with Ran to forgive him for his part in the battle that killed his family, the child reveals that he feels no animosity towards the Marine. "What you did had to be done.... My people knew that and they marched bravely, singing, to their deaths ... because they knew it also brought death to our enemies!" Ran continues, "No, I do not hate you! Many of your Marine brothers died to save my country.... You all good men ... and you fine guy, Howie!"[54] Ran Wo, with skin that has not been rendered in any shade of sickly yellow, absolves Burns of any culpability in his family's death, freeing the young soldier from his guilt and allowing him to recover his mobility.

Combat Kelly No. 30 (April 1955) featured "Victory in the Village," in which the series' title character not only defends a Korean village from the Commies but also instills a sense of internationalism in the isolation-minded Korean elders. In Hatong, a Korean village under the iron rule of "General Chang," a young boy named Kil Ki witnesses the arrival of Combat Kelly and his troop of "Doggies." While Kil Ki is overjoyed that the U.N. forces liberated their village, his grandfather is suspicious. "Yes, Kil Ki, but they too are foreigners!" the old man explains. "And Korea has been robbed and enslaved by foreigners for centuries! They will be no different! ... Now they come to deal with us! But we must be brave.... As we were when the Communists took our village!"[55] Even after the American soldiers refuse any of the villagers' property without sufficient payment, the elders are still suspicious. Their fears are allayed, however, when they observe American troops refusing to defile a Buddhist temple to set up their command post (unlike the Communists) and sacrificing their own comfort in order to clothe, feed, and provide medical care to the town's children. While on patrol, the Americans are warned of an ambush by Kil Ki, whom Kelly saves from death at the hands of an enemy soldier. After burying the child's pet goose (who Kelly was not able to save from the devious Reds), Combat and Kil Ki witness an American medical supply helicopter being shot down by North Korean forces. In a show of gratitude, and as an apology for the initial suspicion they harbored against the Americans, all of the villagers line up gladly to donate blood for the soldiers wounded in the helicopter attack. As the tale ends, Kil Ki and Combat are seen saluting American and Republic of Korea flags, side-by-side as symbols "of a friendship bound by blood!"

"To the Victors" (*Battle Cry* No. 14, September 1954) details the suffering of peasants in the Korean village of Punsang. While American forces are portrayed as "the good guys," the reader's sympathy is directed towards the villagers who, after both North Korean and American forces are withdrawn, must retrieve and rebuild what they can from the burned out husk that was once their village. Such a conclusion is contrasted with the idyllic images of peasant happiness before the war, as provided in the story's splash page.

In *Fightin' Marines* No. 5 (April 1952), American soldier extraordinaire Tripoli Shores belongs to a group of "Fugitives from the Firing Squad," and only escapes due to the aid of a captured South Korean translator. The December 1954 issue of DC's *G.I. Combat* (No. 19) featured two stories that present an internationalist message to its readers. In "Red Invasion," American troops fight alongside the forces of Nationalist China when a contingent of Red Chinese soldiers attempts to take advantage of a mock naval battle/training exercise, seizing the island of Formosa. Chiang Kai-shek's forces are never stereotyped, in either appearance or language, and, upon the story's end, are praised by the Americans as valiant allies who eventually will retake the mainland "from those stinkin' Reds!"[56]

"No Escape," found in the same issue of *G.I. Combat,* relates the experiences of Johnny Yang and Frank Hoi, two Korean-American soldiers on the front, who volunteer to go undercover behind enemy lines in a spy operation. After their ruse is discovered, the pair embarks on a death-defying journey to return to the American side of the battleground. The duo, who refer to themselves proudly as Korean-Americans, fill their escape with witty banter and jokes that are no different from that espoused by any of the countless Caucasian soldiers fighting the Korean War in the comics. Upon returning successfully to their base, they have only one thing on their minds, the one thing any red-blooded American would: which team is currently ahead in the World Series.

Frontline Combat No. 4, published by EC Comics in January–February of 1952, provided "Air Burst," which is unique in its treatment of Communist Chinese soldiers, who are the tragic protagonists of the short tale. Chinese soldiers Lee and "Big Feet" are escaping an American advance across the fields of Korea when their contingent is strafed by enemy planes, leaving only the two alive, and Lee severely wounded. "Big Feet," pleading with his friend not to die on him, after all they had been through the last few years, valiantly struggles to carry his wounded comrade to American lines in the hopes of surrendering and ending the hellish existence of constant warfare. They are felled, however, by one of their own booby-traps intended for American pursuers, realizing only at the end that life is too valuable to be used as playthings by commanders and generals. The two soldiers are portrayed in a sympathetic light, showing a camaraderie and concern for each other that any American soldier would display as well.

"Corpse on the Imjin!" appearing in EC's *Two-Fisted Tales* No. 25 (January–February 1952), offers a short, brutal minute in the lives of two soldiers — one American, one North Korean. Eating on a river bank, the American is attacked by a starving enemy soldier; their respective weapons out of reach, the two struggle until the American gains the upper hand and drowns his rival in the river, demonstrating ferocity and a will to survive matched only by the desperation and hunger that drove the Korean to attack. The final monologue of the tale emphasizes the realization that, aside from man-made barriers such as nationalistic and ideological adherences, there is not a great deal that separates one man from another. "Have pity for a dead man! For he is now not rich or poor, right or wrong, bad or good! Don't hate him! Have pity.... For he has lost that most precious possession that we all treasure above everything.... He has Lost his life! Lightning flashes in the Korean hills, and on the rain swollen Imjin, a corpse floats out to sea."[57]

Internationalism, Jimmy Woo and the Yellow Claw

Marvel Comics' precursor, Atlas Comics, provided what appears to be the lone example of a heroic Asian character who was not a sidekick or back-up player, but the star of a title — Chinese-American F.B.I. agent Jimmy Woo. Jimmy Woo first appeared in the inaugural issue of *The Yellow Claw,* one of the rare titles named after a super-villain — a super-villain who in this case is a direct literary descendent of Sax Rohmer's Fu Manchu. Perhaps an attempt to appeal to more conservative elements following Wertham's accusation of all comics being unbridled sources of liberal extremism and "un–Americanness," *The Yellow Claw* premiered in October of 1956. Once again the traditional Oriental villain is recast in a new light, in that the Yellow Claw is a worldwide criminal mastermind as well as a Communist agent. The narrator warns: "In an ancient Manchu palace hidden in a mist-filled valley deep among the foothills of the Tibetan Alps, America's greatest menace waited.... A legendary Oriental mystic whose very name alarmed those who were familiar with his strange and terrible powers! Read now of.... The Coming of THE YELLOW CLAW."[58] While battling an enemy clearly in the yellow peril vein, Jimmy Woo's position as the protagonist of the series offered hope of a lessening of yellow peril stereotypes, as if the battles between the Claw and Woo were reflections of a real-world attempt to destroy such "Fu Manchu" imagery.

The first issue's story begins in Yuunan province, China (the base of Mao Zedong's power during the Chinese Civil War), wherein leaders of the "Chinese Communist High Command" are planning "the next phase of our campaign of world domination ... the invasion of Formosa." Fear of America's Seventh Fleet in the Taiwan Straits has made the planned invasion almost an impossibility until the gathered leaders, under the guidance of "General Mao Sung," decide to enlist the aid of an "ancient mystic" known only as the Yellow Claw. Terrified villagers run in fear of the Claw's name wherever Sung attempts to find him, until a beautiful young woman named Suwan, claiming to be the

The titular villain of this short-lived series was obviously a progeny of Fu Manchu, yet even *The Yellow Claw* contains small bits of cross-cultural acceptance in the form of FBI hero Agent Jimmy Woo (*The Yellow Claw* No. 1, October 1956, ™ and © Marvel Entertainment).

Claw's grandniece, offers to guide them to her master. Upon arrival at the Claw's palace, complete with statues of Buddha and ornate Manchu decorations, the Maoist envoys are assured by the Claw himself of his dedication to their cause; his willingness to travel to America to destroy it from within; and of his mystic powers far beyond human understanding. Gazing into his crystal ball at the end of the introductory story, the Yellow Claw sees his greatest enemy, the one individual capable of foiling his schemes: Chinese-American F.B.I. operative Jimmy Woo.

Based in a curio shop in Chinatown, and enlisting the aid of a former commandant of Auschwitz, the Yellow Claw begins his plans of sabotage and fifth columnist activities. In "The Yellow Claw Strikes!" the Claw frees a convicted felon whose services he requires in attaining sensitive government documents. However, once informed by Jimmy Woo that the Claw is serving the Communist cause, the criminal's patriotism emerges and he sacrifices himself to thwart the Claw's plans. The third story of the inaugural issue reveals Suwan's role in the Yellow Claw's plan — that of unwilling accomplice made to serve her mad uncle through hypnotism. Suwan also serves as a potential love interest for the protagonist. When Jimmy is captured by the Yellow Claw, it is Suwan who engineers his escape, allowing him to report back to the F.B.I. that they have an ally inside the madman's criminal empire. In subsequent stories the Yellow Claw utilizes both magic and modern science, such as his allying with a powerful alien entity and his use of a "shrinking ray," to better infiltrate the offices of highly-placed government officials ("U.F.O.— The Lightning Man!" and "The Microscopic Army," *The Yellow Claw* No. 3, February 1957).

The character of the Yellow Claw is a near identical twin of Fu Manchu. Indeed, Atlas editor Stan Lee, who created the character, stated rather bluntly in an interview, "We fashioned him after Fu Manchu."[59] The Yellow Claw has a sickly yellow visage with pointed ears, deceitfully slanted eyes, and a snake-like mustache. His form is clothed in a long Chinese robe with high collar, topped off with a Mandarin cap, and his hands end in long, pointed fingers. Jimmy Woo's relationship with Suwan, and her reluctance to aid in her uncle's diabolical schemes, mirrors that of Kâramanèh, a servant of Fu Manchu's who falls in love with, and eventually marries, Manchu's nemesis, Dr. Petrie. Suwan also bears a literary resemblance to Fu Manchu's daughter, Fah lo Suee, who was brainwashed by her father at times and often rebelled against him (usually in the hopes of usurping him). Suwan would appear to be an amalgamation of the two. The Yellow Claw, like Fu Manchu, takes advan-

Illustration from *The Yellow Claw* No. 1 (October 1956, ™ and © Marvel Entertainment).

tage of both ancient sorcery and modern Western science in order to achieve his ends.

In direct contrast to the Yellow Claw, Jimmy Woo is not a traditional Asian stock character, speaking in Engrish or belonging to some ancient mystic cult. Nor is he an avatar for a homogeneous Anglo-American culture, as was the case with Fu Manchu's adversary, Sir Denis Nayland Smith. Jimmy Woo is Chinese, like the Yellow Claw, yet no attention is drawn to that fact over the course of the comic, with the exception of it being noted that Woo has many contacts in Chinatown. White officers take orders from him, and he is the one that leads the charge into the Yellow Claw's headquarters. While Nayland Smith was working to save white civilization, Jimmy Woo is working to protect his country and everyone inhabiting it, regardless of their ethnicity. *The Yellow Claw* lasted only four issues (with the villain appearing sporadically in later decades, and Jimmy Woo finding new life in the Marvel Comics of the twenty-first century). Such a short life-span could be attributed to the comic reading public's inability to digest an Asian superhero (the first popular minority superhero, Marvel's the Black Panther, was still over a decade away). It could also be surmised, however, that the problem rests not with Woo but with the Yellow Claw himself. As was the case with other yellow peril characters, it is entirely possible that a Fu Manchu derivative had simply lost much of its appeal among comic readers. The belief on publisher Martin Goodman's and editor Stan Lee's parts that a Chinese-American hero could lead to a viable franchise should indicate that, in their eyes, the reading public had changed to a degree that such an undertaking was at least possible, as well as potentially profitable.

The depictions of Asians that were prevalent in the 1920s and 1930s pulps existed through World War II, though augmented to fit the enemy of the time — the Japanese. After the war this imagery continued in the form of America's newest menace, international Communism, and specifically Asian Communists. America's newfound internationalist stature promoted the notion that not all Asians were evil, hungry, Fu Manchu–like monsters out for blood. Rather, many of them were not as different from Americans as once supposed, and they too valued traditional American values such as freedom and individualism.

With the end of the Second World War, a period of relative peace was thought to be at hand after decades of both war and economic stagnation. As Eric F. Goldman chronicled in *The Crucial Decade*, there was a general optimism that swept the country after Japan's surrender, "a zest in today, wondrous hopes for tomorrow."[60] This optimism would eventually be brought back to reality, however, through the emerging animosity developing between the United States and the Soviet Union. The ideological battlefield on which the Cold War was fought took form in dozens

Illustration from *The Yellow Claw* No. 1 (October 1956), ™ and © Marvel Entertainment.

of ways, one of the most illustrative being that of the popular literature of the time, comic books in particular. Comic books supplanted one hated enemy with another, tying Communism to the defeated Nazism, and carrying much of its imagery over to the "Red Hordes" of Eastern Europe. With the "loss" of mainland China to Communists, comic books again reinvented older stereotypes. The yellow peril, a casualty (to a degree) of America's newfound internationalism, found new life in the form of the Red Chinese and Communist Koreans. In short, with the defeat of the Third Reich and Imperial Japan, popular escapism presented a "new fascist" in the form of International Communists, drawing on decades-old imagery of both Europeans and Asians. These "new Nazis" fell perfectly into place, with stereotypes and depictions seemingly tailor-made for them. Over the years, however, many things in the American worldview had changed, and nativist imagery had changed as well. Did the fanged Oriental and barbaric Hun motifs of the 1920s through the 1940s continue into the 1950s? Yes. Were they, during the Cold War, used solely to denounce ethnic or national origins? No. Ideology, as opposed to ethnicity, began to claim a larger portion of what was, or what was not, considered "American"— not completely, but to a much greater degree than previously.

Domestically, the ethnic composition and understanding of race in America were experiencing changes, as they always have and always will. Despite the continuation of many laws that hindered immigration, there was a large influx of Japanese and Koreans into the American citizenry through the marriage of "war brides" after both the Second World War and the Korean War, although the number of native-born Asian-Americans had been growing for a number of years.[61] As of the 1940 Census, the majority of Chinese-Americans were actually born in the United States, and this was a trend that continued through the following decades.[62] Many Chinese were allowed citizenship in America as an act of asylum, as refugees following the Chinese Communist Party's victory in 1949. Anthropologists and sociologists were arguing, as early as 1950, that Chinatowns as separate, racially-segregated enclaves would vanish as Asians of all backgrounds were gradually welcomed into a more inviting and heterogeneous American society; while this utopian ideal was certainly not the case, it still speaks to the general optimism concerning race relations in America at the time.[63]

In regards to racism and eugenics, if these disciplines' association with Hitler's Nazi Germany did not discredit them as legitimate avenues of scientific thought for the majority of Americans before and during the war, the War Crimes proceedings in Nuremberg in 1945–1946 certainly did.

The horrors of the concentration camps, and the Nazi regime's affectivity in murdering Jews, Catholics, Romani, Communists, homosexuals, and a host of other "undesirables" acted as a final "nail in the coffin" regarding eugenics and scientific racism in respected academic circles. American anthropologist Ashley Montagu, who had done so much to challenge scientific racism in the 1930s and 1940s, was tasked by the United Nations Educational, Scientific and Cultural Organization to formulate an official United Nations stance on the issue of race, and to hopefully further bury any inkling toward racial prejudices, a treatise eventually titled *The Race Question* and released in 1950. The United Nations' *Declaration of Universal Human Rights* (1948) and other post-war actions supported by the United States echoed the sense of international cooperation and racial interdependence that had helped fuel the war effort, and had been such an integral part of the war's popular media.

After World War II this spirit of internationalism fostered the understanding that not all Asians were emissaries of the yellow peril and that not all Chinese were tong-men and servants of Fu Manchu. Not all Eastern Europeans, those condemned as "undesirable immigrants" as recently as the 1920s, were bomb-wielding, wild-eyed anarchist radicals and Communists. As the American mindset was increasingly molding itself into a revision of the "us" versus "them" mentality, the need for abandoning the nativist, Anglo-Saxon-centric imagery of years past was both a necessity and a hallmark of the tolerance that the Soviets so often accused the West of not embracing. Racism and nativism still existed in America during the Cold War and have existed long since. Arguably-racist imagery still appeared in comic books for years to come. Nonetheless, the change in tone, tolerance, and acceptance in popular escapist literature from the 1920s to the 1950s cannot be overlooked, in both the magnitude of change that occurred within that frame of time and its progression in the works that would follow.

Conclusion

"'Yes, we have white folks out there, about one in every ten thousand, and they don't think anything of it and neither do we. You can't hide from the universe. You're going to be tramped under with color—all the colors of the rainbow!' And he understood then that that was exactly what they feared."—*All the Colors of the Rainbow* (1957)

The fear that the townspeople experience upon seeing green-skinned ambassadors from the Galactic Federation in Leigh Brackett's "All the Colors of the Rainbow" (*Venture Science-Fiction,* November 1957) embodies a conversation that had been a part of American history almost since the nation's inception. It focused on a fear of change, a fear called nativism that combined with already-present xenophobic and racial undertones, resulting in literary (as well as physical) attacks against anyone deemed to be *them*, as opposed to an imagined homogenous *us*. The aliens (called "green niggers" by the bigoted, armed mob) are hated and brutally assaulted by the nativist crowd in a way that mirrored the manner in which many Asians, Eastern Europeans and others were assaulted in the pages of early twentieth century inexpensive escapism.[1] The short story's condemnation of both nativist sentiments and the individuals who still retain them parallels a change in regards to the treatment of such groups in popular fiction, albeit a change that occurred ever so slowly.

An obsession with defining what was "American" permeated the nation's popular culture following the end of the First World War. Fears that America would be contaminated by European ideologies such as socialism and communism, and of impending onslaughts from the hordes of the East, worked their way into the literature, politics, and social discourse of the era. The pulp magazines of the 1920s continued this discourse in a fictional setting. This fiction provides invaluable information as to what was considered wholesome and "American," and what was not. Physical differences, religious and cultural backgrounds, an inability to speak

"American" English — these attributes, and many more, defined the caricature of the "other" in the pulps of the 1920s, and would appear throughout succeeding decades. Racist in nature, and fueled by domestic and international events that seemed to confirm such stereotypes, the imagery applied to "undesirable" Europeans and "untrustworthy" Orientals. This attitude was the product of rapid changes within and outside the country that led Americans to mourn the loss (or predicted loss) of what was considered traditionally "American." Whether a monstrous fiend determined to destroy the white race, such as Fu Manchu, or the stereotypical, unemotional gumshoe of Charlie Chan and his imitators, the message was the same. They are, at the very least, unable to be assimilated into the American culture, and at worst threaten the very survival of the country and even of Western Civilization itself. There were, however, kernels of tolerance and even acceptance within these texts, which would grow more apparent in the events and warfare that defined the later years of the 1930s and the early 1940s. Was racism a contributing factor? Absolutely; it would be nonsensical to assume otherwise. But, just as assuredly, there is another factor at work — the death of one America and the beginning of another, more multicultural in composition and outlook. With the growing urbanization of America and increased globalization, traditional America seemed under assault in the minds of those who would not, or could not, tolerate such a change.

The literature of the pulps, with many focusing on race as the essential divisor between intelligent or mentally deficient, progressive or socially backwards, good or evil, continued through the isolationism of the post–World War I era and into the Second World War. It emerged, however, fundamentally altered and not nearly as simplistic as it had once been. These were events that no American, no matter how nativist, could avoid. As time went on, the pulps and comic books reserved the most virulent depictions of racial differences for the newer, ideological enemies. Groups that would have formerly been designated atheistic Slavs or Yellow Emperors suddenly became allies, many of whom stood alongside their Anglo-American counterparts. Such a retreat from nativism appeared in the comic books of the late 1940s and early Cold War years, as the demonization formally reserved for the "Japs" and the Nazis was recycled to reference Red Chinese and European Communists. Ideology overshadowed race as the deciding aspect as to who was "the other."

The unifying factor through all of these years was nativism, in one form or another, and to one degree or another. Often, nativism and racism are terms used interchangeably, but such usage is flawed, although the two are not necessarily mutually exclusive either. There were factors that entered into the social and political equation that produced nativism, however unfounded those stereotypes arising from those factors might have been. The media certainly did its part over the years, reporting (and often embellishing) events at home and abroad. From the Boxer Uprising in China, to the tong wars of New York, to the theoretical innate belligerence of Europeans — the public clamored for sensationalism, and the presses delivered at the expense of the innocent. Americans, filled with stories of Boxers murdering Christians, or of Russian radicals bombing orphanages and murdering thousands in the name of socialism, were almost certain to overlay their opinions of ethnic minorities with manufactured memories of such events. Witnessing the building of an Eastern Orthodox Church, or a Buddhist temple in areas that had retained a Protestant Christian majority for centuries, was bound to unnerve many (out of ignorance if for no other reason). Were worries of a socialist takeover of the United States by a small band of Yiddish-speaking socialists, or fears concerning a "yellow pope" stamping out American Christianity unwarranted? Of course, and ludicrously so. But they were fears nonetheless, which is not the same as out-and-out racism. Similar situations are evident today. Early twenty-first concerns over immigration (legal or otherwise) in America represent a strain of Zolberg's "legitimate nativism." There are Americans today, from all manner of ethnic, religious and racial backgrounds, for whom immigration and its related issues cause major anxiety. Are all such individuals racist? No, although it would be unwise to rule out racism's part in swaying some peoples' opinions. Overall, however, it is safe to say that many present-day Americans are concerned with issues, among them immigration, that are nativist to a degree but cannot be called pure racism.

Concluding this work in the 1950s is not an attempt to say that nativist-centric imagery was gone forever, or that the process of nativism-into-multiculturalism was concluded by the beginning of the 1960s — far from it. Despite the continued liberalization of America's immigration policy, such as the 1965 Hart-Celler Act (which finally abolished the quota system entirely), nativism existed as a strong force throughout the nation.[2] Methods of characterizations that had lasted for decades, almost a century in some cases, would not be dispelled easily or quickly. The end of the 1950s through to the present day displays a continuation of the process, although the most profound changes occurred during the earlier decades of the century. This development would continue in the comic books; the pulps, for the most part, aside from the digest versions of *Astounding*

Science-Fiction (now known as *Analog*) and a few other titles, had either ceased to exist or had been reformatted into men's magazines, as was the case with *The Argosy* and *Adventure*.

Nativist imagery in the comic books continued to recede to some degree. The period that is usually referred to as the "Silver Age of Comics" coincided with a period of continued change in America's approach to race relations and nativism. The resurrection of the superhero was initiated by DC's *Showcase* No. 4 (October 1956), followed by *Showcase* No. 22 (October 1959), which premiered updated versions of the 1940s heroes, The Flash and Green Lantern, respectively. These characters began a rejuvenation of the superhero as a staple of American popular culture that has not abated since. By the first appearances of the Fantastic Four and Spider-man (*Fantastic Four* No. 1, November 1961; *Amazing Fantasy* No. 15, August, 1962), comic books were seeing sales and popularity levels that rivaled those of the 1940s. The newer characters had more "foibles" and deeper personalities than the rather stiff heroes of the Second World War. These characters approached societal issues, such as race, in ways that had never been attempted in years past.

The fanbase that sprang up around comic books in the 1960s and '70s was of a different mold than the medium's target audience in the past. They were children of post–World War II prosperity, the first generation born after the Second World War. Many were well-educated, and comic book publishers were finding their audience growing not among children but among college students and young adults who demanded more from the popular literature. Characters were not as rigid and two-dimensional as had been the case in years past. A teenage Spider-Man wrestled with his conscience daily, even considering using his gifts for crime in order to resolve his elderly aunt's financial woes. Captain America, returned from the battlefields of World War II (his 1950s adventures attributed to an imposter), now wrestled with guilt over the death of his former partner; sought psychoanalytical help when faced with hallucinations; and struggled to find his place in a world where he seemed to be nothing more than a relic. DC Comics' Batman, despite being the star of his eponymous camp television show, was later removed from the science fiction storylines he had inhabited since the end of the 1940s and restored to his original role as a mysterious and brooding vigilante. Superman, long-time champion of truth, justice and the American way, found himself starring in more stories that spoke to the loneliness and isolation he felt regarding his abilities, in addition to his status as an alien on Earth. Writers such as Stan Lee, Roy Thomas, and Denny O'Neil used literary devices and approaches to comic narration never seen in comic books before. Artists such as Bill Steranko, Neal Adams, Barry Windsor-Smith, and Frank Miller pushed the envelope of comic creativity. These creators, and a multitude more, either participated in or were influenced by the changes occurring in the comics in the 1960s and 1970s.

The comic industry also began to reexamine its history of the archetypal white hero. As was the case with other real-world issues, the comic books grappled with the issues of racism and nativism. In *Green Lantern* No. 76 (April 1970), writer Denny O'Neil and artist Neal Adams re-envisioned the character as a symbol of law and order, the protector of the establishment. The Green Lantern teamed with the Green Arrow, who had recently been remade into a voice for the liberal, anti-establishment left, a hero who was sick of all the other costumed crusaders doing nothing to aid the average person. In the first issue of their team-up title, Green Lantern is approached by an elderly black man, who asks him a simple question:

> I been readin' about you.... How you work for the blue skins ... and how on a planet someplace you helped out the orange skins ... and you done considerable for the purple skins! Only there's skins you never bothered with! The Black skins! I want to know.... How come?! Answer me that, Mr. Green Lantern!"

In response, the Emerald Crusader, after a brief pause, can only look down and reply, "I ... can't..."[3] This story was the start of a brilliant run by the O'Neil/Adams team, which took the duo across the country in an old pickup truck, combating the ills of society such as racism and religious fanaticism, and fighting for the average American.

Characters of ethnically-diverse backgrounds who were the feature of anthology titles or the stars of their own series appeared in the comics as early as the 1960s. African-American characters were the first to significantly challenge the hold on superheroics previously reserved primarily for Caucasians. Marvel's the Black Panther appeared in 1966 (*Fantastic Four* No. 52, July 1966), receiving his first ongoing title in 1973. Another African-American hero, Luke Cage, appeared in 1972 (*Luke Cage—Hero for Hire* No. 1, June 1972) and remains a vital part of Marvel Comics continuity today. In December of 1971, DC introduced John Stewart (*Green Lantern* Vol. 2, No. 87), an African-American Green Lantern who has maintained tremendous popularity into the twenty-first century, most notably as a star of DC's animated television show *Justice League* (later *Justice League Unlimited*), beginning in 2001. In 1983, Marvel's Tony Stark, the secret identity of the armored hero Iron Man, took time off to recover from alcoholism and was replaced by African-American Jim Rhodes, a lifelong friend of Stark. Following the return of the original Iron Man, Rhodes was given his own suit of armor, known as War Machine, and has remained a mainstay of the franchise, portrayed by Academy Award–winning actor Don Cheadle in 2010's *Iron Man 2*. In the early 1990s, under the banner of its *2099* imprint, Marvel Comics introduced a future version of Spider-Man who happened to be Hispanic, Miguel O'Hara. What is noticeable is an obvious lack of Asian-American and Eastern European characters receiving the same treatment. Unfortunately, they continued on, in many titles for many years, as exotic Orientals or European barbarians, not gaining a great deal of footing during the social upheavals in America during the 1960s and 1970s.

While strides were made in the 1960s–80s, there still remained a large amount of ethnic stereotypes in comic books. In "The Strength of the Sumo!" (*Tales of Suspense* No. 61, January 1965), Captain America battles a Sumo wrestler—in Vietnam, as opposed to Japan—and contends with Viet-Cong that speak more like "ancient Celestials" than modern, Marxist revolutionaries, showcasing a mangling of cultures that harkens back to the "Mongolians" occupying dime novel Chinatowns at the turn of the century. Marvel Comics' Shang-Chi, the Master of Kung Fu (first appearing in April 1974), while still a very popular superhero, was still a "master of kung-fu," which many would consider a stereotype in and of itself. Shang-Chi, still appearing in Marvel Comics today, is the son of Fu Manchu (a fact that has not been greatly publicized in recent years); and his sister, Fah Lo Suee, was portrayed in the traditional dragon lady role, a characterization she had maintained for half a century previously. The Yellow Claw appeared in Marvel Comics titles through the '60s and '70s, albeit as a more international villain associated less and less with the Chinese in particular as the years went on. One of Iron Man's first enemies was "the Mandarin," and the Blackhawks' Chop-Chop appeared relatively unaltered until a mid–1970s reboot of the franchise. In the 1990s, the central villain of the entire Valiant Comics* universe was Toyo Harada, a Japanese businessman bent on world domination who only lacked the long mustache and dragon robes of Fu Manchu and other "yellow emperors"— a reminder of the reinvigorated yellow peril that swept America in the late

---

*Not to be confused with the modern *Valiant Entertainment*, which began publication in the spring of 2012.

1980s and early 1990s regarding the economic ascendency of Japan. The stereotypes may have lessened to a degree, but they were still there — and would remain there, for the most part, until a new group of creators, more diverse in both creativity and ethnicity, began to take larger parts in the industry in the late 1980s and early 1990s.

Now, in the twenty-first century, any sort of racist or nativist imagery in comic books is seen as intolerable, as it is in any other medium. Many minority characters can be found in modern comic books — not as generic stereotypes, but heroes in their own right. Jimmy Woo, Atlas' Chinese-American hero of the 1950s, is now among Marvel's popular stable of characters, having been revived in 2006 to lead a team of other "resurrected" Atlas heroes (*Agents of Atlas*, and related titles); he also had a role in the 2010 animated series *The Avengers: Earth's Mightiest Heroes*. In the 2005–2006 mini-series *Infinite Crisis*, the newest incarnation of DC's superhero the Blue Beetle, appeared in the form of Jaime Reyes, an Hispanic teenager. Recently, Aquaman has been joined by Jackson Hyde, an African-American youth who has taken the mantle of Aqualad (*Brightest Day* No. 10, June 2010). Also in August of 2011, Marvel Comics, in its alternate reality *Ultimate Comics* imprint, introduced the new Spider-Man — a half Black/half Hispanic teenager named Miles Morales. As part of the 2011 revamp of DC Comics' properties, African-American hero Cyborg has been reintroduced as a top-tier character and placed alongside Superman, Batman, and Wonder Woman in an all-new Justice League (*Justice League* No. 1, September 2011). With the 2011 reboot also came a Batman native to the Democratic Republic of the Congo, the star of his own ongoing series, *Batwing*. The Marvel Comics series *Captain America Corps* introduces a future version of the Captain, a man of Japanese and Hispanic ancestry named Kiyoshi Morales (August 2011). These characters may be few in number, but they still present a divergent course from the traditional Anglo-American hero of years past. Perusing modern comic books, one would be hard-pressed to find many titles, superhero or not, that were not ethnically or culturally diverse in one form or another. Still, however, it is obvious that the two groups examined in this work, Eastern Europeans (who, admittedly, have lost a good amount of their "brute" identity since the fall of the Berlin Wall) and especially Asians, are under-represented in comic books today.

Searching for stereotypes, or a lack thereof, in comic books today can have its potential pitfalls, as the lines may become blurred between what one is looking for and what is actually there. For example, is Amadeus

Cho, partner to Marvel superheroes the Hulk and Hercules, and one of the most intelligent individuals on Earth, conforming to the stereotype of the Asian "model minority" and mathematical genius — or is he simply a super-intelligent character who just happens to be Asian (which, given his characterization, is more than likely the case)? A question of concern: Will it reach the point where we are searching for stereotypes and depictions that are not actually present, thereby recreating them and guaranteeing their continuation into the next century? Do modern comic narratives featuring superheroes fighting against Communist-loyalists and holdouts from the Cold War present a reappearance of the barbaric Eastern European stereotype, or do they simply continue the trend of demonizing characters in relation to their ideology and not their ethnicity? Or will some stereotypes persist in American popular media, regardless of the degree to which they are despised and regardless of attempts to erase them once and for all? Perhaps these are inquiries only posterity can answer.

The change in the definition of what the archetypical American hero represents is mirrored by a similar change that has occurred in the American populace as a whole over the course of the twentieth century. Since its inception, beginning with the dime magazines, through the pulps and into the comic books of today, American popular and inexpensive literature has acted as a kind of cultural *pomerium* designating, among other things, what the majority of the population respects and considers part of "Americanness." Unfortunately, in the past that included imagery that is deemed racist today. That, however, is an over-simplification of the past that does not take into account the myriad changes that were sweeping the nation through the entirety of those years. And that has been the purpose of this work — to examine the horrendous depictions that accompanied nativist imagery; to suggest some possible reasons for their existence outside of simple racism (but not excluding it as a factor); and to show a change over time — to demonstrate that America was, and is, in the process of shedding such imagery and sentiments as the years go on.

Chapter Notes

Preface

1. Dr. Jeremiah W. Jenks, W. Jett Lauck, and Rufus D. Smith, *The Immigration Problem — A Study of American Immigration Conditions and Needs* (New York: Funk and Wagnalls Company, 1922), 262.

2. Excellent and expertly-researched sources of information by the authors listed include, but are not limited to: Mike Ashley, *The Time Machines — The Story of the Science-Fiction Pulp Magazines from the Beginning to 1950* (Liverpool: Liverpool University Press, 2000); Sam Moskowitz, *Under the Moons of Mars — A History and Anthology of "the Scientific Romance" in the Munsey Magazines, 1912-1920* (New York: Holt, Rinehart and Winston, 1970); John Locke, *Pulp Fictioneers: Adventures in the Storytelling Business* (Silver Spring: Adventure House, 2004); Ron Goulart, *Cheap Thrills: An Informal History of the Pulp Magazines* (New Rochelle: Arlington House, 1972); Ed Hulse, *The Blood 'n' Thunder Guide to Collecting Pulps* (Morris Plains: Murania Press, 2007).

3. Tony Goodstone, ed., *The Pulps: Fifty Years of American Pop Culture* (New York: Chelsea House Publishers, 1970), xv.

4. Robert Sampson, *Yesterday's Faces Volume 3: From the Dark Side* (Bowling Green: Bowling Green State University Popular Press, 1987), 8.

5. William F. Wu, *The Yellow Peril — Chinese Americans in American Fiction, 1850-1940* (Hamden: Archon Books, 1982), 183.

6. Erin A. Smith, "How the Other Half Read: Advertising, Working-Class Readers, and Pulp Magazines," *Book History* 3 (2000): 204-230. Smith, in her opening paragraph of this article, uses two descriptors of pulps (that they were works intended to be discarded upon reading, and that the "majority" of pulps featured covers with scantily-clad women) that owe more to the popular conception of the pulp than to actual experience with the medium. One can peruse the first forty or so years of *Argosy's* publication and not find any scantily-clad females on the covers. Later pulps in the weird fiction and detective veins, and more so the men's magazines of the 1960s, certainly employed such marketing tactics; however, a demarcation between one type of pulp and another is still required.

7. Archer Jones, "The Pulps: A Mirror to Yearning," *The North American Review* 246, no. 1 (Autumn 1938): 35-47. In his article Jones states that advertising accounted for less than 10 percent of the pulp industry's revenue, with the majority of profits coming from actual magazine sales at the newsstands and through subscriptions.

8. Erin A. Smith, *Hard-Boiled: Working-Class Readers and Pulp Magazines* (Philadelphia: Temple University Press, 2000).

9. Gerald Early and Alan Lightman, "Race, Art and Integration: The Image of the African American Soldier in Popular Culture During the Korean War," *Bulletin of the American Academy of Arts and Sciences* 57, no. 1 (Autumn 2003): 32-38. Jeffrey A. Brown, *Black Superheroes, Milestone Comics, and Their Fans* (Jackson: University Press of Mississippi, 2001). Arie Kaplan, *From Krakow to Krypton: Jews and Comic Books* (Philadelphia: Jewish Publication Society, 2008).

10. Les Daniels, *Marvel: Five Fabulous Decades of the World's Greatest Comics* (New

York: Harry N. Abrams, Incorporated, 1993), 52.
 11. Dr. Michael J. Vassallo, "Introduction" to *Marvel Masterworks: Golden Age U.S.A. COMICS Vol. 1* (New York: Marvel Publishing, Inc., 2007), vii.
 12. Richard Reynolds, *Super-Heroes: A Modern Mythology* (Jackson: University Press of Mississippi, 1994), 8.
 13. Mike Benton, *The Illustrated History: Superhero Comics of the Golden Age* (Dallas: Taylor Publishing Company, 1992), 55.
 14. Bradford W. Wright, *Comic Book Nation: The Transformation of Youth Culture in America* (Baltimore: Johns Hopkins University Press, 2001), 42–43.
 15. David Hajdu, *The Ten-Cent Plague: The Great Comic Book Scare and How It Changed* America (New York: Farrar, Straus and Giroux, 2008), 47.
 16. Arie Kaplan, *From Krakow to Krypton: Jews and Comic Books* (Philadelphia: Jewish Publication Society, 2008), 58.
 17. Brian N. Fry, *Nativism and Immigration: Regulating the American Dream* (New York: LFB Scholarly Publishing LLC, 2007), 5.
 18. Loren Baritz, ed., *The Culture of the Twenties* (Indianapolis: The Bobbs-Merril Company, Inc., 1970), 51.
 19. Robert F. Zeidel, *Immigrants, Progressives, and Exclusion Politics: The Dillingham Commission* (Dekalb: Northern Illinois University Press, 2004), 138.
 20. Robert G. Lee, *Orientals: Asian Americans in Popular Culture* (Philadelphia: Temple University Press, 1999), 45.
 21. Aristide R. Zolberg, *A Nation by Design: Immigration Policies in the Fashioning of America* (New York: Russell Sage Foundation, 2006), 16.
 22. Zolberg, *A Nation by Design*, 17.

Introduction

 1. Thomas H. Hunt, *Ideology and U.S. Foreign Policy* (New Haven: Yale University Press, 1987), 46.
 2. Ibid., 49.
 3. Thomas, J. Curran, *Xenophobia and Immigration, 1820–1930* (Boston: Twayne Publisher, 1975), 12.
 4. Ibid., 79.
 5. John Soennichsen, *The Chinese Exclusion Act of 1882* (Santa Barbara: Greenwood, 2011), 15.

 6. Ibid., 55–57.
 7. Ibid., 132.
 8. Dr. Jeremiah W. Jenks, W. Jett Lauck, and Rufus D. Smith, *The Immigration Problem—A Study of American Immigration Conditions and Needs* (New York: Funk and Wagnalls Company, 1922), 231.
 9. Curran, *Xenophobia and Immigration*, 90.
 10. Ibid., 89.
 11. Harold Irwin Cleveland, *Massacres of Christians by Heathen Chinese and Horrors of the Boxers* (New Haven: Butler and Alger, 1900), 537–540.
 12. John Higham, *Strangers in the Land—Patterns of American Nativism, 1860–1925* (New York: Atheneum, 1988), 77.
 13. Jerry Israel, *Progressivism and the Open Door—America and China, 1905–1921* (Pittsburgh: University of Pittsburgh Press, 1971), 6.
 14. Albert C. Stevens, ed. *The Cyclopedia of Fraternities* (New York: Hamilton Printing and Publishing Company, 1899), 317.
 15. Jane E. Robbins, M.D., "The Foreign-Born American," *The Outlook* (August 18, 1906): 891–893.
 16. Israel, *Progressivism and the Open Door*, 33.
 17. For excellent insight into the history of the dime novel, and its subsequent fandom and nostalgia, see Edmund Pearson, *Dime Novels; or, Following an Old Trail in Popular Literature* (Port Washington: Kennikat Press, 1968 [1929]).
 18. Ann Sophia Winterbotham Stephens, "Malaeska, the Indian Wife of the White Hunter," *The Ladies' Companion*, February 1839, 192.
 19. For more information regarding the birth of the story papers, see Quentin Reynolds, *The Fiction Factory, or from Pulp Row to Quality Street—The Story of 100 Years of Publishing at Street and Smith* (New York: Random House, 1955).
 20. Philip Reade, "Tom Edison, Jr.'s Electric Sea Spider, or the Wizard of the Submarine World," *The Nugget Library* 134, February 11, 1892, 4.
 21. Philip Reade, "Tom Edison, Jr.'s Sky-Scraping Trip; or, Over the Wild West Like a Flying Squirrel," *The Nugget Library* 102, July 16, 1891, 11.
 22. A. L. Pinkerton, "Dick Ferret—De-

tective, and the Opium Fiends; or, Saved from a Terrible Fate," *The Nugget Library* 146, March 24, 1892, 9.

23. A New York Detective, "The Bradys and the Drug Slaves; or, the Yellow Demons of Chinatown," *Secret Service — Old and Young King Brady, Detectives* 157, January 24, 1902, 27.

24. Nicholas Carter," *Nick Carter's Close Call; or, the Way of the Doomed* (New York: Street and Smith, 1907), 85.

25. For more information on, and insight into, the American propensity to form internalized opinions regarding historical events portrayed in popular culture that we never, and could not have ever, experienced, see Alison Landsberg, *Prosthetic Memory: The Transformation of American Remembrance in the Age of Mass Culture* (New York: Columbia University Press, 2004).

26. William Ward, *Jeff Clayton's Fatal Shot; or, Solving the Great Chinatown Mystery — Adventure Series No. 73* (Cleveland: Arthur Westbrook Company, 1911), 129. It is interesting to note that the year of this novel's release, 1911, is the same year that the Qing dynasty was indeed overthrown, and the Republic of China established by Sun Yat-sen and his Kuomintang, or Nationalist, party.

27. Ibid., 161.

28. For fascinating insight into the Taiping Rebellion, with a unique approach that places focus on Hong Xiuquan himself, see Jonathan D. Spence, *God's Chinese Son — The Taiping Heavenly Kingdom of Hong Xiuquan* (New York: W.W. Norton and Company, 1996).

29. A. L. Pinkerton, "Dick Ferret — Detective," 6.

Chapter I

1. George Britt, *Forty Years — Forty Millions: The Career of Frank A. Munsey* (Port Washington: Kennikat Press, 1972), 82.

2. Nathan Vernon Madison, "The Life and Works of Frank Andrew Munsey — The Man Who Made the Argosy," *Blood 'n' Thunder* (Summer 2011): 62–86.

3. Quentin Reynolds, *The Fiction Factory, or from Pulp Row to Quality Street — The Story of 100 Years of Publishing at Street and Smith* (New York: Random House, 1955).

4. A.E. Apple, "Mr. Chang, Man Trapper," *Detective Story Magazine*, October 25, 1924, 39.

5. Robert J. Pearsall, "The Escape," *Adventure*, August 18, 1920, 166.

6. For fascinating insight into the origins of both the pulp magazine industry, and the various publishers and creators who occupied it, see Ron Goulart, *Cheap Thrills: An Informal History of the Pulp Magazines* (New Rochelle: Arlington House, 1972.)

7. Diana Preston, *The Boxer Rebellion* (New York: Walker and Company, 2000), x.

8. Peter Huston, *Tongs, Gangs, and Triads — Chinese Crime Groups in North America* (Boulder: Paladin Press, 1988), 30.

9. Huston, 27–44; Victor Nee and Brett de Bary Nee, *Longtime Californ'*: *A Documentary Study of an American Chinatown* (Stanford: Stanford University Press, 1986), 68.

10. Roger Daniels, *Asian America — Chinese and Japanese in the United States Since 1850* (Seattle: University of Washington Press, 1988), 24–25.

11. Thomas Sowell, *Ethnic America: A History* (New York: Basic Books, Inc., 1981), 147.

12. "Crime," *Time*, Time Magazine Archives for September 21, 1925. *Time* magazine, on its official website, provides an amazing archive of past articles and issues, dating back to the earliest years of the twentieth century.

13. Thomas S. Duke, *Celebrated Criminal Cases of America* (San Francisco: James H. Barry, 1910), 652; Mary Ting Yi Lui, *The Chinatown Trunk Mystery — Murder, Miscegenation and Other Dangerous Encounters in Turn-of-the-Century New York City* (Princeton: Princeton University Press, 2005).

14. "It is at night only that you may see the Mongol quarter of New York in its quickened phases, for there the people come to life with darkness and disappear with the dawn."— William Brown Meloney, "Slumming in New York's Chinatown — a Glimpse into the Sordid Underworld of the Mott Street Quarter, Where Elsie Sigel Formed Her Fatal Associations," *Munsey's*, September 1909, 818.

15. Herbet Asbury, *The Gangs of New York: An Informal History of the Underworld* (New York: Capricorn Books, 1970 [1928]), 289.

16. For a more detailed account of the Bow Kum incident, see Asbury, *The Gangs of New York*.

17. Robert Sampson, *Yesterday's Faces: A Study of Series Characters in the Early Pulp Magazines — Volume 3: From the Dark Side* (Bowling Green: Popular Press, 1987), 14.

18. A. E. Apple, "Mr. Chang's Tong War," *Street & Smith's Detective Story Magazine*, December 27, 1930, 1.

19. This is one of the instances of the pulps not sticking too close to reality, as there was no such rebellion going on in China at the time. Glaring inaccuracies can also be seen in the author's reference to "the Period of Giants, back in the fabled era that proceeded the twenty-two thousand years of authentic Chinese history." Again, in the case of popular culture, it is not necessarily important what was true or what was not, but rather what the public believed, or was willing to accept, to be the truth. Or, at the very least, what made for a smashing story.

20. Sidney Herschel Small, "Fireflies of Death," *Detective Fiction Weekly*, January 9, 1932, 19.

21. Robert Sampson, *Yesterday's Faces — Volume 5: Dangerous Horizons* (Bowling Green: Popular Press, 1991), 201.

22. Robert Wallace, "The Tomb of Death," *The Phantom Detective*, November 1934, 17.

23. Howard Phillips Lovecraft, "The Horror at Red Hook," *Necronomicon — The Best Weird Tales of H.P. Lovecraft*, ed. by Stephen Jones (London: Orion Books, 2008), 151.

24. L. Sprague De Camp, *Lovecraft: A Biography* (New York: Ballantine Books, 1976), 101.

25. Lemuel L. DeBra, "The Mystery of the Missing Hands," *The Blue Book Magazine*, December 1920, 63.

26. W.F. Hammond, "Lakh-Dal, Destroyer of Souls," *Amazing Stories*, March 1928, 1185.

27. Harold J. Ashe, "Combating 'Crime Wave' in Tibet," *Argosy All-Story Weekly*, November 24, 1928, 493.

28. For fascinating insight into the penal system of China during its revolutionary and republican periods, see Frank Dikötter, *Crime, Punishment, and the Prison in Modern China* (New York: Columbia University Press, 2002).

29. George F. Worts, "The Crime Circus," *Argosy All-Story Weekly*, October 6, 1928, 411.

30. Worts, "The Silver Fang," *Argosy All-Story Weekly*, January 12, 1929, 700.

31. J. Allan Dunn, "The Pagan Ruby," *Argosy All-Story Weekly*, October 13, 1928, 497.

32. Dale T. Knobel, *"America for the Americans"— The Nativist Movement in the United States* (New York: Twayne Publishers, 1996), 250.

33. Ibid., 245.

34. Ibid., 252. The law, however, was overturned by the United States Supreme Court three years later.

35. Emma Goldman, *Anarchism and Other Essays* (New York: Mother Earth Publishing Association, 1910), 20.

36. Horace Howard Herr, "A Daughter of the White Star," *Argosy All-Story Weekly*, May 28, 1921, 297.

37. Hector Gavin Grey, "Steel Skeletons," *The Phantom Detective*, May 1935, 111.

38. Lemuel L. DeBra, "Crooks Is Crooks," *The Blue Book Magazine*, January 1921, 87.

39. Nels Leroy Jorgensen, "The Tale of the Bat-Dragon," *The Danger Trail*, June 1927, 181.

40. Daniel J. Kevles, *In the Name of Eugenics — Genetics and Uses of Human Heredity* (Berkeley: University of California Press, 1986), 160.

41. "Literary Notes," *Harvard Graduates' Magazine* vol. XIV, 1905–1906, 546.

42. Richard Elwood Dodge, *Advanced Geography* (Chicago: Rand McNally and Company, 1920), 79.

43. Maryland, *Course of Study — Baltimore County, Maryland Public Schools — Grades I to VIII* (Baltimore: Warwick and York, Inc., 1921), 200.

44. Harmon B. Niver, *Complete Geography* (New York: Hinds, Hayden and Eldredge, Inc., 1922), 104.

45. Ohio State University, College of Education, Bureau of Educational Research, *Educational Research Bulletin — Volumes II* (Columbus: Bureau of Educational Research, 1923), 150.

46. Nina Jay Smith Beglinger, *Constructive Lessons in English for the Foreign Born* (Boston: Gorham Press, 1922), 160.

47. Ibid., 160.

48. After all survivors of plague had

been shot on sight, "then began the great task, the sanitation of China. Five years and hundreds of millions of treasure were consumed, and then the world moved in — not in zones, as was the idea of Baron Albrecht, but heterogeneously, according to the democratic American program. It was a vast and happy intermingling of nationalities that settled down in China in 1982 and the years that followed — a tremendous and successful experiment in cross-fertilization. We know today the splendid mechanical, intellectual, and artistic output that followed."— Jack London, "The Unparalleled Invasion," ed. I.F. Clarke, *The Tale of the Next Great War, 1871–1914 — Fictions of Future Warfare and of Battles Still-to-Come* (Syracuse: Syracuse University Press, 1995), 270.

49. Madison Grant and Henry Fairfield Osburn, *The Passing of the Great Race; or, the Racial Basis of European History* (New York: Charles Scribner's Sons, 1922), 218.

50. Ibid., 221.

51. Knobel, *"America for the Americans,"* 259.

52. Sax Rohmer, *The Insidious Dr. Fu Manchu* (New York: Robert M. McBride and Company, 1920), 71–72.

53. Arthur Benjamin Reeve, *The Romance of Elaine* (New York: Harper and Brothers Publishers, 1916), 11, 13.

54. John Charles Beecham, *The Yellow Spider* (New York: W. J. Watt and Company, 1920), 140.

55. T. T. Flynn, "The Evil Brand," *Dime Detective Magazine*, November 15, 1934, 40.

56. William Doughty, "The Kalgan Road," *Oriental Stories*, February–March 1931, 344.

57. Apple, "Mr. Chang, Man Trapper," 8.

58. Erle Stanley Gardner, "The Warlords of Darkness," *Adventure*, July 1934, 5.

59. Lee, *Orientals: Asian-Americans in Popular Culture*, 17.

60. George C. Hull, "The Hidden Emperor," *The Thrill Book*, April 15, 1919, 37.

61. "White Man," Lyn Fox, *Man Stories*, October 1930, 17.

62. David H. Keller, "The Hidden Monster," *Oriental Stories*, Winter 1932, 414.

63. Robert E. Pinkerton, "Yellow Ghosts," *Argosy All-Story Weekly*, October 13, 1928, 439.

64. Philip Francis Nowlan, *Armageddon 2419 A.D.* (New York: Ace Books, 1972), 10.

65. Robert E. Howard, "Skull-Face," *Moon of Skulls — The Weird Works of Robert E. Howard, Volume 2*, ed. by Paul Herman (Rockville: Wildside Press, 2005), 12.

66. Ibid., 29.

67. The intimacy in which the "weird fiction" trio worked is evident in the antagonist's name, as it is extremely close to the creature for which H.P Lovecraft is best known for — the evil monstrosity found in the Cthulhu Mythos.

68. Lothrop Stoddard, *The Rising Tide of Color — Against White World Supremacy* (New York: Charles Scribner's Sons, 1921), 289.

69. Higham, *Strangers in the Land*, 272.

70. Howard, "Skull-Face," *Moon of Skulls — The Weird Works of Robert E. Howard, Volume 2*, 26.

71. Fred MacIsaac, "Those Lima Eyes," *Argosy All-Story Weekly*, January 8, 1927, 163.

72. Edgar Rice Burroughs, *The Martian Tales Trilogy* (New York: Barnes and Noble, 2004), 58.

73. Warren Hastings Miller, "The Dancer of Djogyakarta," *Oriental Tales*, Winter 1932, 31.

74. Robert G. Lee, *Orientals: Asian-Americans in Popular Culture* (Philadelphia: Temple University Press, 1990), 108.

75. Nikki L. M. Brown and Barry M. Stentiford, *The Jim Crow Encyclopedia* (Westport: Greenwood Publishing Group, 2008), 275.

76. G.K. Chesterton, *Eugenics and Other Evils* (London: Cassell and Company, 1922), 142.

77. Knobel, *"America for the Americans,"* 251, 253.

78. Baritz, *The Culture of Twenties*, 70.

79. F. H. Hankins, "Book Notes," *The Journal of Social Forces* 3 (November 1924): 184.

80. Catherine Ross Nickerson, ed., *The Cambridge Companion to American Crime Fiction* (Cambridge: Cambridge University Press, 2010), 140.

81. Lemuel L. DeBra, "The Broker of Marriages," *The Blue Book Magazine*, November 1920, 53.

82. Horace Howard Herr, "A Daughter of the White Star," *Argosy All-Story Weekly*, May 28, 1921, 467.

83. Clarence Reynolds, "Fifty Murders for the Love of Sweet Flower," *True Strange Stories*, November 1929, 32.

84. Frank Owen, "Della Wu — Chinese Courtesan," *Oriental Stories*, February–March 1931, 417.

85. E. R. Hagemann, "Ramon Decolta, a.k.a. Raoul Whitfield, and His Diminutive Brown Man: Jo Gar, the Island Detective," in *Jo Gar's Casebook*, ed. by Keith Alan Deutsch (Norfolk: Crippen and Landru, 2002), 21.

86. "Camp-Fire," *Adventure*, August 18, 1920, 178.

87. "The Souk," *Oriental Stories,* February–March 1931, 292.

88. "The Souk," *Oriental Stories,* Summer 1932, 425.

Chapter II

1. In the name of its Asian Co-Prosperity Sphere, the Japanese forces besieged Nanjing, an under-defended and thoroughly-shelled capital that Generalissimo Chiang Kai-shek had already abandoned following his relocation of China's capitol farther inland, to the city of Chongqing, in advance of the Japanese army. The undermanned city soon fell, and the Japanese descended upon its civilians, embarking upon a vicious melee of rape, torture and murder. For more information on the Japanese atrocities in China, see Honda Katsuichi, *The Nanjing Massacre: A Japanese Journalist Confronts Japan's National Shame* (Armonk: M.E. Sharpe, 1999).

2. For excellent insight into the years between the world wars, see Piers Brendon, *The Dark Valley — A Panorama of the 1930s* (New York: Vintage Books, 2002).

3. Elazar Barkin, *The Retreat of Scientific Racism — Changing Concepts of Race in Britain and the United States Between the World Wars* (Cambridge: Cambridge University Press, 1992), 332.

4. Edwin Black, *War Against the Weak — Eugenics and America's Campaign to Create a Master Race* (New York: Four Walls Eight Windows, 2003), 395.

5. Ashley Montagu, *Man's Most Dangerous Myth — The Fallacy of Race* (New York: Columbia University Press, 1945), 5–7.

6. Carleton Stevens Coon's *The Races of Europe* (New York: Macmillan Company, 1939) is full of detailed measurements of subjects' heads, from a variety of ethnicities, comparing one group to another, and analyzing the differences between subgroups that belong to larger "familial" groups.

7. Barkan, 337.

8. In his first appearance (*Action Comics* no. 1 — June 1938), Superman saves an innocent woman from execution, beats a wife-batterer into submission, and journeys to Washington D.C. to face a corrupt politician. In his inaugural story (*Detective Comics* no. 27 — May 1939), Batman solves a case involving a wealthy "captain of industry" who has murdered his business partners for monetary gain.

9. Ron Goulart, *Great American Comic Books* (Lincolnwood: Publications International, Ltd., 2001), 117.

10. Maxwell Grant, "The Golden Pagoda," *The Shadow* March 1, 1938, 7.

11. Curtis Steele, *Operator #5 — Blood Reign of the Dictator* (Wildside Press, 2004), 7.

12. Curtis Steele, *Operator #5 — Invasion of the Crimson Death Cult* (Wildside Press, 2005), 106.

13. Frederick C. Painton, "The Invasion of America," *Argosy Weekly*, July 16, 1938, 4.

14. Ibid., 17.

15. Arthur Leo Zagat, "Tomorrow," *Argosy Weekly*, May 27, 1939, 26.

16. Ibid., 30.

17. Arthur Leo Zagat, "Children of Tomorrow," *Argosy Weekly*, June 17, 1939, 5.

18. Willy Ley, "Atlantropa — The Improved Continent," *Marvel Science Stories*, February 1939, 99.

19. Oscar J. Friend, "Experiment with Destiny," *Thrilling Wonder Stories*, October 1939, 69.

20. Ibid., 72.

21. Robert Moore Williams, "The Fifth Column of Mars," *Amazing Stories*, September 1940, 11–12.

22. Frederic Arnold Kummer, Jr., "Blitzkrieg — 1950," *Amazing Stories*, September 1940, 85.

23. Ibid., 93.

24. Ibid., 99.

25. Jay Hamilton, "We Bomb Tokyo!," *Argosy Weekly*, September 27, 1941, 7.

26. Robinson MacLean, "Nazi Terror Over New York," *Argosy Weekly*, October 4, 1941, 6.

27. Ibid., 8.

28. Ibid., 13.

29. E. Hoffmann Price, "Peril in the Pacific," *Argosy Weekly*, December 14, 1941, 19.

30. The publication date printed on the cover was not exactly when the issue was released. This was true with the pulp magazines, going as far back as the first issue of *The Golden Argosy*, released on December 2, 1882, but actually dated a week later. In pulps and comics, the publication date and the actual date that the issue arrived on newsstands varied a good deal, so that an issue dated "October 1940" was more than likely released to the public at some point in September or possibly even late August, depending on the publisher.

31. Arie Kaplan, *From Krakow to Krypton: Jews and Comic Books* (Philadelphia: Jewish Publication Society, 2008), 4.

32. *Famous Funnies* is considered the first *successful* monthly comic book; an earlier title, *Comic Monthly*, first appeared in 1921 and also contained popular newspaper strips, but unfortunately folded within a year. Ron Goulart, *The Comic Book Reader's Companion—An A-to-Z Guide to Everyone's Favorite Art* Form (New York: HarperCollins, 1993), 36, 60.

33. To avoid any possible confusion regarding National Allied Publications and the several entities it incorporated into itself in the 1940s, all titles produced by National Allied, and its related branches, will henceforth be referenced simply as "DC Comics" or "DC."

34. Ian Gordon, *Comic Strips and Consumer Culture, 1890–1945* (Washington: Smithsonian Institution Press, 1998).

35. Mike Ashley, *The Time Machines—The Story of the Science-Fiction Pulp Magazines from the Beginning to 1950* (Liverpool: Liverpool University Press, 2000), 80. Sam Moskowitz, *Explorers of the Infinite—Shapers of Science Fiction* (Westport: Hyperion Press, 1974), 328.

36. An excellent example of this can be seen in an illustration Marchioni created for a February 1936 issue of *Astounding Stories*, reprinted in Everett F. Bleiler and Richard J. Bleiler, *Science-Fiction—The Gernsback Years* (Kent: Kent State University Press, 1998), 618.

37. "The Shield—G-Man Extraordinaire," *Pep Comics* 3 (M. L. J. Publications, April 1940).

38. "Professor Supermind and Son," *Popular Comics* 60 (Dell Publishing, February 1941).

39. "Super-American—One Man Against the Mad Dogs of Europe!," *Fight Comics* 15 (Fight Stories, Inc., October 1941). Being a hero now in the public domain, the Super-American has appeared in other titles throughout the latter half of the twentieth century; this 1941 debut was one of four appearances during the "Golden Age."

40. *Superman Sunday Classics—Strips 1–183: 1939–1943* (New York: Sterling Publishing Company, 1999), 190.

41. Les Daniels, *Marvel: Five Fabulous Decades of the World's Greatest Comics* (New York: Harry N. Abrams Company, 1993), 18.

42. While National Allied, home of Superman and Batman, did not get too violent in their dealings with Nazis, other heroes often did not hold back. Comic historian Ian Gordon also points out that Superman and Batman were more associated with bond drives and home-front support, as opposed to other "frontline" characters.—Ian Gordon, *Comic Strips and Consumer Culture, 1890–1945* (Washington: Smithsonian Institution Press, 1998), 141.

43. "Case No. 1—Meet Captain America," *Captain America Comics* 1 (Timely, March 1941).

44. John Higham, *Strangers in the Land—Patterns of American Nativism, 1860–1925* (New York: Atheneum, 1988), 210.

45. Ibid., 218.

46. Dana R. Marsh, "Ace of Intrigue," *Spy Novels Magazine*, 1935, 42.

47. "Harold F. Cruikshank, "Drome of the Living Dead," *Daredevil Aces*, November 1934, 106; Capt. Kerry McRoberts, "The Flying Kitchens," *Lone Eagle*, September 1933, 115.

48. T. W. Ford, "Prisoners of the Piane," *Flying Aces*, March 1930, 185; Gordon Carrol, "The Last Dispatch," *Adventure*, January 1934, 77.

49. Robert J. Hogan, "The Squadron of Death Flies High!," *G-8 and His Battle Aces*, December 1942, 1.

50. Don Hutchison, *The Great Pulp Heroes* (Oakville: Mosaic Press, 1996), 68–70.

51. Grant Stockbridge, "The Spider and Hell's Factory," *The Spider*, October 1943, 5.

52. Harold Lavine, *Fifth Column in America* (New York: Doubeday, Doran and Company, Inc., 1940), 4.
53. George Britt, *The Fifth Column Is Here* (New York: Wilfred Funk, Inc., 1940), 2.
54. Ibid., 118.
55. Kenneth R. Seppi, *The Magnificent Superheroes of Comics Golden Age* (Effingham: Vintage Features, 1979), 45, 61.
56. "Civil War," *Pep Comics* 28 (M. L. J. Publications, June 1942).
57. "The American Eagle," *Exciting Comics* 23 (Standard, December 1942).
58. In recoiling from one of Captain Marvel's punches, Captain Nazi kills an elderly man and permanently cripples the man's grandson, Freddy Freeman. Moved by the young boy's spirit and courage, Captain Marvel endows him with some of his own abilities, so that whenever Freeman shouts his benefactor's name, he is transformed into Captain Marvel, Jr., a miniature version of his namesake and perpetual enemy of Captain Nazi.— *Whiz Comics* 25 (Fawcett, December 1941).
59. "Captain Terror," *U.S.A. Comics* 4 (Timely, December 1941).
60. John W. Dower, *War Without Mercy—Race and Power in the Pacific War* (New York: Pantheon Books, 1986), 79.
61. "The Cat-Man and the Kitten," *Cat-Man Comics* 22 (Holyoke, December, 1943).
62. D.C. Comics, *D.C. Rarities Archives Volume 1* (New York: D.C. Comics, 2004), 96.
63. "The Claws of the Red Dragon," *Detective Comics* 8 (D.C. Comics, October 1937).
64. Big Little Books were small (3½ × 4½ inches), thick adaptations of comic strip characters wherein one page held text, while the next page offered an image, usually from the adapted work, and so on, with each novel telling a story in roughly 300 to 400 pages; they were first produced by the Whitman Publishing Company in 1932 and lasted into the 1960s.— Ron Goulart, *Great American Comic Books* (Lincolnwood: Publications International, Ltd., 2001), 16.
65. Roger Daniels, *The Politics of Prejudice—The Anti-Japanese Movement in California and the Struggle for Japanese Exclusion* (Gloucester: University of California, 1966), 3.
66. Ibid., 2.
67. For fascinating insight into a culture that can only come from someone firmly immersed in it, see the works of famed Japanese history professor and one-time American ambassador to Japan Edwin O. Reischauer. Specifically, see E. O. Reischauer, *The United States and Japan* (Cambridge: Harvard University Press, 1965).
68. Daniels, *The Politics of Prejudice*, 70.
69. Russell O. Wright, *Chronology of Immigration in the United States* (Jefferson: McFarland and Company, Inc., 2008), 74.
70. Robert Carse, "The Secret Behind the Stab in the Back by Japan," *Argosy*, April 1, 1942, 6.
71. A few such reports include: *Life* Magazine's printing of photographs of massacred Chinese civilians being looted by Japanese troops in its December 1, 1937, edition, and *Time* Magazine, in its November 7, 1938, issue, carrying stories describing the "brutal horrors perpetuated in the native quarters" of Hankow, Nanjing, and Shanghai. Both magazines carried sections describing the brutality Americans suffered following the fall of Bataan, in the Philippines, to the Japanese in 1942.
72. "The Unknown," *National Comics* 38 (Quality, January 1944).
73. Greg Sadowski, *Supermen! The First Wave of Comic Book Heroes 1936–1941* (Seattle: Fantagraphics Books, 2009), 141.
74. Sadowski, *Supermen!*, 143.
75. "The Fighting Yank," *The Fighting Yank* 9 (Standard, August, 1944).
76. "Minute Man and the Fumes of Fear!" *Master Comics* 29 (Fawcett, August 1941).
77. "U.S. Rangers," *Rangers Comics* 16 (Fiction House, April, 1943).
78. "The Blue Beetle," *The Blue Beetle* 15 (Holyoke, October, 1942); "The Cat-Man and the Kitten," *Cat-Man Comics* 22 (Holyoke, December, 1943).
79. Daisuke Miyao, *Sessue Hayakawa: Silent Cinema and Transnational Stardom* (Durham: Duke University Press, 2007), 3.
80. Earl H. Leaf, "How Japan Debauches Chinese Girls," *Argosy*, February 7, 1942, 44.
81. Leaf, "How Japan Debauches Chinese Girls," 47.
82. Walter C. Brown, "Black Pigeons," *Adventure*, May 1942, 61.
83. Louis C. Goldsmith, "The Streamlined Dragon," *Argosy*, March 7, 1942, 25.

84. "Loops and Banks," *Military Comics* 1 (Quality, August 1941); "Dick Storm in China," *Top Notch Comics* 3 (M.L.J. Publications, February 1940).
85. "Japan's First Victim," *The United States Marines* Vol. 1, No. 3 (Magazine Enterprises, Spring 1944).
86. "Japan's First Victim"
87. "Legless Ace," *Pioneer Picture Stories* Vol. 1 No. 4 (Street and Smith Publications, September, 1942).
88. "Traitor's Reward," *Air Ace Comics* Vol. 2 No. 2 (Street and Smith Publications, March 1944).
89. The fact that no such royal family with any political, or even figurative, power existed in China at this point was apparently not a hindrance.
90. "The League of the Unicorn," Captain America Comics 13 (Timely, April 1942).
91. "The Unknown," *National Comics* 38 (Quality, January 1944).
92. "The Junior Rangers," *Headline Comics* 2 (American Boy's Comics, March 1943).
93. "Blackhawk," *Military Comics* 1 (Quality, August 1941).
94. Ron Goulart, *The Comic Book Reader's Companion — An A-to-Z Guide to Everyone's Favorite Art Form* (New York: HarperCollins, 1993), 137.
95. "The Four Musketeers," *Air Ace Comics* Vol. 2 No. 3 (Street and Smith Publications, May 1944).

Chapter III

1. Richard A. Schwartz, *The 1950s — An Eyewitness History* (New York: Facts on File, 2003), 422.
2. To add an even deeper sense of loss to the takeover of China by Communist forces, historian Eric F. Goldman points out that for many in the United States it seemed to be America's mission to Christianize the Chinese, as missionaries had been traveling there for centuries, especially during the era of the Qing's "Unequal Treaties" with the Western nations. To some, the loss of China to the atheist Communists was seen as a failure on America's part to bring Christianity to the Orient. — Eric F. Goldman, *The Crucial Decade — America, 1945–1955* (New York: Alfred a Knopf, 1956), 116.

3. This story was later reprinted in the April, 1953 issue of *Adventure*. In 1942, Popular Publications, owners of *Adventure*, bought *Argosy* from the Frank A. Munsey Company; ads for one magazine appeared in the other, and stories obviously traveled between the two, as well.
4. Milton Lesser, "He Fell Among Thieves," *Fantastic Adventures*, March 1952, 55.
5. In many parts of the *Seduction of the Innocent*, the accusations of Wertham are either laughable, or horribly frightening, depending on the reader. While Wertham is correct that many comic books did feature scenes of violence that were arguably too harsh for young children (and many are shocking even by today's standards), some of the author's contentions, however, seem somewhat questionable: from blowing up a single panel of a comic strip to show what Wertham believes to be the figure of a nude woman within an illustration of a man's shoulder "for children who know how to look," to a question as to how familiar he actually was with the subject matter — at one point, Wertham refers to a character named the Blue Beetle, who changes from man into beetle, and back again, and claims that it is "Kafka for the kiddies!" Such a character never existed; the Blue Beetle was a police officer who donned a blue costume to battle crime while not on the beat. Fredric Wertham, M.D., *Seduction of the Innocent* (New York: Main Road Books, 2004 [1954]), 185, 106.
6. M.J. Heale, *American Anticommunism — Combating the Enemy Within 1830–1970* (Baltimore: The Johns Hopkins University Press, 1990), xii.
7. Ibid., 14.
8. Russell O. Wright, *Chronology of Immigration in the United States* (Jefferson: McFarland & Company, Inc., 2008), 59, 75.
9. A New York Detective, "The Bradys After the Bomb Throwers; or, Smashing the Anarchist League," *Secret Service — Old and Young King Brady, Detectives* 1283 (August 24, 1923), 15.
10. Wright, *Chronology of Immigration in the United States*, 78.
11. William Ward, *Jeff Clayton's Red Mystery; Or, The Nihilist Conspiracy — Adventure Series No. 65* (Cleveland: Arthur Westbrook Co., 1910), 61.

12. Ward, *Jeff Clayton's Red Mystery*, 62.
13. Sarolea, in his optimistic view concerning the outcome of the "Bolshevik experiment," wrote that "Even as in the material sense Russia will soon become once again the granary of the European continent, so in a political and moral sense Russia is likely to prove, in a not distant future, the mainstay of European law and order, and the most uncompromising enemy of all collectivist impostures."—Charles Sarolea, *Impressions of Soviet Russia* (London: Eveleigh, Nash & Grayson, 1924), 276.
14. Kenneth D. Ackerman, *Young J. Edgar—Hoover, The Red Scare, and the Assault on Civil Liberties* (New York: Carroll & Graf Publishers, 2007), 45.
15. *Unmasking the C.I.O.*'s definitions of "Nazi" and "Fascism" are rather interesting, as they equate the two terms to general, American anti–Communist sentiment": "NAZI—A powerful European enemy of Communism. There is no Nazi Party in America. The Communists use it interchangeably with 'Fascist' branding all opposing communism as either Nazi or Fascist—instead of using the correct word AMERICAN. They say you are a 'Nazi' if you do not support the Communist program." "FASCISM—A powerful European enemy of Communism. There is no Fascist Party in America. The communists call every American movement that opposes Communism, 'Fascism' simply because they could not resist it with the support of the people if they called it by its correct name 'Americanism.'"—Martin Luther Thomas, *Unmasking the C.I.O.* Los Angeles: Christian American Crusade, 1934), 16–17.
16. S. Andrew Wood, "Red Terror," *Blue Book Magazine*, May 1933, 21.
17. Everett F. Bleiler and Richard J. Bleiler, *Science-Fiction—The Gernsback Years* (Kent: The Kent State University Press, 1998), 12.
18. For more information on the Futurians, and a history of early SF fandom overall, see: Sam Moskowitz, *The Immortal Storm—A History of Science Fiction Fandom* (Westport: Hyperion Press, Inc., 1974).
19. Interestingly, in the second story, "The Airlords of Han," Rogers' enemies are "retconned" from Asians (as was the case in the first story) to being the by-products of a cross-breeding program between Asians and extraterrestrials, and it is this strain of outer space genes that is the cause of the Han's bloodthirsty warmongering and not any sort of intrinsic evil on the part of Asians, themselves. Despite this change, the enemy is still referred to as the Han, the traditional name of the majority, native ethnic population of China. Bleiler and Bleiler, *Science-Fiction—The Gernsback Years*, 311.
20. Marshall B. Tymn and Mike Ashley, ed. *Science Fiction, Fantasy and Weird Fiction Magazines* (Westport: Hyperion Press, 1974).
21. Nat Schachner, "Redmask of the Outlands," *Astounding Stories*, January 1934, 2.
22. Mr. Davies' praise of Stalin would make even the best Soviet propagandist smile approvingly: "He greeted me cordially with a smile and with great simplicity, but also with a real dignity. He gives the impression of a strong mind which is composed and wise. His brown eye is exceedingly kindly and gentle. A child would like to sit in his lap and a dog would sidle up to him.... He has a sly humor. He has a very great mentality.... If you can picture a personality that is exactly opposite to what the most rabid anti–Stalinist anywhere could conceive, then you might picture this man."—Joseph E. Davies, *Mission to Moscow* (New York: Simon & Schuster, 1941), 356.
23. Joe Abrams, "The Way of a Cossack," *Adventure*, March 1943, 5.
24. R.W. Daly, "Patrols are Everywhere," *Adventure*, March 1943, 50.
25. Michael Barson and Steven Heller, *Red Scared! The Commie Menace in Propaganda and Popular Culture* (San Francisco: Chronicle Books, 2001), 45.
26. "Zip Comics' Hall of Fame—Marshal Timoshenko," *Zip Comics* No. 35 (M.L.J. Publications, March 1943).
27. "The picture of the Soviet Union as a new imperialism against which we must defend ourselves exists only in the heads of professional anti–Soviet propagandists.... On [acknowledging] that necessity the possibility of peace and the immediate future of democracy depend. That is the inexorable condition for realizing the possibility that Stalin has repeatedly affirmed of Soviet democracy living side by side with capitalist democracy, each developing into higher forms, and working together to achieve peace, security and social progress for all

the people of the earth."—Harry F. Ward, *Soviet Democracy* (New York: Soviet Russia Today, 1947), 47.

28. Roger Daniels, *Guarding the Golden Door—American Immigration Policy and Immigrants Since 1882* (New York: Hill and Wang, 2004), 104.

29. "Back from the Dead!," *Young Men* 24 (Atlas, December 1953).

30. "The Hour of Doom," *Captain America* 78 (Atlas, September 1954).

31. "The Deserters to Red Doom," *T-Man Comics* 26 (Quality, June 1955).

32. "How Stalin Hopes We Will Destroy America," *How Stalin Hopes We Will Destroy America* (Pictorial Media, Inc., 1951).

33. "Is This Tomorrow," *Is This Tomorrow* (Catechetical Guild, 1947).

34. "Is This Tomorrow."

35. "Operation Vengeance," *Atomic War!* 2 (Junior Books, December 1952).

36. "World War III Unleashed," *World War III* 1 (Ace Magazines, March 1952).

37. "The Stranger from the Stars," *Strange Adventures* 3 (D.C. Comics, December 1950).

38. For a more complete understanding of what separated the various strains of Communism present during the Cold War from one another, see: Gary K. Bertsch and Thomas W. Ganschow, *Comparative Communism—The Soviet, Chinese, and Yugoslav Models* (San Francisco: W.H. Freeman and Company, 1976).

39. The ideology based upon Kim Il-sung's programs, known as *Juche*, now bears little resemblance to traditional Marxism, and the North Korean Constitution drafted in 1972 officially removed Marxism-Leninism as the guiding ideology of the nation, and replaced it with *Juche*, often translated as "self-reliance," Stalin's idea of "socialism in one country" taken to the extreme. For an excellent understanding of *Juche*, "Kimilsungism," and of North Korea as a whole, see: Bradley K. Martin, *Under the Loving Care of the Fatherly Leader—North Korea and the Kim Dynasty* (New York: Thomas Dunne Books, 2004).

40. Daniels, *Guarding the Golden Door*, 113.

41. Daniels, *Guarding the Golden Door*, 118.

42. Wright, *Chronology of Immigration in the United States*, 99.

43. Daniels, *Guarding the Golden Door*, 125.

44. "The Ape of Pung-Noi!" *Battle Stories* 10 (Fawcett, July 1953).

45. "Playing with Fire!," *Captain America* 78 (Atlas, September 1954).

46. Beginning in 1941, National Allied filed suit against Fawcett Comics over the Captain Marvel character, claiming it infringed on their copyright of Superman, although the fact that *Captain Marvel* titles were outselling those featuring *Superman* throughout the 1940s should be taken into consideration as a possible motive for litigation. The case went to trial in 1948, and finally ended in a settlement in 1953, at a time when superhero comics were no longer as profitable as they once were. Fawcett agreed to pay damages to National Allied, in addition to promising to never publish Captain Marvel stories again. After superheroes rebounded in popularity, DC Comics acquired the rights to all of Fawcett's characters, and began a new Captain Marvel series, entitled *Shazam!* in 1973.—Goulart ed., *The Encyclopedia of American Comics—From 1897 to the Present* (New York: Facts on File, 1990), 70.

47. "Captain Marvel Battles the Red Crusher," *Captain Marvel Adventures* 139 (Fawcett, December 1952).

48. "Captain Marvel Fights the Mongol Blood-Drinkers," *Captain Marvel Adventures* 140 (Fawcett, January 1953).

49. "The Marvel Family Fights the Mightiest Mongol," *The Marvel Family* 81 (Fawcett, March 1953).

50. "The Hermit Girl," *Joe Yank* 9 (Standard, December 1952).

51. "Kid Hero," *War Battles* 2 (Harvey Comics, April 1952).

52. "Massacre at Manghowon!," *Battlefield* 6 (Atlas, December 1952).

53. "Village of Sealed Lips," *Battle Stories* 10 (Fawcett, July 1953).

54. "The Gunner and the Kid!," *Tell It to the Marines* 10 (Toby Press, November 1954).

55. "Victory in the Village," *Combat Kelly* 30 (Atlas, April 1955)—This issue also features a full-length story detailing the exploits of the all-black 91st and 92nd Infantry Divisions of World War I.

56. "Red Invasion," *G.I. Combat* 19 (DC Comics, December 1954).

57. "Corpse on the Imjin!," *Two-Fisted*

Tales 25 (EC Comics, January–February 1952), reprinted in Michael Barrier and Martin Williams, ed. *The Smithsonian Book of Comic-Book Comics* (New York: Smithsonian Institution Press and Harry N. Abrams, Inc., 1981), 310.

58. "The Yellow Claw," *Yellow Claw* 1 (Atlas, October 1956).

59. Les Daniels, *Marvel — Five Fabulous Decades of the World's Greatest Comics* (New York: Harry N. Abrams, Incorporated, 1993), 80.

60. Goldman, *The Crucial Decade*, 14.

61. Ellis Cashmere, ed., *The Encyclopedia of Race and Ethnic Studies* (New York: Routledge, 2004), 43.

62. Richard T. Schaefer, ed., *The Encyclopedia of Race, Ethnicity, and Society — Volume III* (Thousand Oaks: Sage Publications, 2008), 283.

63. Ibid., 287.

Conclusion

1. Leigh Brackett, "All the Colors of the Rainbow," *Venture Science-Fiction*, Nov. 1957, 112.

2. Russell O. Wright, *Chronology of Immigration in the United States* (Jefferson: McFarland & Company, Inc., 2008), 106.

3. "No Evil Shall Escape My Sight," *Green Lantern/Green Arrow* 76 (DC Comics, April 1970).

Bibliography

Collections

Comic Book Collection, Library of Congress
Dr. William Blake, Jr. Collection of True Life 1940s Era Comics, James Branch Cabell Library, Virginia Commonwealth University
Nathan Vernon Madison Collection of Periodicals and Comic Books, 1870–Present
Pulp Fiction Collection, Library of Congress
Special Collections and Archives, James Branch Cabell Library, Virginia Commonwealth University

Story Papers

Golden Days
Golden Argosy, The
Might and Main Library
New Nick Carter Weekly
Nugget Library, The
Secret Service
Tip Top Weekly

Dime Novels
(Thick Books)

Carter, Nicholas. *Nick Carter's Close Call; or, the Way of the Doomed — New Magnet Library No. 1059*. New York: Street and Smith Corporation, 1907.
Ward, William. *Jeff Clayton's Fatal Shot: or, Solving the Great Chinatown Mystery — Adventure Series No. 73*. Cleveland: The Arthur Westbrook Company, 1911.
_____. *Jeff Clayton's Red Mystery; or, the Nihilist Conspiracy — Adventure Series No. 66*. Cleveland: The Arthur Westbrook Company, 1910.
_____. *Jeff Clayton's Surprise; or the Lure of the Red Dragon — Adventure Series No. 51*. Cleveland: The Arthur Westbrook Company, 1909.

Pulp Magazines

Aces
Action Stories
Adventure
The All-Story
Amazing Stories
Argosy
Argosy All-Story Weekly
Astounding Stories/Science Fiction/Analog
Black Mask
The Blue Book Magazine
Complete Detective Novel Magazine
The Danger Trail
Dare-Devil Aces
Detective Fiction Weekly
Detective Story Magazine
Detective Tales
Doc Savage Magazine
Famous Fantastic Mysteries
Fantastic Adventures
Flying Aces
G-8 and His Battle Aces
The Lone Eagle
Man Stories
Marvel Science Stories
Marvel Stories
Oriental Stories
Phantom Detective
The Shadow
The Spider
Spy Novels Magazine
Strange Detective Mysteries
The Thrill Book
Thrilling Detective
Thrilling Mystery
Thrilling Wonder Stories

Top Notch
True Mystic Crimes
True Strange Stories
Unknown
Venture Science Fiction (Vol. 1)
Weird Tales
Wu Fang

COMICS

Action Comics
Air Ace
Astonishing
Atomic War!
Batman
Battle Cry
Battle Attack
Battle Stories
Battlefield
Black Cobra
Black Terror Comics
The Blue Beetle
Captain America Comics
Captain Battle Comics
Captain Marvel Adventures
Cat-Man Comics
Charlie Chan
Combat Casey
Combat Kelly
Comic Novel
Daredevil Comics
Detective Comics
Exciting Comics
Fight Comics
Fightin' Marines
Fighting Yank
Frontline Combat
G.I. Combat
G.I. in Battle
G.I. Joe
Headline Comics
How Stalin Hopes We Will Destroy America
Human Torch
Is This Tomorrow
Joe Yank
Kid Komics
Marvel Boy
Marvel Family
Marvel Mystery Comics
Master Comics
Military Comics
Men's Adventures
Mystic Comics
National Comics
Pep Comics
Phantom Lady
Popular Comics
Rangers Comics
Secret Voice, The
Strange Adventures
Sub-Mariner Comics
T-Man
Tell It to the Marines
Terry and the Pirates
Top-Notch Comics
True Comics
United States Marines
U.S.A Comics
U.S. Paratroops — Surprise Attack!
World War III
World's Finest Comics
Yellow Claw
Young Men
Zip Comics
Zip-Jet

SHORT ARTICLES/ ACADEMIC JOURNALS

Curran, Thomas J. "Assimilation and Nativism." *International Migration Digest* 3, no. 1 (Spring 1966): 15–25.

Early, Gerald, and Alan Lightman. "Race, Art and Integration: The Image of the African American Soldier in Popular Culture During the Korean War." *Bulletin of the American Academy of Arts and Sciences* 57, no. 1 (Autumn 2003): 32–38.

Farmer, Paul. "On the Basis for Literary Appreciation." *The English Journal* 34, no. 5 (May 1945): 280–282.

Jones, Archer. "The Pulps: A Mirror to Yearning." *The North American Review* 246, no. 1 (Autumn 1938): 35–47.

Lusk, Hugh H. "The Real Yellow Peril." *The North American Review* 186, no. 624 (November 1907): 375–383.

Madison, Nathan Vernon. "The Life and Works of Frank Andrew Munsey — The Man Who Made the Argosy." *Blood 'n' Thunder* (Summer 2011): 62–86.

Murphy, Paul L. "Sources and Nature of Intolerance in 1920s." *The Journal of American History* 51, No. 1 (June 1964): 60–76.

O'Conner, Thomas F. "The National Organization for Decent Literature: A Phase in American Catholic Censorship." *The Library Quarterly* 65, no. 4 (October 1995): 386–414.

Peterson, Bill E., and Emily Gerstein. "Fighting and Flying: Archival Analysis of Threat, Authoritarianism, and the North American Comic Book." *Political Psychology* 26, no. 6 (Dec., 2005): 887–904.

Singer, Marc. "Black Skins' and White Masks: Comic Books and the Secret of Race." *African American Review* 36, no. 1 (Spring 2000): 107–119.

Smith, Erin A. "How the Other Half Read: Advertising, Working-Class Readers, and Pulp Magazines." *Book History* 3 (2000): 204–230.

Watt-Evans, Lawrence. "The Other Guys—A Gargoyle's Eye-View of the Non-EC Horror Comics of the 1950s." *Alter Ego* 3, no. 97 (October 2010): 3–33.

Zorbaugh, Harvey. "Comics—There They Stand!" *Journal of Educational Sociology* 18, no. 4 (December 1944): 196–203.

Books

Ackerman, Kenneth D. *Young J. Edgar: Hoover, the Red Scare, and the Assault on Civil Liberties*. New York: Carroll and Graf Publishers, 2007.

Ashley, Michael, ed. *The History of the Science Fiction Magazine—Vol. 1, 1926–1935*. Chicago: Henry Regnery Company, 1976.

_____. *The Time Machines—The Story of the Science-Fiction Pulp Magazines from the Beginning to 1950*. Liverpool: Liverpool University Press, 2000.

Baritz, Loren, ed. *The Culture of the Twenties*. Indianapolis: The Bobbs-Merril Company, Inc., 1970.

Barkan, Elazar. *The Retreat of Scientific Racism—Changing Concepts of Race in Britain and the United States Between the World Wars*. Cambridge: Cambridge University Press, 1992.

Barrier, Michael, and Martin Williams, eds. *A Smithsonian Book of Comic-Book Comics*. New York: Smithsonian Institution Press and Harry N. Abrams, Inc., 1981.

Barson, Michael, and Steven Heller. *Red Scared! The Commie Menace in Propaganda and Popular Culture*. San Francisco: Chronicle Books, 2001.

Beecham, John Charles. *The Yellow Spider*. New York: W.J. Watt and Company, 1920.

Beglinger, Nina Jay Smith. *Constructive Lessons in English for the Foreign Born*. Boston: The Gorham Press, 1922.

Behdad, Ali. *A Forgetful Nation—On Immigration and Cultural Identity in the United States*. Durham: Duke University Press, 2005.

Benton, Mike. *The Illustrated History: Superhero Comics of the Golden Age*. Dallas: Taylor Publishing Company, 1992.

Black, Edwin. *War Against the Weak—Eugenics and America's Campaign to Create a Master Race*. New York: Four Walls Eight Windows, 2003.

Bleiler, Everett F., and Richard J. Bleiler. *Science-Fiction—The Gernsback Years*. Kent: Kent State University Press, 1998.

Bolino, August C. *From Depression to War: American Society in Transition—1939*. Westport: Praeger Publishers, 1998.

Bradley, Patricia. *Making American Culture: A Social History, 1900–1920*. New York: Palgrave Macmillan, 2009.

Brendon, Piers. *The Dark Valley: A Panorama of the 1930s*. New York: Alfred A. Knopf, 2000.

Britt, George. *The Fifth Column Is Here*. New York: Wilfred Funk, Inc., 1940.

_____. *Forty Years—Forty Millions: The Career of Frank A. Munsey*. Port Washington: Kennikat Press, 1972 [Reprint].

Brown, Jeffrey A. *Black Superheroes, Milestone Comics, and Their Fans*. Jackson: University Press of Mississippi, 2001.

Buckley, Thomas H. *The United States and the Washington Conference, 1921–1922*. Knoxville: University of Tennessee Press, 1970.

Capozzola, Christopher. *Uncle Sam Wants You: World War I and the Making of the Modern American Citizen*. New York: Oxford University Press, 2008.

Cashman, Sean Dennis. *America in the Twenties and Thirties: The Olympian Age of Franklin Delano Roosevelt*. New York: New York University Press, 1989.

Choy, Philip A., Lorraine Dong, and Marlon K. Hom, eds. *The Coming Man—19th Century American Perceptions of the Chinese*. Seattle: University of Washington Press, 1994.

Chudacoff, Howard P., and Judith E. Smith. *The Evolution of American Urban Society, Third Edition*. Englewood Cliffs: Prentice Hall, 1988.

Clements, Paul H. *The Boxer Rebellion—A Political and Diplomatic Review*. New York: AMS Press, 1967.

Cleveland, Harold Irwin. *Massacres of*

Christians by Heathen Chinese and Horrors of the Boxers. New Haven: Butler and Alger, 1900.

Connelly, Mark, and David Welch, eds. *War and the Media: Reportage and Propaganda, 1900–2003.* London: I.B. Tauris and Co. Ltd., 2005.

Constitutional Educational League. *Communism's Iron Grip on the CIO—Taken from a Speech by Hon. Clare E. Hoffman, Congressman from Michigan in the House of Representatives Tuesday, June 1, 1937.* New Haven: The Constitutional Education League, 1937.

Cox, J. Randolph. *The Dime Novel Companion: A Source Book.* Westport: Greenwood Press, 2000.

Curran, Thomas J. *Xenophobia and Immigration, 1820–1930.* Boston: Twayne Publishers, 1975.

Daniels, Les. *DC Comics: Sixty Years of the World's Favorite Comic Book Heroes.* Boston: Bulfinch Press, 1995.

_____. *Marvel: Five Fabulous Decades of the World's Greatest Comics.* New York: Harry N. Abrams, Inc., 1993.

_____. *Superman: The Complete History—The Life and Times of the Man of Steel.* San Francisco: Chronicle Books, 1998.

Daniels, Roger. *Guarding the Gold Door—American Immigration Policy and Immigrants Since 1882.* New York: Hill and Wang, 2004.

_____. *The Politics of Prejudice—The Anti-Japanese Movement in California and the Struggle for Japanese Exclusion.* Gloucester: University of California, 1966.

Davies, Joseph E. *Mission to Moscow.* New York: Simon and Schuster, 1941.

De Camp, L. Sprague. *Lovecraft—A Biography.* New York: Ballantine Books, 1976.

Denning, Michael. *Mechanic Accents—Dime Novels and Working-Class Culture in America.* New York: Verso Publishing, 1987.

Dodge, Richard Elwood. *Dodge's Advanced Geography.* Chicago: Rand McNally and Company, 1920.

Dower, John W. *War Without Mercy—Race and Power in the Pacific War.* New York: Pantheon Books, 1986.

Duke, Thomas S. *Celebrated Criminal Cases of America.* San Francisco: James H. Barry, 1910.

Dumenil, Lynn, and Eric Foner. *The Modern Temper: American Culture and Society in the 1920s.* New York: Hill and Wang, 1995.

Dunar, Andrew J. *America in the Fifties.* Syracuse: Syracuse University Press, 2006.

Feiffer, Jules. *The Great Comic Book Heroes.* New York: The Dial Press, 1965.

Fry, Brian N. *Nativism and Immigration: Regulating the American Dream.* New York: LFB Scholarly Publishing LLC, 2007.

Gibson, Walter. *The Shadow and the Golden Master.* New York: The Mysterious Press, 1984.

Goldman, Eric F. *The Crucial Decade—America, 1945–1955.* New York: Alfred A. Knopf, 1956.

Gong, Eng Ying, and Bruce Grant. *Tong War!* New York: Nicholas L. Brown, 1930.

Goodstone, Tony, ed. *The Pulps: Fifty Years of American Pop Culture.* New York: Chelsea House Publishers, 1970.

Gordon, Ian. *Comic Strips and Consumer Culture, 1890–1945.* Washington: Smithsonian Institution Press, 1998.

Goulart, Ron. *Cheap Thrills: An Informal History of the Pulp Magazines.* New Rochelle: Arlington House, 1972.

_____. *Comic Book Culture—An Illustrated History.* Portland: Collector's Press, Inc., 2000.

_____. *The Comic Book Reader's Companion.* New York: HarperCollins, 1993.

_____. *Great American Comic Books.* Lincolnwood: Publications International, Ltd., 2001.

_____. *Great History of Comic Books.* Chicago: Contemporary Books, Inc., 1986.

Goulart, Ron, ed. *The Encyclopedia of American Comics—From 1897 to the Present.* New York: Facts on File, Inc., 1990.

Grant, Madison, and Henry Fairfield Osburn. *The Passing of the Great Race; or, the Racial Basis of European History.* New York: Charles Scribner's Sons, 1922.

Hajdu, David. *The Ten-Cent Plague: The Great Comic Book Scare and How It Changed America.* New York: Farrar, Straus and Giroux, 2008.

Harvey, Robert C. *The Art of the Comic Book: An Aesthetic History.* Jackson: University Press of Mississippi, 1996.

_____. *Children of the Yellow Kid—The*

Evolution of the American Comic Strip. Seattle: The Frye Art Museum, 1998.

Haynes, John Earl. *Red Scare or Red Menace?—American Communism and Anticommunism in the Cold War Era.* Chicago: Ivan R. Dee, Inc., 1996.

Heale, M. J. *American Anticommunism—Combating the Enemy Within, 1830–1970.* Baltimore: Johns Hopkins University Press, 1990.

Hendershot, Cyndy. *Anti-Communism and Popular Culture in Mid-Century America.* Jefferson: McFarland and Company, Inc., 2003.

Higham, John. *Strangers in the Land—Patterns of American Nativism, 1860–1925.* New York: Antheneum, 1988.

Howard, Robert E., *Moon of Skulls—The Weird Works of Robert E. Howard, Volume 2.* Edited by Paul Herman. Rockville: Wildside Press, 2005.

Hunt, Michael H. *Ideology and U.S. Foreign Policy.* New Haven: Yale University Press, 1987.

Huston, Peter. *Tongs, Gangs and Triads—Chinese Crime Groups in North America.* Boulder: Paladin Press, 1995.

Hutchison, Don. *The Great Pulp Heroes.* Oakville: Mosaic Press, 1996.

Israel, Jerry. *Progressivism and the Open Door—America and China, 1905–1921.* Pittsburgh: University of Pittsburgh Press, 1971.

James, Pearl, ed. *Picture This: World War I Posters and Visual Culture.* Lincoln: University of Nebraska Press, 2009.

Jenks, Dr. Jeremiah W., W. Jett Lauck, and Rufus D. Smith. *The Immigration Problem—A Study of American Immigration Conditions and Needs.* New York: Funk and Wagnalls Company, 1922.

Jones, Gerard. *Men of Tomorrow: Geeks, Gangsters, and the Birth of the Comic Book.* New York: Basic Books, 2004.

Kaplan, Arie. *From Krakow to Krypton: Jews and Comic Books.* Philadelphia: The Jewish Publication Society, 2008.

Karasik, Paul, ed. *Fletcher Hanks: I Shall Destroy All the Civilized Planets!* Seattle: Fantagraphics Books, 2007.

Katsuichi, Honda. *The Nanjing Massacre—A Japanese Journalist Confronts Japan's National Shame.* Armonk: M.E. Sharpe, 1999.

Kennedy, David M. *Freedom from Fear: The American People in Depression and War, 1929–1945.* New York: Oxford University Press, 1999.

Knobel, Dale T. *"America for the Americans"—The Nativist Movement in the United States.* New York: Twayne Publishers, 1996.

Krensky, Stephen. *Comic Book Century: The History of American Comic Books.* Minneapolis: Twenty-First Century Books, 2008.

Lake, David A. *Entangling Relations: America Foreign Policy in Its Century.* Princeton: Princeton University Press, 1999.

Lavine, Harold. *Fifth Column in America.* New York: Doubleday, Doran and Company, Inc., 1940.

Lesser, Robert. *Pulp Art: Original Cover Paintings for the Great American Pulp Magazines.* New York: Metro Books, 2009.

Lovecraft, Howard Phillips. *Necronomicon—The Best Weird Tales of H.P. Lovecraft.* Edited by Stephen Jones. London: Orion Books, 2008.

Lui, Mary Ting Yi. *The Chinatown Trunk Mystery—Murder, Miscegenation and Other Dangerous Encounters in Turn-of-the-Century New York City.* Princeton: Princeton University Press, 2005.

MacMillan, Margaret. *Paris 1919—Six Months That Changed the World.* New York: Random House Trade Paperbacks, 2003.

McDougall, William. *Is America Safe for Democracy?* New York: Charles Scribner's Son, 1921.

Miyao, Daisuke. *Sessue Hayakawa: Silent Cinema and Transnational Stardom.* Durham: Duke University Press, 2007.

Montagu, Ashley. *Man's Most Dangerous Myth—The Fallacy of Race.* New York: Columbia University Press, 1945.

Moskowitz, Sam. *Explorers of the Infinite—Shapers of Science Fiction.* Westport: Hyperion Press, 1974.

_____. *The Immortal Storm—A History of Science Fiction Fandom.* Westport: Hyperion Press, Inc., 1974.

_____. *Strange Horizons—The Spectrum of Science Fiction.* New York: Charles Scribner's Sons, 1976.

Moskowitz, Sam, ed. *Science Fiction by Gaslight—A History and Anthology of Science Fiction in the Popular Magazines, 1891–1911.* Westport: Hyperion Press, Inc., 1974.

Mudgridge, Ian. *The View from Xanadu: William Randolph Hearst and United States Foreign Policy.* Montreal: McGill-Queen's University Press, 1995.

Northrop, Henry Davenport. *China; the Orient and the Yellow Man.* Publisher Unknown, 1900.

Nowlan, Philip Francis. *Armageddon 2419 A.D.* New York: Ace Books, 1972.

Pearson, Edmund. *Dime Novels; or, Following an Old Trail in Popular Literature.* Port Washington: Kennikat Press, 1968 [1929, Little, Brown and Company].

Penzler, Otto, ed. *The Black Lizard Big Book of Pulps.* New York: Vintage Books, 2007.

Perrett, Geoffrey. *America in the Twenties: A History.* New York: Simon and Schuster, 1982.

Prasso, Sheridan. *The Asian Mystique—Dragon Ladies, Geisha Girls, and Our Fantasies of the Exotic Orient.* New York: Public Affairs, 2005.

Preston, Diana. *The Boxer Rebellion.* New York: Walker and Company, 2000.

Pullen, John J. *Patriotism in America: A Study of Changing Devotions, 1770–1970.* New York: American Heritage Press, 1971.

Reeve, Arthur Benjamin. *The Romance of Elaine.* New York: Harper and Brothers, Publishers, 1916.

Reischauer, E.O. *The United States and Japan.* Cambridge: Harvard University Press, 1965.

Reynolds, Quentin. *The Fiction Factory, or from Pulp Row to Quality Street—The Story of 100 Years of Publishing at Street and Smith.* New York: Random House, 1955.

Reynolds, Richard. *Super-Heroes: A Modern Mythology.* Jackson: University Press of Mississippi, 1994.

Rohmer, Sax. *The Insidious Dr. Fu Manchu.* New York: Robert M. McBride and Company, 1920.

Sabin, Roger. *Comics, Comix and Graphic Novels: A History of Comic Art.* London: Phaidon Press Ltd., 1996.

Sadowski, Greg, ed. *Supermen! The First Wave of Comic Book Heroes, 1936–1941.* Seattle: Fantagraphics Books, 2009.

Said, Edward W. *Orientalism.* New York: Pantheon Books, 1978.

Sampson, Robert. *Yesterday's Faces—Volume III: From the Dark Side.* Bowling Green: Bowling Green State University Popular Press, 1987.

_____. *Yesterday's Faces—Volume V: Dangerous Horizons.* Bowling Green: Bowling Green State University Popular Press, 1991.

Sarolea, Charles. *Impressions of Soviet Russia.* London: Eveleigh, Nash and Grayson, Ltd., 1924.

Savage, William W. *Commies, Cowboys, and Jungle Queens: Comic Books and America, 1945–1954.* Hanover: Wesleyan University Press, 1998.

Schwab, Orrin. *Redeemer Nation: America and the World in the Technocratic Age—1914 to the Present.* Salt Lake City: American Book Publishing, 2004.

Schwartz, Julius. *Man of Two Worlds: My Life in Science Fiction and Comics.* New York: Harper Collins Publishers, 2000.

Schwartz, Richard A. *The 1950s: An Eyewitness History.* New York: Facts on File, Inc., 2003.

Seppi, Kenneth R., ed. *The Magnificent Superheroes of Comic's Golden Age.* Effingham: Vintage Features, 1979.

Smith, Erin A. *Hard-Boiled: Working-Class Readers and Pulp Magazines.* Philadelphia: Temple University Press, 2000.

Soennichsen, John. *The Chinese Exclusion Act of 1882.* Santa Barbara: Greenwood, 2011.

Spence, Jonathan D. *God's Chinese Son—The Taiping Heavenly Kingdom of Hong Xiuquan.* New York: W.W. Norton and Company, 1996.

Steele, Curtis. *Secret Service Operator #5—Blood Reign of the Dictator.* Wildside Press, 2004.

_____. *Secret Service Operator #5—Invasion of the Crimson Death Cult.* Wildside Press, 2005.

_____. *Secret Service Operator #5—Winged Hordes of the Yellow Vulture.* Wildside Press, 2005

Stevens, Albert, C. *The Cyclopedia of Fraternities.* New York: Hamilton Printing and Publishing Company, 1899.

Stoddard, Lothrop. *The Rising Tide of Color—Against White World Supremacy.* New York: Charles Scribner's Sons, 1921.

Superman Sunday Classics—Strips 1–183: 1939–1943. New York: Sterling Publishing Company, 1999.

Thomas, Martin Luther. *Unmasking the C.I.O.* Los Angeles: The Christian American Crusade, 1934.

Thomas, Roy, and Peter Sanderson. *The*

Marvel Vault. Philadelphia: Running Press Book Publishers, 2007.

Thompson, Don, and Dick Lupoff. *The Comic-Book Book—Recalls the Great Comic-Book Features of the Past*. Carlstadt: Rainbow Books, 1998.

Treacy, Rev. Gerald C. *God and Liberty Against Satan and Slavery—A Simplified Edition of the Encyclical "Divini Redemptoris"—Atheistic Communism—By Pope Pius XI*. New York: The Paulist Press, 1943.

Tymn, Marshall B., and Mike Ashley, eds. *Science Fiction, Fantasy and Weird Fiction Magazines*. Westport: Greenwood Press, 1985.

Utley, Jonathan G. *Going to War with Japan: 1937–1941*. Knoxville: University of Tennessee Press, 1985.

Ward, Harry F. *Soviet Democracy*. New York: Soviet Russia Today, 1947.

Watkins, T.H. *The Great Depression: America in the 1930s*. Boston: Little, Brown and Company, 1993.

Wertham, Fredric M.D. *Seduction of the Innocent*. New York: Main Road Books, 2004 [1954].

Whitfield, Raoul. *Jo Gar's Casebook*. Edited by Keith Alan Deutsch. Norfolk: Crippen and Landru Publishers, 2002.

Wright, Bradford W. *Comic Book Nation: The Transformation of Youth Culture in America*. Baltimore: Johns Hopkins University Press, 2001.

Wright, Russell O. *Chronology of Immigration in the United States*. Jefferson: McFarland and Company, Inc., 2008.

Wu, William F. *The Yellow Peril: Chinese Americans in American Fiction, 1850–1940*. Hamden: Archon Books, 1982.

Zeidel, Robert F. *Immigrants, Progressives, and Exclusion Politics: The Dillingham Commission, 1900–1927*. DeKalb: Northern Illinois University Press, 2004.

Zolberg, Aristide R. *A Nation by Design: Immigration Policies in the Fashioning of America*. New York: Russell Sage Foundation, 2006.

INDEX

Action Comics 102, 182
Adventure 24, 28, 40, 42,-45, 70, 84, 86, 92, 100, 111, 125, 126, 136, 147–151, 163–165, 205
All Story Weekly 42, 43, 80
Amazing Stories 42, 57, 58, 74, 98, 99, 103, 150, 160, 161
Americanization 22, 61, 83, 113, 157
Argosy 27, 30, 40–42, 47, 50, 52, 53, 59–62, 64, 68, 73, 77, 79, 80, 84, 92, 94–97, 100–102, 111–114, 118, 125, 126, 135–137, 148, 150, 151, 159, 160, 162, 163, 205
Argosy All-Story Weekly see *Argosy*
"Armageddon 2419 A.D." 74, 161
Astounding Stories 42, 149–152, 161, 204
Atlas Comics 168–170, 175, 176, 181, 183, 184, 188, 190, 191, 195, 197, 208
Atomic War! 174, 175

Batman 93, 103, 118, 122, 140, 168, 179–181, 184, 205, 208
Battlefield 181, 191
Beadle Dime Novels 27, 28
Black Mask 86
Blackhawk 133, 142–144, 207
Blue Book 42, 45, 49, 84, 111, 126, 149, 160
Bow Kum 50, 81, 85
Boxer Rebellion 4, 11, 19, 23, 24, 36, 37, 46, 125
Brackett, Leigh 202
Burroughs, Edgar Rice 42, 80, 108

Captain America 7, 93, 108, 109, 116, 120, 121, 128, 140, 166, 168–171, 183, 184, 190, 191, 205, 207, 208
Captain America Comics 108, 109, 128, 140, 166, 168
Captain Battle 108, 118, 137, 138
Captain Marvel 142, 184–187
Cat-Man Comics 121, 128, 132
Chinatown 19, 32–35, 37, 38, 46, 48–50, 52, 54, 72, 84, 85, 122, 132, 133, 156, 197, 198, 200, 207
Chinese 2, 5, 15–20, 23, 25, 26, 31–40, 43, 46–90, 92, 93, 96, 99, 109, 121–124, 128, 132–138, 140, 142–144, 147, 149, 150, 158, 160, 161, 177–179, 181, 187–191, 194–201, 203, 207, 208
The Claw 108, 129
Combat Kelly 181, 193
Comics Novel 168, 169
Communists 15, 36, 40, 48, 116, 138, 146–201, 203, 209
Complete War Novels 126

Daredevil Comics (Lev Gleason) 108, 129, 130
DC Comics 102, 103, 118, 121, 151, 152, 180, 182, 184, 185, 206, 208
"Della Wu, Chinese Courtesan" 81, 85, 86
Detective Comics 121, 122
Detective Fiction Weekly 70
Detective Story Magazine 42, 52, 69, 75
dime novels 2, 23–25, 27, 28, 34, 37, 38, 41, 42, 46, 49, 74, 167
dragon ladies 3, 8, 78, 82, 132, 134, 181, 188, 189

EC Comics 8, 152, 176, 181, 194
eugenics 8, 66, 83, 90, 120, 200
Exciting Comics 116, 119
exotic love interests 76, 78–81, 133

Famous Fantastic Mysteries 151
Famous Funnies 102
Fantastic Adventures 150, 151
Fawcett Comics 168, 183, 184
Fifth Column 98, 101, 106, 109, 113, 115–117, 162, 174, 183, 197
Fight Comics 102, 106, 143
Fighting Yank 117, 128, 129, 131, 140, 142
The Future Eve 80, 81

gender 3, 8, 76, 78–82, 132–134, 181, 188, 189
Germans 7, 13, 21, 22, 24, 40, 86–88, 90, 91, 93, 94, 98, 100, 101, 105–117, 120, 121, 133, 145, 147, 154, 157, 162–166, 175, 200
Gernsback, Hugo 57, 58, 161
G.I. Combat 181, 194
Golden Argosy 30, 41; see also *Argosy*
Grant, Madison 57, 66, 67, 76, 87, 90, 110, 145

Hayakawa, Sessue 124, 133
Headline Comics 117, 128, 142
Herr, Howard Horace 62
Hitler, Adolf 7, 88, 95, 96, 98, 101, 107–109, 114, 115, 119, 129, 142, 162, 170, 171, 173, 200
"Horror at Red Hook" 55
How Stalin Hopes We Will Destroy America 172, 173
Howard, Robert E. 42, 55, 75
Human Torch 107, 108, 116, 120, 169, 170, 183, 184, 190

The Insidious Dr. Fu Manchu 67
internationalist, or transplanted heroes 133–145, 190–199
Is This Tomorrow 174

Japan 2, 4–6, 11, 23, 34, 39, 40, 64, 65, 71, 78, 84, 87–101, 107–109, 121–141, 144, 145, 147, 149, 165, 169, 177, 178, 185, 188, 189, 192, 199, 200, 207, 208
Jeff Clayton 35, 37, 39, 46, 156–158
Jo Gar 86

Kâramanèh 79–81, 197
Kiang-Ho 31, 32
Kirby, Jack 93–103
Know-Nothings 14
Korean War 6, 8, 147, 149, 150, 178, 188, 194, 200
Koreans 6, 8, 39, 40, 89, 92, 138, 139, 147, 149, 150, 178, 179, 183–185, 187–195, 200

Lee, Stan 197, 199, 205
London, Jack 65, 214
Lovecraft, Howard Phillips 42, 55, 57

MacIsaac, Fred 79
Malaeska 28–30
Marvel Boy 168, 175, 176
Marvel Comics 6, 103, 107, 195, 198, 206–208

Marvel Mystery Comics 107, 108, 152
Marvel Science Stories 98, 107
Mission to Moscow 162, 219
Mr. Chang 52, 69, 70, 89, 137
Mr. Wong 133, 134
Mr. Woo 62, 63
M.L.J. Publication 104, 107, 119, 128, 164
Munsey, Frank Andrew 27, 41, 42, 100, 149

Namor *see* Sub-Mariner
Nazis 7, 25, 88, 90–92, 95, 99, 101, 102, 105–109, 113, 118–122, 127, 129, 133, 142–145, 147, 149, 162–164, 166–173, 176, 177, 181, 187, 189, 190, 200, 203
Nick Carter (character) 34, 35, 37, 38
Nugget Library 26, 27, 31–33, 74

Operator #5 94, 95, 101
Oriental Stories 24, 51, 54, 56, 72, 81, 86

Pearsall, Robert J. 44
Phantom Detective 53, 54, 59, 60, 63, 69, 72, 73
Popular Comics 102, 105
Popular Publications 74, 100
Professor Supermind & Son 105

Quality Comics 142, 171

Rohmer, Sax 4, 30, 42, 44, 45, 51, 67, 89, 122, 123, 145, 148, 195
Russians 2, 13, 40, 62, 90, 111, 112, 124, 143, 146, 148, 150, 154, 156, 157, 159, 160, 162–166, 168, 172, 173, 175, 204

scientifiction 57, 93
Secret Service 30, 33, 34, 38, 155, 156
Seduction of the Innocent 152
The Shadow 24, 42, 53, 73, 75, 73, 103, 114, 160
The Shield 104, 107, 122, 130
Short Stories 42, 100, 111
"Skull-Face" 75, 76, 79
Small, Sidney Herschel 52, 70
Stalin, Joseph 95, 107, 148, 160, 162–165, 171–173, 175, 178
Standard Publications 116, 117, 181
Stoddard, Lothrop 76
story papers 25, 27, 30, 32, 34, 37, 38, 41, 42, 46, 167
Street & Smith 42, 52, 75, 102, 120, 139, 144, 160
Sub-Mariner 107, 108, 116, 120, 167, 169, 183
Super-American 102, 105, 106

Superman 93, 102, 103, 107, 119, 121, 134, 135, 144, 168, 176, 179–182, 184, 205, 208

Taiping Rebellion 17, 25, 36, 37, 46–48, 125, 157
Tell It to the Marines 188, 192
Terry and the Pirates 122, 132, 187
The Thrill Book 42, 71
Thrilling Wonder Stories 98
Timely Comics 6, 107, 153, 169
Tom Edison, Jr. (character) 31, 32
tongs 34, 35, 46, 48, 49, 50, 52, 54, 57, 59, 69–75, 84, 85, 89, 93, 95, 122, 123, 128, 145, 156, 159, 193, 201, 204
True Mystic Crimes 49, 50, 52

U.S. legislation 18, 82, 110, 158, 179, 204
United States Marines Comics 122, 141
U.S.A. Comics 6, 119, 120

Weird Tales 42, 54, 55, 75, 79
Wertham, Frederic 152, 153, 195
Wheeler-Nicholson, Malcolm 102, 107, 151, 159
Wong, Anna May 77, 78, 134
World War II 2, 7, 8, 40, 87–149, 164, 166, 169, 172, 177–179, 181, 183, 187, 189, 191, 192, 199, 201, 205
World War III 172, 175
Worts, George F. 53, 60

The Yellow Claw 177, 190, 195–199, 207
Young Men 169, 170

Zagat, Leo 96, 97, 125

www.ingramcontent.com/pod-product-compliance
Ingram Content Group UK Ltd.
Pitfield, Milton Keynes, MK11 3LW, UK
UKHW041944140426
5217IPUK00014B/653